PONTIAC
THE PERFORMANCE YEARS

MARTYN L. SCHORR

Dedications

For my son, Stuart, daughter, Collier, and my wife and best friend, Sharon.

To the memory of Paul Zazarine, who passed away on January 3, 2011. Paul was the consummate Pontiac aficionado and an author, editor, and photojournalist who had mastered his craft and helped shape the muscle car hobby. He was also a great friend and fellow Sarasota Cafe Racer.

Copyright © 2011 by PMPR, Inc.

Published by:

www.stanceandspeed.com

All rights reserved. With the exception of quoting brief passages for the purposes of review, no part of this publication may be reproduced without prior written permission from the publisher.

The information in this book is true and complete to the best of our knowledge. All recommendations are made without any guarantee on the part of the author or publisher, who also disclaim any liability incurred in connection with the use of this data or specific details.

We recognize, further, that some words, model names, and designations mentioned herein are the property of the trademark holder. We use them for identification purposes only. This is not an official publication.

Version History
Stance & Speed edition published January 2011
Originally published as three volumes of the Quicksilver Supercars series:
Pontiac: The Performance Years Volume 1, ISBN 0-940346-12-5;
Volume 2, ISBN 0-940346-20-6; and *Volume 3*, ISBN 0-940346-24-9

Schorr, Martyn L.
Pontiac: The Performance Years

ISBN-10 0983060622
ISBN-13 9780983060628

Design, layout, and scanning by Tom Heffron

Contents

INTRODUCTION 6
PUBLISHER'S NOTE 9
ROUTE OF THE SILVER STREAK 10
CHIEF OF THE SHOW CARS 16
1955: THE START OF SOMETHING BIG 18
TURBINE PROGRAM IGNITES THE FIREBIRD 20
1956: MOVING RIGHT ALONG! 22
PONTIAC CHALLENGES THE WORLD 24
1957: PONTIAC STANDS FOR PERFORMANCE 26
AMERICA'S ROAD CAR 28
BONNEVILLE: WHAT'S IN A NAME? 30
1958: NO MORE NICE-GUY STUFF 32
1959: WIDE TRACK CITY 34
THE 389 ARRIVES 36
THE ULTIMATE FIREBIRD 38
1960: THE CLEAN AND MEAN APPROACH 43
1961: WIDE-TRACKING TO THE TOP! 45
1962: THE YEAR OF THE SUPER-DUTY 47
THE SUPER-DUTY SAGA 49
"YOU DON'T HEAR THAT SOUND ANYMORE" 54

TEMPEST IN A TEAPOT	56
GRAND PRIX X-400 (1962)	58
ROYAL ROUTE OF THE SILVER STREAK	60
ROYAL'S RACING LEGEND	62
RACING IMPROVES THE BREED	63
1963: THE SUPER-DUTY BEAT GOES ON	66
MYSTERY MANIFOLD	69
1963 SUPER-DUTY REFERENCE GUIDE	70
GRAND PRIX X-400 (1963)	79
THE CAMMER CONSPIRACY	81
1964: THE YEAR OF THE SUPERCAR	83
A DEVICE FOR SHRINKING TIME AND DISTANCE	85
BIRTH OF THE SUPERCAR (GTO 1964-1974)	88
THE ORIGINAL TIN INDIANS	93
STRICTLY FOR SHOW	96
GRAND PRIX X-400 (1964)	98
1965: PERFORMANCE SPOKEN HERE!	100
1966: THE CHOICE IS PONTIAC	103
1967: THE SUPERCAR AND PONYCAR SHOW!	105
THE FIRST-GENERATION FIREBIRD	108
THE SIX THAT ROARED	113
1968: CAR OF THE YEAR	118
BIRTH OF THE TRANS AM	121
PONTIAC FIREBIRD SPRINT TURISMO	124
1969: HERE COMES THE JUDGE!	125
GRAND PRIX, THE DRIVER'S CAR	129
GRAND PRIX STEAMER	133
CIRRUS!	136
1970: THE FUN OF DRIVING	138
PONTIAC'S MAGNIFICENT FIVE	142

THE SECOND-GENERATION FIREBIRD	145
1971: THE WRITING'S ON THE WALL!	148
FIREBIRD CAFE RACER, STAGE 1	152
THE ULTIMATE GRAND PRIX	154
1972: THE END IS NEAR!	155
THE GREAT REAR SPOILER DEBATE!	158
FIREBIRD CAFE RACER, STAGE 2	159
1973: SAVED BY THE SUPER-DUTY!	161
SD-455: THE MYTH AND THE MAGIC!	165
HOW TO DOCUMENT AN SD-455	171
FIREBIRD CAFE RACER, STAGE 3	174
1974: THE END IS HERE!	176
END OF AN ERA	179
GTO SPOTTER'S GUIDE AND HIGH-PERFORMANCE PONTIAC REFERENCE GUIDE (1964-1974)	181
THE GRAND AM THAT NEVER WAS!	190
PONTIAC WAGONMASTER!	192
THE BANSHEE TRILOGY	194
THE FIREBIRD PHENOMENON	196
DESIGNING THE THIRD-GENERATION FIREBIRD	201
HIGH-OUTPUT TRANS-AM (1983/1984 MODEL)	205
PONTIAC SETS THE PACE	206
THE FIERO STORY	208
CHEATING THE WIND	213

Introduction
WELCOME TO PONTIAC: THE WAY IT WAS!

"Everything old is new again!" That's what I determined automotive enthusiasts were craving in the early-1980s when I published The *Quicksilver Supercar Series*. The most exciting products that General Motors, Ford, and Chrysler produced were not the new ones in dealerships. Enthusiasts wanted to read about the era—the 1950s, 1960s and early-1970s—that defined Motown's wheel-to-wheel competition.

The early-1980s were grim times for new performance cars. It really didn't matter which brand you chose; engines were emasculated and laden with power-robbing smog controls, styling was in a state of flux, performance options were scarce, and quality was certainly not Job One!

Once again I feel that everything old is new again, but not because Detroit has abandoned performance enthusiasts—quite the contrary. Today's performance cars are quicker, faster, handle better, are far more economical, and are safer than the vintage iconic models lusted for by enthusiasts and collectors. There remains, however, a great deal of curiosity and romance attached to the nameplates and cars that *owned* the streets and tracks in days gone by.

The *Quicksilver Supercar Series* was very successful because it focused the golden age of performance cars. For some readers it was all new, an education in the how and why Detroit marketed muscle. For others it was a nostalgic look back at the "good old days." The three volumes of PONTIAC: The Performance Years were among the most successful titles we published.

This special, limited edition represents a compilation of the best of Volumes I, II, and III of the original series published in the early-1980s. Out of print for nearly three decades, original copies are highly collectible and coveted by Pontiac historians and enthusiasts. *PONTIAC: The Performance Years* is packed with a treasure trove of period photography and information from Pontiac Engineering, specialty marketers like Royal Pontiac (Bobcat), and factory and private racecar builders.

Pontiac is the brand that brought us the GTO in 1964 and created a whole new market segment: Supercars. First an option in 1964-1965 and then a full model line in 1966, the GTO was the first of the Supercar genre and was supported by incredibly creative marketing programs, in-your-face advertising, and almost endless option lists. Today we call vintage GTOs and competitive mid-size models with high-profile trim and large displacement, high-horsepower engines "musclecars." Back then, though, it was the Supercar Sixties, and Pontiac started it all!

During these years I had the great fortune to be editor of *Hi-Performance CARS* Magazine and editorial director of the Magnum Automotive Group: *Speed & Supercar, Super/Stock & FX, Supercar Annuals,* and other motorcycle and auto titles.

I had the pleasure of spending time with Pontiac engineers responsible for the GTO and high-performance engines and suspensions, as well as Jim Wangers, who consulted on Pontiac's performance advertising (the best in the field) and was responsible for all those great GTO promotions that helped establish Pontiac as the youth-market, performance brand.

I also enjoyed spending time with the guys at Ace Wilson's Royal Pontiac and racing one of their Bobcat GTOs.

Nothing beat test-driving the hottest Pontiacs (and some prototypes breathed on by guys like Herb Adams) every year at GM's Milford Proving Grounds. When most of the enthusiast magazines were heavily weighted toward Chevrolet editorial, I turned *Hi-Performance CARS* into one of Pontiac's biggest media supporters.

My love affair with Pontiac pre-dated the GTO. It started in 1961 when I road tested a new four-speed, 389/348 tri-power '61 Bonneville convertible for *Hi-Performance CARS*. I remember being blown away by this big car's performance and road manners and wanting to own one. After the test session I called friends at Pontiac Public Relations and asked them to help me secure a discount with a local dealer on a Coronado Red, 348-horsepower Bonneville hardtop coupe with automatic. It was one of the best cars I've owned!

It was not, however, my first Pontiac. That was the '51 Pontiac that I inherited from my family in the mid-1950s. It was two-tone blue with skirts, bull-nosed hood, shaved deck, and lots of chrome on its Mallory-sparked Straight Eight. My third and final Pontiac was a '73 GTO with 455-inch engine and every option, including sunroof, that Pontiac offered. It appeared on the cover of the April 1973 issue of *Hi-Performance CARS*.

PONTIAC: The Performance Years showcases the brand's history and performance heritage, starting with its first modern V-8 in 1955: a 287-inch, four-barrel rated at 200 horsepower. In 1956 displacement grew to 317 cubic inches and four-barrel engines were rated at 227 horsepower. Later in the model year, a high-compression, dual-quad competition-only engine was introduced. In 1957 Pontiac upped the ante with a 347 cubic inch variant. Hot tri-power street and track versions pumped out 290 and 317 horsepower. Like Chevrolet with its fuelie Corvette, Pontiac debuted Rochester fuel injection for its hot engine in 1957.

Detroit's legendary horsepower race was in full swing by the late 1950s and Pontiac was a front-runner. In 1958 you could order an over-styled Pontiac Bonneville coupe or convertible with a 370-inch V-8 rated at 300-hp (tri-power) or 310-hp (FI). A tri-power Bonneville paced the 1958 Indy 500.

A new 389-inch V-8 in 1959 signaled the start of Pontiac's meteoric rise to the top on roundy-round tracks, drag strips, and, of course, the street. That's when the factory started its yard-long high-performance option lists, leading the way to Super-Duty 389s and 421s, and then 389-400 and 455-inch engines in the GTO.

Unfortunately Pontiac is now considered an "orphan" brand, making books like this one even more important. On April 27, 2009, Fritz Henderson, GM CEO, announced the end of Pontiac; nothing new would be coming from the brand that started the Supercar Revolution. Even with the G8 (a four-door GTO iteration that could hold its own against European sport sedans) and Solstice (Miata-beater sports car) in the showrooms, Pontiac was abandoned by GM. A sad day indeed for Pontiac enthusiasts.

How much do I still love Pontiac? After selling my '61 Bonneville in 1967, more than 40 years ago, I still wish I had it. First loves don't die easily!

Martyn L. Schorr

Publisher's Note

Pontiacs have always held a special place in my heart, probably because of the popularity of the Firebird and Trans Am during my formative years in the late 1970s. Pontiac's standing wasn't even diminished by the absolutely atrocious LeMans sedan that my family owned during that period.

Consider the wide range of interesting Pontiacs over its history, though, and it's clear that Pontiac always was one of the most intriguing American car brands. It pains me to say "was." Pontiac deserved a better fate than it got. Perhaps a little more Solstice and G8 and a little less Montana and Aztek would have saved it; we'll never know for sure.

Nevertheless, it's worth cherishing the great cars that Pontiac delivered over the years. That's what *Pontiac: The Performance Years* does, with lots of in-depth, period coverage of the earliest performance Pontiacs of the 1950s through the Firebirds and Fieros of the early 1980s. There's plenty of GTO and Trans-Am in these pages, as well as engine specs, drag racing exploits, concept cars, and more. Join me in celebrating Pontiac—may it rest in peace!

Peter Bodensteiner
Founder, Stance & Speed

ROUTE OF THE SILVER STREAK

A short course on the history of Pontiac—from buggies to high-output aero Trans-Ams and sophisticated GT sedans

TO TRACE the history of Pontiac Motor Division to its beginning it is necessary to go back to the gay nineties and to the nostalgic days of the dashboard and whip socket!

Edward M. Murphy, a successful young businessman organized the Pontiac Buggy Company in Pontiac, Michigan, in 1893. During the following ten years, his company gained an enviable reputation for fine carriage work.

It was in the early 1900s that the farsighted Murphy began to look with interest at the smoking, sputtering horseless carriages that appeared occasionally on the streets. Sensing the potential of the automobile which still was branded as an impractical and temporary novelty, he acquired the rights to a two-cylinder engine designed by A.P. Brush, a famous motor pioneer who already had established his reputation in the field of engineering by designing a successful one-cylinder Cadillac and Brush car.

Murphy equipped a section of his buggy works for car production and on August 28, 1907, he founded the Oakland Motor Car Company. The initial investment of $200,000 in the new automobile manufacturing concern is less than the cost of some of the machines which now equip sprawling plants at Pontiac!

Murphy produced the two-cylinder Oakland for a year. However, it did not sell, so in 1908 he introduced the Oakland Model K, a four-cylinder car that was powerful for its time and competitively-priced. A total of 278 four-cylinder Oaklands were produced in 1908 and 491 in 1909.

The growing young Oakland Motor Car Company attracted the attention of William Crapo Durant, one of the organizing geniuses behind the then-forming business which was to become General Motors.

Durant, through his agents, entered into negotiations with the Oakland stockholders and on April 9, 1909, Oakland

1926 Pontiac

Pontiac's Plastic Fantastic

joined General Motors taking its place beside Buick and Oldsmobile. Cadillac joined GM later that year and Chevrolet was added in 1918.

In September, 1909, E.M. Murphy died at age 45. L.L. (Lee) Dunlap, a long-time friend and business associate of Murphy's succeeded Murphy and Oakland continued its growth.

In 1910, production of the Model K Oakland boomed to 4,639, mainly on the basis of its hill-climbing ability. Three years later, Oakland introduced its first Six along with a fast Four that was equipped with a self-starter.

After World War I, Oakland pioneered closed bodies in the light car field and skeptics shook their heads. In 1923, Oakland introduced long-lasting, fast-drying Duco lacquer to the auto industry.

In 1925, rumors spread of a new companion car to the Oakland line. Ben H. Anibal, who had been chief engineer for Cadillac, was engaged by General Manager A.R. (Al) Glancy to design a completely new light, six-cylinder car.

Pontiac, the Chief of the Sixes, made its bow at the New York Auto Show in January, 1926. Little did Oakland executives dream at the time that the Pontiac would one day supersede the parent.

The new automobile became as aggressive and powerful in its field as did the colorful Indian chief who over 200 years ago banded together the Ottawas, Chippewas, Pottawatomis and Miamis into a powerful confederation.

Embodying many features of high-priced automobiles, yet costing little more

Breakaway Auto Show Classic

1964 GTO—The First Supercar

1969 Trans-Am Convertible

In 1933, Harry J. Klingler was named general manager of Pontiac, and it was decided to put a Six back in the line, retaining the Eight as well. The 1935 models were the first to bear the Silver Streak identification; and sales doubled calling for further factory expansion.

Pontiac produced 330,061 units of its 1941 model, thus becoming the largest producer in its price class and the fifth largest in the nation. After an outstanding war production record, Pontiac returned to passenger car production in 1945.

To satisfy growing demands, a vast expansion program was launched in 1945 to increase productivity capacity by 50 percent. Pontiac's iron foundry was greatly enlarged. Layout of the engine plant was altered to provide for more machines and heavier production. A new building was erected for increased production of rear axles, and for heat treating of steel forgings to make them tougher and more durable. Pontiac's than the least-expensive lines, Pontiac immediately captured public favor and in 1926 a total of 76,742 units were built.

Popularity of Pontiac became so great that Oakland was discontinued in 1932. Pontiac is one of the few companion cars to survive the rigors of competition and today holds the distinction of being the only line introduced by General Motors after formation of the corporation.

Soon after the introduction of Pontiac, it was evident that the original factory site near the center of the city of Pontiac was too small, so 246 acres were acquired on the northern edge of the city for a new plant.

The new facility was to be known as the "daylight plant" because the extensive use of glass skylights provided natural illumination. It was considered a miracle in the construction industry that within 90 days after ground was broken cars were being produced in the new plant.

A new Fisher Body Division plant was built nearby, connected by an overhead closed bridge—a convenience not available to many manufacturers who had to truck-in their bodies.

electroplating system, one of the largest automatic setups in the new warehouse for handling past-model parts, was put into service.

In 1951, Klingler became vice president in charge of vehicle production for GM and Arnold Lenz was appointed general manager of Pontiac. Lenz served as general manager until his tragic death in 1952.

R.M. Critchfield succeeded Lenz as general manager and under his guidance Pontiac embarked on the most extensive enlargement and modernization program since 1927. A new car finish building was completed and the engine plant was completely modernized to produce V-8 engines in record volumes. Production for 1955 established a new high of 581,860 cars.

A new era started for Pontiac in 1956 when Semon E. (Bunkie) Knudsen took over the reins as general manager. Knudsen, son of William S. Knudsen, a former GM president, at the time was the youngest general manager at age 43. He proceeded without fanfare to make over the Pontiac image.

With a new engineering group headed by E.M. (Pete) Estes, the new Pontiacs were methodically developed. Starting with the 1959 models, an image of a youthful car with appeal across the spectrum of new car buyers emerged.

In the fall of 1960, following intensive research, development and testing, Pontiac introduced the completely new Tempest series. Unique in conception and fresh in styling, the Tempest became an immediate success and was recognized as the outstanding engineering achievement of the year.

When Knudsen moved to Chevrolet as general manager in 1961, Estes headed Pontiac. Under his direction the division continued to grow in sales volume and facilities.

With the addition of the Tempest, the division moved into third place in sales in 1961. Long regarded as the hot-spot in automobile sales, third place has a reputation of being hard to keep. Several car manufacturers have occupied the position over the years only to lose out to another make.

Pontiac continued its dominance of third place during the Sixties as sales records were shattered.

The division also moved ahead in plant construction and in 1964 three new projects were announced. All were completed the following year and added some 1½ million square feet to Pontiac's home production facilities.

These include a 180,000 square-foot addition to the foundry for new core-making machines, water-cooled cupolas and a new finishing room to make Pontiac's foundry the most modern in the industry.

Also added was a service parts warehouse containing 1,070,000 square feet under one roof to consolidate storage of service parts. A one-story storage and shipping building, 800 feet long and 330 feet wide, to expedite shipments to other Pontiac assembly plants was completed in 1964.

Estes followed Knudsen's footsteps to Chevrolet as general manager in 1965 and John Z. DeLorean was named to Pontiac's top position, moving up from chief engineer of the division.

Before the introduction of its 1966 models, Pontiac announced a completely new overhead camshaft engine as standard equipment on all 1966 Tempest models. This was the first time such an engine had been used in an American passenger car.

In January, 1967, Pontiac unveiled the Firebird. Aimed at the youthful sports car market, it was offered with the OHC-6 and with a 400 cubic-inch V-8 engine.

1968 was another milestone year for Pontiac. Production and sales records were shattered as 943,253 cars were produced for an all-time high. Pontiac's GTO was chosen Car of the Year by

1970 Bonneville—14,000,000th car

1973 GTO—Top
Performance Car Of The Year

1973 Grand-Am—The First GT Sedan

Motor Trend magazine for "... being so successful in confirming the correlations between safety, styling and performance." The presentation of the Golden Calipers trophy marked the fourth time Pontiac had won the trophy, more than any other manufacturer.

Contributing to the GTO success was the innovative energy-absorbing Endura front bumper developed by Pontiac engineering. Hailed as an industry first and projected as a pacesetter for others to copy, the car and bumper attracted nationwide publicity.

Sales boomed in 1968. For the first time, the specialty cars—Tempest, Grand Prix and Firebird—exceeded those of the traditional line. When the final tallies were in, 910,997 Pontiacs had been sold.

The '69 Grand Prix was a phenomenal success as its sales more than tripled over the previous model year to 105,000. Car Life magazine awarded the Grand Prix its "Car of the Year" award.

In February, 1969, F. James McDonald returned to Pontiac as general manager, replacing DeLorean who moved up to Chevrolet in the same capacity.

McDonald (who had served as Pontiac's works manager from 1965-'68) returned after spending one year to the day at Chevrolet as director of manufacturing operations.

The division's new 300,000 square-foot ulta-modern administration building opened in early 1970. The five-level structure, headquarters the general manager and the sales, accounting, data processing, purchasing and public relations departments.

In March, 1971, Pontiac entered the compact car market with the low-priced, stylish Ventura II. Built on a 111-inch wheelbase, the Ventura II was offered in two-door and four-door models.

In April, 1971, Pontiac dedicated a new multi-million dollars vehicle emissions control and carburetor testing facility. The two-story, 43,000-square-foot building is being used by Pontiac engineers working on the development of vehicle emissions controls of components in the power train and the fuel system.

The 1971 calendar year saw Pontiac take firm hold on third place in the auto industry's sales race. Pontiac dealers sold 710,352 cars to capture the hotly-contested third spot in sales for the 10th time in the last 11 years.

In 1972, Pontiac featured a new energy-absorbing bumper on all full-size cars. The system consisted of two telescoping steel boxes which contain urethane positioned between the bumper and the frame of the car. Since the urethane blocks were not damaged by an impact, the bumper could be struck numerous times during the life of the car and continue to absorb energy.

On October 1, 1972, Martin J. Caserio became general manager of Pontiac replacing Mr. McDonald who was named Chevrolet general manager. Mr. Caserio had been general manager of the GMC Truck & Coach Division since 1966.

The 1973 Pontiac lineup was highlighted by a totally-redesigned intermediate series, topped by the stunning Grand Am. This fine road touring car featured a "soft nose" front end made of flexible rubber-like urethane for protection. Pontiac sales of 854,343 for the 1973 model year were the second-best in history. The GTO received CARS Magazine's Top Performance Car of the Year Award from Editor Martyn L. Schorr.

1980 Turbo Trans-Am—Indy Pace Car

Third Generation Trans-Am

The 1974 Pontiac lineup featured significant engineering improvements in energy-absorbing bumpers and a new Radial Tuned Suspension package.

By 1974 the major construction was completed on a multi-million dollar program to clean up smoke emissions from the Pontiac Casting Plant. Five modern arc-melt furnaces and four electric induction holding furnaces with the latest dust collecting units were installed. Two remaining coke-fired cupolas had modern emissions control equipment installed making them as clean as the electric furnaces.

Introduction of the sub-compact Astre, bold restyling of the compact Ventura and extensive use of Radial Tuned Suspension with steel-belted radial tires highlighted introduction of the 1975 Pontiacs. Rectangular headlamps were utilized on the Bonneville and Grand Ville Brougham for the first time. Pontiac continued its strong emphasis on customer satisfaction by extending its First 100-Day Survey program to all retail purchasers of new Pontiacs. The survey was introduced on a sample basis during the 1973 model year. The survey seeks customer reaction to the new car, and to the dealership and its service. The survey is a domestic industry exclusive for Pontiac.

Pontiac's Golden Anniversary model lineup for 1976 included a new sporty sub-compact, the Sunbird, and a new top-of-the-line entry, the Bonneville Brougham. Usage of rectangular headlamps was expanded to include the intermediate LeMans, the Grand Prix and the new Sunbird. The new Pontiacs showed the positive results of Pontiac engineers' continuing efforts to improve fuel economy.

On October 1, 1975, Alex C. Mair was appointed general manager of Pontiac, succeeding Mr. Caserio, who became General Motors vice president and group executive in charge of the automotive components—electrical group. Mr. Mair had been general manager of the GMC Truck & Coach Division since 1972, and previously had been director of engineering for the Chevrolet Motor Division.

Pontiac's 1977 model lineup was headlined by the introduction of the completely-redesigned full-size cars, plus Pontiac's two new engines. Catalina, Bonneville, Bonneville Brougham, Catalina Safari and Grand Safari models all were redesigned—shorter and lighter than their predecessors, they continued to offer as much or more interior and luggage compartment space as earlier models. The new engines—a 2.5-litre (151 cid) cast-iron L-4 and a 4.9-litre (301 cid) V-8—were designed from the outset to provide improved durability and reliability as well as outstanding fuel economy.

Pontiac introduced a new car mid-year in 1977. The Phoenix was added to the Pontiac lineup as the top-of-the-line compact car. It joined the Pontiac Ventura as the only American compact cars to offer a four-cylinder engine. Among other features, the Phoenix offered the first U.S. headlamps completely designed under the metric measurement system.

Complete redesign of the mid-size LeMans and Grand LeMans and of the personal luxury Grand Prix, the return of the Grand Am and continuing engineering and fuel economy improvements were the highlights of Pontiac's 1978 model lineup. The LeMans, Grand LeMans an Grand Prix were all shorter and lighter than their predecessors, providing significant increases in fuel economy while retaining traditional levels of roominess and comfort. New front and rear design treatments and several new interior trims were offered in the 1978 full-size Pontiacs. The Grand Am was reintroduced with distinctive features that included a soft, flexible rubber front end panel. The Phoenix replaced the Ventura and the Sunbird replaced the Astre as Pontiac's compact and subcompact cars, respectively, for the 1978 model year.

In April, 1978, the completely remodernized manufacturing office building was dedicated. Occupying the new building are Industrial Engineering, Manufacturing Staff, Reliability Staff, Plant Engineering and Production Engineering.

Pontiac Motor Division sold more new cars—871,391—during the 1978 model year than in any previous model year in its history. Firebirds, led by the performance-oriented Trans-Am, continued to be among the most popular cars in the auto industry, setting an all-time model year sales record of 175,607. Pontiac's sporty little Sunbird also set a sales record.

The 1979 model lineup for Pontiac was highlighted by Firebird's new front and rear styling and a new "crossflow" cylinder head designed four-cylinder engine for the Sunbird for improved performance. The 1979 model year marked the first full year since the Thirties that Pontiac offered genuine wire wheels on certain models. Four wheel power disc

1984 6000 STE

Turbo-Injected OHC— 10,000th Experimental Engine

brakes were introduced as an option on Firebird Formula and Trans-Am models. The Grand Safari wagon was renamed the Bonneville Safari to more closely identify it with the Pontiac family of cars. The 400-cubic-inch V-8 was discontinued for all Catalina and Bonneville models in the division's efforts to increase its fuel economy average and help General Motors meet stringent federal fuel economy standards.

On November 6, 1978, Robert C Stempel became Pontiac general manager, succeeding Alex C. Mair who was named vice president and group executive in charge of the technical Staffs Group at the GM Technical Center in Warren, Michigan. Mr. Stempel was formerly Director of Engineering for Chevrolet Motor Division.

Pontiac introduced its first front-wheel-drive car in April, 1979, with a totally redesigned "efficiency-sized" Phoenix. Available in a two-door coupe and five-door hatchback sedan, the Phoenix lineup included the base car, a luxury LJ or a new sporty SJ option. A transverse-mounted 2.5-litre (151 cid) four-cylinder L-4 "crossflow" engine was standard in Phoenix with an optional 2.8-litre (173 cid) 60-degree transverse V-6 two-barrel engine available. The 1980 Phoenix was smaller and tightly packaged on the outside, but larger in many respects on the inside, compared to the 1979 Phoenix.

The remainder of Pontiac's 1980 model lineup, introduced in October, 1979, included major styling changes to full-size Pontiacs and a revised engine lineup for more fuel efficiency while maintaining good performance. A GM 4.9-litre (301 cid) four-barrel V-8 turbocharged engine, produced by Pontiac Motor Division, was introduced as an option federally for Firebird Trans-Am and Formula models and a GM 4.3-litre (265 cid) V-8 engine, also produced by Pontiac, was introduced as a down-sized version of the Pontiac-produced 4.9-litre (301 cid) V-8. A white Limited-Edition Pontiac Turbo Trans-Am was chosen as the Official Pace Car for the 64th running of the Indianapolis 500 race, May 25, 1980.

In August, 1980, William E. Hoglund, who had been comptroller of General Motors, returned to Pontiac as general manager, replacing Stempel who was appointed managing director for Adam Opel AG in Germany.

A major design change for Grand Prix and a new General Motors Computer Command Control system for all Pontiac carlines (except with diesel) to meet stricter 1981 emission standards highlighted Pontiac's 1981 product lineup. The '80 Sunbird was carried over through the end of the 1980 calendar year.

The '81½ Pontiac T1000 made its debut at the Chicago Auto Show in February. Targeted at the price-conscious family buyer in need of inexpensive entry level transportation, Pontiac T1000 models were available as a three-door or five-door hatchback.

Introduced in May, 1981, Pontiac's 1982 J2000 models were totally new, efficiently functional front-wheel-drive sub-compact cars. Built on a 101.2-inch wheelbase, the J2000 was available on a two-door coupe, four-door sedan, three-door hatchback or four-door station wagon. Standard powertrain for all J2000 models was a 1.8-litre (112 cid) L-4 two-barrel with a four-speed manual transaxle. Pontiac J2000 models were promoted as appealing to both traditional and the important "new values" buyers as a car that was functional but yet offered a blend of flair and excitement in the best Pontiac tradition.

Pontiac Motor Division produced over 700,000 four-cylinder engines during the 1981 model year. During the summer of 1981, the division opened a new engine facility, Plant 55, where it produced additional GM 2.5-litre four-cylinder engines. Pontiac was one of the first in the industry to use microwave measurement for accurately timing these engines built in the new plant. Other technological innovations used in the 712,000-square-foot, 200 million dollar plant, included a functional check that performed several tests, a signature analysis torque rate system and a computer Management Information System.

The world-famous Bonneville nameplate adorned a more fuel efficient luxury car in Pontiac's 1982 fall product introductions. The Pontiac-produced 1982 2.5-litre four-cylinder engine underwent major technological improvements, including elimination of the conventional carburetor, and offered improved driveability and fuel economy through advanced technology of electronic fuel injection (EFI).

All-new ultra-aerodynamic Firebirds and contemporary five-passenger front-wheel-drive Pontiac 6000 models joined the 1982 Pontiac lineup in January.

Available in three distinct models—the sporty Firebird coupe, the performance-oriented Trans-Am and the new sophisticated luxury S/E—each had its own specific identity. Firebird featured a 2.5-litre EFI engine, S/E had a 2.8-litre V-6 and the Trans-Am was powered by a 5.0-litre four-barrel V-8 engine; all models had a standard four-speed manual transmission. Extensive wind tunnel testing on the Firebird resulted in an excellent drag coefficient which made the car one of the most aerodynamic cars ever produced.

Although the Pontiac 6000 was based on the General Motors X-car platform and powertrain, it was a completely different car inside, outside and underneath with ride and handling characteristics that made it internationally competitive. Available in first level and LE series as a spacious four-door sedan or contemporary two-door coupe, the Pontiac 6000 was powered by a fuel-injected 2.5-litre four-cylinder engine with three-speed automatic transmission as standard equipment. The dramatic wedge shape of the 6000 was the result of many hours of aerodynamic tuning the surface, contour and detail, making the 6000 one of the most aerodynamic sedans available in America.

In April, 1982, Pontiac offered a new overhead cam (OHC), fuel-injected four-cylinder engine for its subcompact J2000 models with an automatic transmission. The OHC-fuel injection engine provided exceptional smoothness with a responsive, fuel efficient performance. A five-speed transmission was added for 1983.

The years 1983 and 1984 put Pontiac back on the performance map with cars like the STE based on the Pontiac 6000 and powered by a high-output V-6, the Trans-Am with aero-trim and high-output V-8 and the two-seat Fiero powered by the 2.5-litre Four. In 1984 the factory debuted engineering prototypes of the Fiero powered by SD-Four and turbocharged and normally-aspirated V-6 powerplants. Racing and high-performance activities once again established Pontiac as the leader in the marketplace.

CHIEF OF THE SHOW CARS

Pontiac's Strato Streak and Strato Star were top attractions of General Motors' dream car show of the Fifties

Heavy front end of the Strato Streak was considered pretty swoopy in 1954. This was considered an aerodynamic car!

The Strato Streak II was the forerunner of the popular Fifties four-door hardtop. Wheelbase of this 'biggie' checks out at 124 inches. Safety switches kept the doors from opening into the windstream when car was moving.

A chrome visor and frame integrate the tail lights and dual exhaust pipes. The vertical exhaust pipes were unique.

THE PONTIAC Strato Streak II, famous General Motors "dream car" featured at major automobile shows, is a four-passenger, four-door "spectator" sports car with no center pillar between the front and rear doors. The futuristic Strato Streak II was the forerunner of the Fifties four-door hardtop model cars.

Long and low, the Strato Streak's aerodynamic lines are emphasized by windsplits which start on the roof and carry down the rear deck and are flanked by vertical twin taillights in each rear fender to give a jet exhaust effect.

The car is 54.5 inches high, 214.3 inches long and 74.5 inches wide on a wheelbase of 124 inches. Modifications in the chassis and body design give passengers ample head and leg room, although the car is considerably lower than a production Pontiac. The body of this car is of fiberglass, finished in iridescent

The Strato Star in a typical show setting. The Star was debuted in 1955 and was powered by the new V-8 engine. Exterior was finished in Metallic Silver.

Flared fenders add to the streamlined look of the Strato Star. Custom wheels, not hubcaps, supply a stream of air to cool the brakes. This was the first of a series of genuine high-performance dream cars.

metallic red.

"In the Strato Streak we have designed a special purpose show car," R. M. Critchfield, Vice President of General Motors and General Manager of Pontiac Motor Division, said in 1955. "It is not being considered for mass production and sale at this time, but in designing and building this spectator sports car our engineers and stylists have experimented with new ideas and new methods which may well influence the features, the appearance and the production of all cars in the future."

Beginning with the panoramic, vertical-pillar windshield, the passenger compartment is virtually surrounded with glass. There is no center pillar between the doors, windshield and backlight pillars are as narrow as possible consistent with required strength, and the wide rear window is supplemented by quadrant-shaped rear sidelights.

Doors are hung from the front and from the rear on each side, with strength provided at the center by rigidity of the frame. The rear doors, since they open into the windstream, are equipped with special locks to prevent their being opened, except when the car is stopped and the Hydra-Matic gear selector in Neutral.

The body construction incorporates a set-back door sill, with the body metal extending down to the road clearance level, thus eliminating the necessity of stepping over the sill as in present cars.

The four seats in the car are bucket-type, upholstered in black patent leather and black and red intertwined nylon cloth. The two front seats swivel 90 degrees for ease of entry and exit. The passenger compartment is ventilated through twin cowl air intakes and elliptical air outlets above the backlight.

Instruments are recessed in nacelles on the panel below a built-in safety cushion, while the windshield wiper and washer controls, heater controls, cigar lighter and ashtray are located in the tunnel between the front seats. The radio is just forward of these controls, the glovebox behind them. In the rear, between the two seats, is a compartment large enough to easily accommodate camera, binoculars and other equipment that might be useful to spectators at sports events. There is also ample trunk space in the rear deck.

Pontiac's famous Silver Streak is carried along the crown of each front fender and the same motif is followed in the chrome-ribbed side vents in each front fender, which are functional in providing extra engine ventilation.

1955— THE START OF SOMETHING BIG

Chevrolet had its Nomad and Pontiac competed with a special two-door station wagon dubbed the Safari. This photo was taken prior to official intro and car is actually a pre-production pilot without Safari ID. Pontiac sold 3,760 units after its late-February 1955 dealer intro. Idea come from 1954 GM Motorama Nomad idea car.

Pontiac gets into the big leagues with a V-8 engine that's packed with performance potential

What could be sportier than a '55 Star Chief convertible with wire wheel hubcaps and wide whites? Pontiac sold 19,762 ragtops in 1955 model year.

THE ORIGINAL 1955 Pontiac V-8 engine was conventional in most respects. Its designers tapped the best features of all the industry's modern V-8's and added a few of their own. Original bore and stroke were 3¾ by 3¼ inches for a displacement of 287 cubic inches. Block and lower end rigidity were assured by using large, well-braced bulkheads at the five main bearings. The combination of the short stroke, with main and rod bearing diameters of 2½ and 2¼ inches respectively, gave a crankpin overlap of .76-inch and a stiff crankshaft. The short 6⅝-inch connecting rods also helped.

The heads had conventional wedge-type chambers giving a compression ratio of 8.00-to-1. The engine required 93-96 octane (Research) fuel to prevent detonation at full throttle. Valve diameters were 1.78 inches on the intakes and 1.50 inches on the exhausts. The valve gear was unusual in using the new ball-joint stamped rocker arms and light tubular pushrods, that were featured on Chevrolet's 265-inch engine. The very light reciprocating weight allows unusually high revs without valve float, with a given combination of lifter and valve spring pressure. The light weight and high column stiffness of a tubular pushrod means less bending and deflection in the valve gear at high rpm, so the motion of the valve more closely follows the motion imparted by the cam lobe. And, the simple height adjustment on the ball-joint rocker studs permits the plungers in the hydraulic lifters to be let out to the ends of their travel, so you can readily adjust hydraulic lifters to be solid lifters in operation. You can't do it with conventional rockers pivoting on a shaft.

The 1955 Pontiac engine also featured a special cooling layout that jetted water onto the inner combustion chamber walls, above the exhaust valves, from a steel tube inserted in the head. A high-capacity water pump put almost twice as much water through the heads as went through the radiator, thus maintaining more even temperature through the engine. All the block and head castings were designed with thin sections for light weight and much attention was given to reducing the numbers of cores needed in the foundry. The production design used only 16 cores for the block and both heads, about half the number used by most V-8 engines. However, the overall engine weight was not too light. The early engines weighed about 680 pounds with all accessories less flywheel. This was much less than the big Olds, Chrysler and Lincoln engines but was about 150 pounds heavier than the similar Chevrolet.

The 1955 engines were rated 180 hp at 4600 rpm with a two-barrel carburetor. It was just a starting point.

Chevrolet stole much of the thunder in 1955 with its new lightweight V-8, but Pontiac was right there with an extremely durable 287-incher that was begging for speed modifications.

During the early-Fifties Pontiac ragtops were the rage with customizers. This trophy-winning Star Chief had full length lakes pipes, chrome-reversed wheels with knock-off spinners and was lowered almost four inches closer to the ground.

TURBINE PROGRAM IGNITES THE FIREBIRD

Before the Firebird belonged to Pontiac,
it was part and parcel of General Motors'
experimental gas turbine project of the Fifties

The late Harley J. Earl, then GM's vice-president in charge of Styling, poses proudly with the Firebird I (1954), right, and the Firebird II (1956). The Firebird I was the first such car built in this country and the Firebird II was the first such vehicle capable of travel on the highway. Earl designed both cars.

The Firebird I was photographed at speed on an abandoned air strip in Arizona in 1955. Millions viewed this car as it was part of GM's show display which toured the U.S., Canada and Europe.

In 1956, GM introduced the Firebird II, an updated four-place version of the Firebird I. It was part of GM's overall concept of highway travel that would be ultra-safe and radar-controlled.

Lined up for acceleration runs on the air strip, the first gas-turbine-powered car built and tested in the U.S., looks more like a jet fighter than a car.

The Firebird II was the first gas turbine car actually suitable for use on conventional highways. Dialed into the radar-controlled highway system, the Firebird II boasted the first all-titanium body.

During GM's 50th anniversary, the Firebird I, Firebird II and the XP-500 (world's first free-piston-powered car, 1956) were part of the Forward From Fifty production.

1956—MOVING RIGHT ALONG!

A dual-quad high-performance engine option
signals Pontiac's direction for the future.

POCI's Len Sokol owns this immaculate '56 Safari. Pontiac built 4,042 Safari models including ten which were equipped with stick transmissions. Trim and paint scheme set this year off from its predecessor. Power change was the big news.

You couldn't get air conditioning when you ordered the 10.0-to-1 compression dual-quad engine. Even though engine package was designed for private parties who wanted to go racing, it offered excellent street performance.

Displacement went up to 317 cubic inches and with new power-package the rating soared to 285 hp. That was with dual-quads and solid-lifter camshaft and kit. Total production of 1956 Pontiacs hit 405,730 units.

For 1956 engine blocks were recored for a 3/16 inch larger bore to get 317 cubic inches. A mild street Power Pack was developed with 8.9-to-1 pistons, four-barrel carb, and a high-lift hydraulic cam with longer duration. It was rated 227 hp at 4,800 rpm and was available only with Hydra-Matic transmission. Also a special engine was developed for high-performance applications. It had dual four-barrel carbs on a new cast-iron manifold, 10-to-1 pistons and a hotter solid-lifter cam with slightly more lift. Pontiac rated the engine at 285 hp at 5,100 rpm. This engine proved to be quite potent on Daytona in the hands of professional racers, but it wasn't seen much on the drag strips.

Safari models like Len Sokol's are rare due to options, condition and because of low production and initial high price for the period. This is one of the finest in the country.

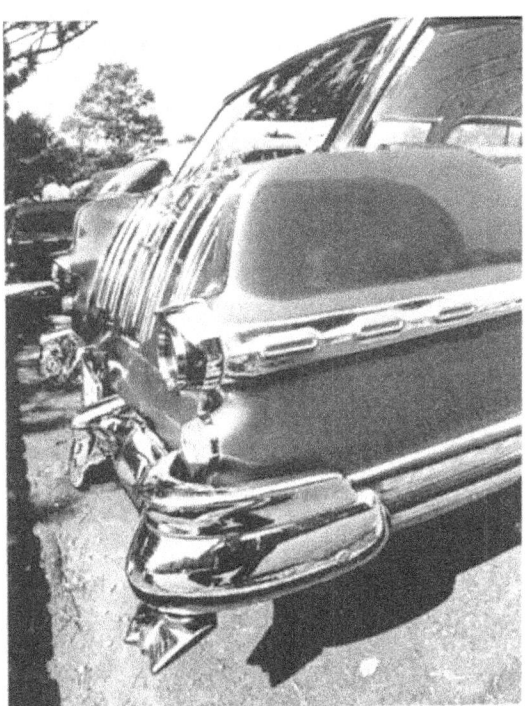

Safari was loaded with chrome trim and goodies, yet overall appearance is tasteful and attractive. License plate is to make sure no one confuses it with a Chevy Nomad!

PONTIAC CHALLENGES THE WORLD

An all-American sports car with aluminum body,
DeDion suspension and a dual-quad
V-8 puts the Chief in the big leagues

Finned ground-hugging sports car boasted the forerunner of the '61 Tempest powertrain along with a 317-inch V-8 rated at 305 hp with dual-quads. Concealed headlamps and grilless front end were quite advanced for the time. Remember, this was 1956!

SPORTS car fans the world over from Le Mans to Mexico have new cause for enthusiasm with the showing of Pontiac's Club de Mer at the auto show. That was Pontiac's pitch in 1956!

An experiment in simplified functional sports car design, the Club de Mer emerges as an exciting automotive pioneer following Pontiac's objective of combining engineering ruggedness with flashing performance. The most sophisticated sports car enthusiast will be thrilled with his first glance at the gleaming Cerulean Blue body of anodized brushed aluminum, and even the most casual automobile viewer will recognize the sweeping twin streaks which contour the hood and stamp it as a member of the famous Pontiac family.

Most striking feature of the two-passenger Club de Mer is the graceful dorsal fin which flashes up from and along the rear deck surface, and which serves not only to add fleetness to its appearance but which also serves practically as a stabilizing influence during operation. The passengers are protected from air by twin bubble windshields. These windshields are so uniquely designed as to deflect the wind up and over the occupants' heads, allowing riders better road vision position while maintaining the low, road-hugging design.

All of the flash of the Club de Mer is not on the exterior alone for this car features a transmission which is mounted behind the passengers and which connects with a DeDion type rear transaxle suspension. The transmission mounted in the rear thus affords much greater leg room for both driver and passenger. It was the forerunner of the '61 Pontiac Tempest powertrain.

The jet age influence is felt in the Club de Mer with the revolutionary design of the grilless front end. At the nose of the car is the air intake aperture for engine cooling which is a chrome-lined slot half engulfing the lower section of the front end. This practical styling innovation allows a long, fast design line from the leading edge of the nose to the trailing tip of the stabilizing fin on the rear deck.

One unique innovation in the front end styling is the exciting treatment of the headlamps, which brings both the highway and parking lamps together in a dual arrangement, one placed directly over the other. To complete the unique design, Pontiac engineers have arranged that the lamp units when not in use will revolve and disappear into the body leaving a completely smooth front surface.

The problem of moving excessive heat from the motor compartment, which often causes valuable loss of horsepower, was solved by Pontiac stylists by stationing heat outlet ports on the sides of the front fenders.

Lowness, which is always an important factor in cars of this design, is another feature of the Club de Mer for it stands only 38.4 inches high from the ground to the top of the windshield, while its length is 180.06 inches overall. Built on a 104-inch wheelbase, the car is powered with a 317-cubic-inch Pontiac Strato-Streak V-8 engine equipped with dual four-barrel carburetors which produces 305 horsepower.

Although definitely designed more for the masculine taste, the Club de Mer takes the back seat to no car in its aesthetic beauty. In addition to the startling Cerulean Blue body of aluminum, the interior is fashioned with an elegant Vermillion Red interior. Seats in the twin-style control cockpit are soft crush grain top leather, and the controls are literally at the driver's fingertips, for they are mounted in line at the forward end of the armrest in the door trim panel. Shifting level, ignition, radio and deck opening level are located on the drive tunnel between the seats.

The Club de Mer is probably one of the safest of its type ever built. It features a spring steel safety-type steering wheel, which is free of protrusions; the cockpit is specially rim-padded and all knobs are protected for assured safety. This scheme is carried even into the location of the instrumentation which is positioned directly in front of the driver so that shift of vision from the road to the instrument panel is minimized.

Mr. S.E. Knudsen, Vice President of General Motors and General Manager of Pontiac pointed out in discussing the Club de Mer in 1956 that it is unlikely the car would ever become a production model.

He said, "The Club de Mer was designed and built, however, to test certain engineering and design features which we, at Pontiac, would conceivably incorporate into our production models in the years to come. The popular four-door hardtop now adopted throughout the industry was originally introduced by Pontiac in our famous Strato Streak dream car at the 1954 GM Motorama.

"It is only through this constant searching for better things, and thinking always in terms of the future, that has enabled us to maintain the fine reputation which Pontiac has earned over its many successful years.

"Our styling experts have managed to design a magnificent competition-type sports car which, because of its exceptional beauty, color, and daring styling, we hope will be of extreme interest to every member of the family, no matter how casual their interest in sports cars," Mr. Knudsen said.

1957 – PONTIAC STANDS FOR PERFORMANCE

This is the kind of stuff that legends are made of

Pontiac sold 19,758 Star Chief Catalina sedans:(hardtops). mostly fitted with consumerish engines and powertrains.

Block used for 347-incher had oversize main bearings and a well-designed crank, so going racing was an easy job for the factory. For circuit racing Pontiac fitted the engines with tri-power and 10.0-to-1 pistons for a 317-hp rating.

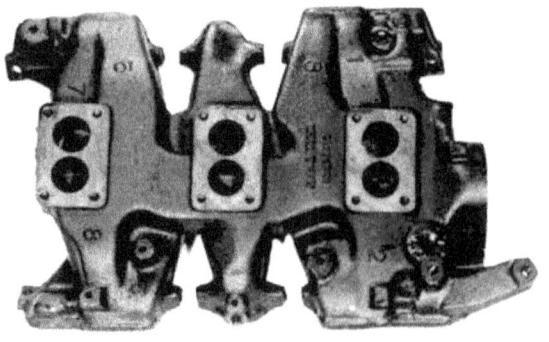

Not happy with the throttle response of the dual-quads on the street, Pontiac engineers came up with three-two barrels and the start of Pontiac's tri-power legend.

With a beefed 347-cubic-inch engine and tri-power induction, the Super Chief Catalina coupe was an instant hit with the street rodders. Production of this model hit 15,494.

PONTIAC started getting serious with the 1957 engines. The bore was kept the same but a new crankshaft was designed with 5/16-inch-longer stroke and 1/8-inch-larger main bearing journals to maintain the overlap rigidity and give more bearing area. Pontiac engineers have always believed in adding bearing area when they increased the displacement substantially. It's a key factor in the reputation the Pontiac engine has for rugged durability under high stresses. The 1957 displacement grew to 347 cubes. In addition the heads were redesigned, with .100-inch-larger intake and exhaust valves (1.88 and 1.60 inches for intakes and exhaust, respectively). Compression ratio was raised to 10-to-1 on the Power Pack engines. The single four-barrel version hit 270 hp at 4,800 rpm.

Pontiac engineers had never been happy with the response of their dual four-barrel system on the street. There was too much venturi area for low speeds with two barrels open on each end and, when they used a progressive throttle linkage that opened only the rear carb at low speeds, the mixture distribution was uneven, hurting response and pushing fuel consumption to the Twilight Zone.

They figured a better answer would be three two-barrel carburetors in line with progressive throttle linkage that opened just the center carb in normal driving. This would give the small venturi area and good mixture distribution needed for city driving and you would still have six barrels ready when you needed it. This was the start of the famous Tri-Power carburetion system. A vacuum throttle linkage was used, pushing the end barrels open by diaphragm force when the center throttles were about two-thirds open. It wasn't quite as responsive as some setups since the end barrels were either wide open or shut, but it was simple to build and tune. The standard Power Pack engine was rated 290 hp with Tri-Power.

For the 1957 racing engine they used the new triple carburetion, 10-to-1 pistons and the hot solid-lifter cam that would give maximum power in the 5,000-5,500 rpm range and be good for at least 6,000 before the valves floated. The engineers figured this kind of performance would be needed to stay competitive on the drag strips and NASCAR tracks, considering the supercharged Fords and fuel-injection Chevys. The valve train used new light mechanical lifters and dual valve springs. Pontiac engineers rated the package at 317 hp at 5,200 rpm.

It should also be mentioned that Pontiac Engineering started to develop the Rochester constant-flow fuel-injection system in 1957. A few were put out to selected dealers in 1957, and the system was listed as optional equipment on the '58 models. But just about the time the project was getting started NASCAR banned all superchargers, fuel injection and multiple carburetion in Grand National racing. That was it!

AMERICA'S ROAD CAR
Fuel injection helps put Pontiac in a class by itself!

Engine compartment of same car with Rochester fuel-injection unit hidden by air filter, housing and other plumbing. New fuelie unit was showcased by Pontiac in its Bonneville convertible and by Chevrolet in the Corvette and two-door sedan (passenger car).

Early factory Bonneville used by Pontiac for promotional purposes. The original buildout was set at 1,500 units for dealer distribution, but only 630 were produced according to most documentation.

Frontal area of '57 Bonneville is massive. They weren't interested in aerodynamics then!

This POCI member went one step beyond and chromed much of the fuel-injection equipment and engine accessories. Screened fresh air intake looks a lot better in chrome than basic black.

THE Pontiac Bonneville, a six-passenger sports convertible powered by a fuel-injection engine, was originally produced in limited quantities for promotional use by Pontiac dealers. The 347-cubic-inch Pontiac fuel-injection V-8 engine delivers over 300 horsepower.

From the massive chrome front bumpers to the louvered rear exhaust ports, the flashy Bonneville measures 215.5 inches. An exciting car-length Star Flight accent panel encases a long rear-fender blister molding that takes its aerodynamic styling from the twin-throat air intake of a jet plane. Ribbed anodized aluminum trim panels on the lower rear-quarter of the Bonneville, continue the flow of the Star Flight molding. Chromed louvers decorate the lower section of the front fenders. The body of the Bonneville is finished in acrylic lacquer. Its custom interior is upholstered in leather.

Production of the Bonneville sports convertibles started early in 1957. Pontiac scheduled its production of the fuel-injected Bonneville convertibles for dealer use only in order to gain valuable field experience with the new fuel injection system before making it available to the public. The Bonneville was available in limited quantity as Pontiac planed to produce only a small volume of the fuel injection engines in 1957.

"We are anxious to determine the performance of our new fuel-injection system under actual field conditions in all sections of the country," stated S.E. Knudsen, then GM Vice-President and General Manager of Pontiac Motor Division. "These engines have shown remarkable economy and performance on dynamometer and proving ground installations. By equipping the new Bonneville convertible with fuel-injection, we provide our dealers with a spectacular show car as well as an opportunity for their service personnel to gain experience with the revolutionary new injection engine before it becomes a standard production item."

BONNEVILLE— WHAT'S IN A NAME?

It all started in 1954 with a Motorama dream car which grew to become a marketing legend

This is the one that started it all in 1954. The Motorama Bonneville Special was fiberglass-bodied, sat 48½ inches high and had gull-wing-style top panels for super easy entry and exit. It was constructed on a 100-inch wheelbase chassis and measures 158.3 inches from bumper-to-bumper. Color is Metallic Red.

THE name "Bonneville" originated with Pontiac's 1954 dream car at the GM Motorama and was taken from the Bonneville Salt Flats in Utah with the permission of the State of Utah.

In June of 1956 a famous race driver, the late Ab Jenkins, broke all previous 24-hour stock car distance records in a 1956 Pontiac by racking up 2,841 miles at Bonneville Salt Flats. Averaging 126.02 mph for the first 100 miles, Jenkins topped the previous record by 219 miles.

Pontiac first introduced the Bonneville in 1957 as a limited-production convertible with a fuel injection engine and special exterior and interior trim as standard equipment. They were manufactured for primarily dealer use only and valuable experience was gained from their performance in all climate and weather conditions.

In 1958 Pontiac put two Bonnevilles into production as its top-of-the-line luxury series; a two-door hardtop sports coupe and a convertible. In 1959 the series was expanded to include two additional models; a superbly styled four-door Vista hardtop and a richly appointed four-door Safari that offered the ultimate in station wagon prestige.

In addition to having special interior styling features these models are distinctive with the Bonneville name plate in gold on the rear fenders, four simulated vents along the rear quarter panels, an attractive emblem on front door panels and special name plates for grille and deck lid featuring the name Bonneville in bold script.

Pontiac continued to use Bonneville as a designation for its top-line, full-size luxury car until the 1982 model year when the name was applied to the top-line mid-size LeMans—Bonneville-G.

The first Bonneville that could be bought was the '57 Bonneville convertible built in limited numbers for dealer promotional use. It showcased the first Pontiac fuel-injection engine. In 1958 the Bonneville was available in convertible and hardtop configurations.

The full-size Bonneville nameplate (and car) was phased out of production at the end of the 1981 model run. Starting in 1982 the Bonneville name was used for a top-line LeMans—Bonneville G.

1958— NO MORE NICE-GUY STUFF!

Pontiac has the most powerful engine on the NASCAR circuit and the makings of a street performance program second to none

The Bonneville became a regular model in 1958, available as a two-door hardtop or a ragtop. It was the first year for bucket seats and Pontiac sold 3,096 convertibles in the model year.

The two-door hardtop Bonneville configuration sold 9,144 units and was magnificently-appointed. Unlike Chevy's Impala, Bonnevilles could be equipped with fuel-injection. Few were, however.

In case you felt that your '58 Pontiac convertible was not long enough, the factory offered a Continental Kit option complete with custom pan, bumper extensions and status lettering.

FOR 1958 the Pontiac engine's bore was increased ⅛-inch, giving 370 cubic inches and compression was pushing to 10.5-to-1 on the top power options. Only a few months before, the AMA anti-racing resolution had put the hex on big factory racing teams. Instead of concentrating on all-out race track equipment there was more attention given to options that would improve street performance. Pontiac engineers designed a new high-rev hydraulic cam, Number 524886.

This cam has 283-degrees duration on the intakes and 293-degrees on the exhaust, with .402-inch lift. It gave a big increase in power and torque for the street without much sacrifice in idling and low-speed flexibility. This was also the year of the "ram-type" streamlined exhaust headers. These swept down to single outlets on each bank, and fed to dual exhaust pipes. The new cam and exhaust manifolds together gave a huge boost in street performance—more than was suggested by the conservative ratings.

For 1958 the standard Power Pack cam was rated 300 hp at 4,600 rpm with Tri-Power carburetion and 10.5-to-1 compression (with 310 hp on the fuel-injection engine). With the new high-performance cam and headers, they rated it a 315 hp at 4,800 rpm with single four-barrel and 330 hp with Tri-Power. (They also had 338 hp at 5,000 with fuel-injection.) These ratings weren't changed when the dealer-installed solid cam kit was used. This helped the cars in the stock classes on the drag strips, and of course the single four-barrel NASCAR cars had an unimpressive 315 hp painted on their hoods. But Smokey Yunick always claimed the 370-cubic-inch Pontiac was the most powerful engine on the racing circuit in the 1958 season, bar none. He could pull 320 horses at 5,100 rpm from the single four-barrel with no trouble at all on his dyno in Daytona Beach.

Photo of blueprinted '58 Pontiac engine block with four-bolt mains was taken at Pontiac Engineering on 3/5/58. It was one of many blocks turned out for testing at Daytona.

The status symbol on this '58 Bonneville coupe is the Fuel-Injection emblem on the lower right side of the trunk lid. A rare bird!

Dynamite Star Chief four-door wagon with tri-power provided the ideal package for the family man who wanted to travel fast. Pontiac built just 2,905 of these four-door cruisers.

Pontiac Engineering test engine fitted with prototype three Rochester two-Jet carburetion.

Fortunately, Pontiac only got involved with one of these Bonneville convertibles for a Hollywood cowboy star. Its only redeeming quality was its tri-power engine!

1959—WIDE TRACK CITY

Pontiac introduces a new level of styling, ride and performance,
and sets the standard for street power

A '59 Pontiac being buffed out at Pontiac's refinishing plant. Paint on '59 models was dried via three-stage bake ovens. Floor conveyors transported each car through 228 feet of ovens in approximately 10 minutes.

Interestingly enough, Pontiac's two-millionth engine was a tri-power high-performance 389 slated for an automatic transmission installation. New 389-incher was the hot setup in 1959 and for many years to come.

PONTIAC was into big internal engine changes in 1959. The stroke was increased 3/16-inch to 3¾ inches and Pontiac engineers once again followed their policy of increasing bearing area and maintaining crankpin overlap when the stroke is lengthened. Main bearing diameter was increased to a massive three inches! This was the largest figure in the history at the time and some of the experts were predicting bearing troubles due to the very high rubbing speed with three-inch journals turning 6,000 rpm. They felt Pontiac should have increased the length rather than the diameter of the bearings. But Pontiac engineers felt that crankshaft rigidity, obtained by the huge crankpin overlap with three-inch main journals, was more important than bearing rubbing speed. They further supplemented this rigidity by using four-bolt main bearing caps, which allowed the block bulkheads to contribute more to bearing stiffness. The factory engineers were proved right, too. No bearing trouble was encountered, and the 1959 and later Pontiac engines proved to be possibly the most reliable in the industry under racing stresses.

Another significant change on the 1959 engine was a switch to larger Rochester two-throat carbs for the Tri-Power carburetion. This increased total venturi area from the 6.65 square inches of the earlier Stromberg carbs to 7.82 square inches. The difference was felt in the breathing, especially above 4,000 rpm. Power ratings of the top engines on the new 389-cubic-inch block were raised 15 hp across the board. This gave 315 hp at 4,600 rpm for the standard Power Pack cam and Tri-Power. With the high-performance hydraulic cam and headers it's 330 hp at 4,800 rpm with single four-barrel, and 345 hp with Tri-Power. The Iskenderian E-2 cam kit was specified for racing, with 270-degrees duration and .420-inch lift. Ratings were not changed when the E-2 cam was used.

When it came to auto shows, Pontiac had a flair for the dramatic!.

Pre-production pilot Bonneville convertible photographed in Pontiac's styling studio. Note fluted grille divider panel.

This was the way to go street racing in 1959. Dynamite Star Chief two-door sedan had room for six adults, a trunk big enough for a spare engine and tri-power 389 power under the hood. Pontiac produced 10,254 two-door models in 1959.

THE 389 ARRIVES

Bunky Knudsen's twin-finned wide-trackers
take charge of the street scene,
boasting new tri-power 389 motors
plus Super-Duty groundshaking options.
And, Pontiac produces its seven-millionth vehicle

The people wanted fins and Pontiac gave them fins—and a lot more. More than 82,000 Bonnevilles were sold in 1959 and Pontiac boasted a 6.33-percent market penetration.

CAPSULE COMMENTS

PONTIAC and performance went hand in hand in the late Fifties and for 1959 the basic V-8 engine was stroked to bring the displacement to 389 cubic inches and the top compression engine still rated at 10.50-to-1. High-performance optional street engines as well as the race-bred versions have beefed blocks with four-bolt mains. Trick engines include the 330-hp single-four-barrel NASCAR and 345-hp Tri-Power drag engine, both fitted with Isky E-2 solid-lifter valve trains. Bob Pemberton's Air Lift Pontiac averaged over 140 mph on the Daytona sand course and, like five other top-running Pontiacs in that race, was disqualified for a very minor infraction. In the Air Lift case it was oversize tires on 15-inch wheels. A '59 Pontiac did cop the Standing Start One-Mile Race at 87 mph.

It was also a big year for NASCAR and Daytona, with the opening of new 2½-mile high-banked Speedway. Thanks to Smokey Yunick turning the wrenches and Fireball Roberts doing the driving, Pontiac became the car to beat. In practice Roberts ran over 145 mph and averaged over 140 mph for the first 125 miles of the race until a faulty fuel pump put him out of the running.

Performance certainly didn't hurt sales, as witnessed by Pontiac's leap from Sixth Place to Third Place in just three years.

Catalina was a big seller—over 230,000—and Plain Jane two-door sedan with new 389 tri-power mill was the hot setup for the street.

1959 PONTIAC HIGH-PERFORMANCE ENGINES

CUBIC INCHES	BORE	STROKE	HORSEPOWER	COMPRESSION	INDUCTION
389	4.06	3.75	280 @ 4400	10-to-1	Two-barrel
389	4.06	3.75	300 @ 4600	10-to-1	Four-barrel
389	4.06	3.75	315 @ 4600	10.5-to-1	Tri-power
389	4.06	3.75	330 @ 4800	10.5-to-1	Four-barrel
389	4.06	3.75	345 @ 4800	10.5-to-1	Tri-power

Downsizing was not one of the major issues in Motown in 1959. It was just fun in the sun!

Vacuum-operated tri-power checked out at up to 345 hp on 389-inch block and was the year's top status symbol.

THE ULTIMATE FIREBIRD

The first space-age-inspired car
from General Motors looked like something
out of Buck Rogers!

THE NAME "Firebird" has, since 1954, become a worldwide symbol of America's advanced automotive thinking. It has come to typify the ceaseless search by stylists and engineers for better ways to transport passengers on highways in greater safety and comfort.

A third car was added to the series in 1959. Like its predecessors, Firebird III was conceived by Harley J. Earl, General Motors Vice President in Charge of Styling and originator of the Dream Car to test advanced automotive ideas. Firebird III was the 37th experimental car since Mr. Earl's famed "Y-Job" began GM's dream car parade in 1936.

In designing Firebird III, Mr. Earl had these objectives:

1. Continue the Firebird tradition of reporting to the public the newest ideas of GM's Technical Center designers.

2. Create a car to demonstrate the important future possibilities offered by GM Research Laboratories' dramatic Unicontrol, Autoguide and Cruisecontrol electronic control systems.

3. Design a car expressive of the thinking of our time: space, science, technology. Go a step beyond the aircraft influences of the previous two Firebirds and draw on the new technology of missiles for inspiration.

"Our attempt in Firebird III was to envision the car which a person may drive to the launching site of a rocket to the moon," explained Mr. Earl. "This concept is not only timely; it matches the car's electronic guidance system which is as thrilling to ground transportation as long-range missiles are to space travel."

Mr. Earl pointed out that the mechanical layout of the car, compartmented in three major sections, resembles a rocket internally, as does the exterior design. However, the arrangement of components is based on sound engineering considerations which make it an outstanding vehicle for the highway as well as the test track.

"On a project of this sort, our function at GM Styling is not merely the embellishment of exterior shapes, but the integration of function and form into a single dramatic design. The shape of Firebird III would mean little without the advanced devices beneath her skin, and vice versa."

Briefly, the three sections carry out their functions as follows:

1. At the front is the *nose compartment* housing the auxiliary 10-horsepower aluminum engine and the many accessories which it powers.

At speed at the Mesa, Arizona, GM Proving Grounds, the Firebird III offered room for two and an automatic guidance system that was certainly revolutionary for 1959. It was the first car designed around a single stick control system which did away with hand and foot controls.

The Firebird III at its birthplace, the GM Tech Center in Warren, Michigan. The radical machine sits just 44.8 inches high at the top of the clean plexi canopies and 57 inches high at the tail. A total of seven fins serves as aerodynamic stabilizers. A rear-mounted Whirlfire gas turbine engine supplies the punch. It was debuted at the GM Motorama of 1959 in New York City.

2. In the center, is *passenger capsule* which seeks in a carefully budgeted space to package two passengers in unparalleled comfort to enjoy the new driving ease afforded them by electronic controls.

3. In the rear portion of the car is the *power compartment* which houses the 225-horsepower Whirlfire gas turbine engine, transmission and other components which propel the car.

"The Unicontrol stick and its elimination of the conventional steering wheel, dashboard and foot pedals opened up a whole new area for the designer," Earl said. "This car illustrates as never before the vital teamwork necessary between stylist and scientist in modern automobile design. There would have been no Firebird III without the skill and imagination of Dr. Lawnrece R. Hafstad and his General Motors Research Laboratories."

Firebird I, introduced in 1954, had its emphasis upon power. It was the first gas turbine passenger car built and tested in the United States.

Firebird II, announced in late-1955, featured highly improved gas turbine design, but had its emphasis upon suspension and chassis—the packaging of the passengers and making them comfortable. It also looked forward to an automatically controlled "Highway Of Tomorrow."

Firebird III introduces improvements in both gas turbine power and passenger comfort, but it incorporates an area scarcely dreamed of when the first Firebird was completed—electronic guidance. It, then, is essentially an *experiment in control.*

"This rapid progress in the Firebird partment satisfies the requirements of efficient operation, as well as the designer's concept of a sleek aerodynamic skin wrapped tightly over the muscles, nerves and brain of the vehicle. Firebird III is a wedding of controlled power and electronic advances with every possible human comfort. It opens new areas of driving pleasure.

In the interest of clarity, it is best to group the styling features of this, the latest of the Firebirds, into two family only goes to show that no one can be sure what will happen to automobiles in even a few years, much less tell you what cars of 25 years from now will be like," Mr. Earl said. "Even as Firebird III goes on display, the creative men and women of General Motors are thinking of improvements for some of its most advanced features."

Firebird III is the first automobile ever designed around a single stick-control system. Taking advantage of the unparalleled driving ease offered by Unicontrol, the device which unifies steering, throttle, and brake into a single fingertip control, GM Styling fashioned a passenger compartment which is an advanced experiment in human engineering. This is the heart of the car.

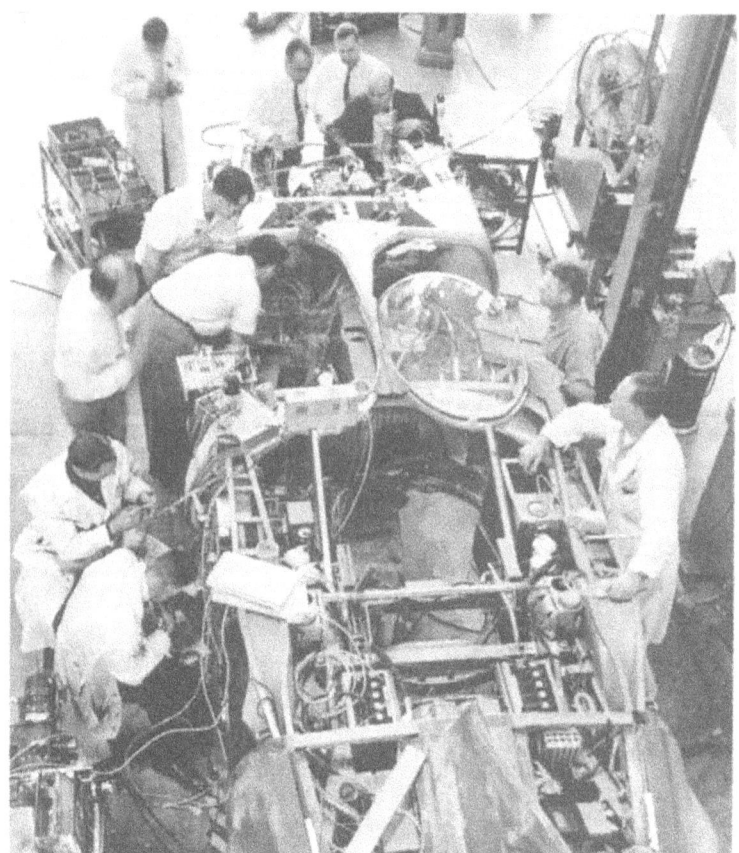

Under construction at the Tech Center, it's hard to tell if the Firebird III is a car or a jet plane!. At the rear is Lawrence R. Hafstad, GM vice-president Research and some of the more than 500 technicians involved in the project.

GENERAL BODY DESIGN

From a wide, extremely flat nose, the body tapers rearward, expanding just enough to clear the front wheels, whose sides are exposed. It then wraps gracefully and compactly around the passenger compartment. Here, twin bubbles sweep over the heads of the two passengers reclining in the lounge-type seats. Flowing on to the rear, the skin expands to its widest section as it envelops the main engine, electronics compartment and fuel tanks. At each side of the body, large scoops direct air into the turbine. As the body encompasses the rear wheels, it is molded into a pair of outward slanting fins, while the rear deck begins to sweep down toward a wide, but slim trailing edge. A large dorsal fin, complemented by two smaller horizontal stabilizers, provides the termination of the air piercing shape.

The underside of the car, which is fully enclosed, also sweeps rearward in a graceful, shallow arc, distorting only around the rear wheels, where narrow fin-shaped air deflectors balance the daring shapes above.

In the tail of the body airfoil, a set of jawlike drag brakes opens to disturb the airflow when desired.

From the sleek nose, through bubble canopy, to the cluster of fins, Firebird III embodies General Motors' latest technical advances into a shape, which, like a missile, shows a deep respect for the medium it is designed to penetrate. For maximum access, all body panels are removable, showing also the designer's respect for the mechanism he is working with.

The body skins are handcrafted fiberglass reinforced plastic, finished mirror-smooth in *"Lunar Sand,"* in GM's new Magic Mirror acrylic lacquer. The flowing forms are proportioned to contrast against the textures of the flexible vinyl bumpers, tires striped in white and gold and the aluminum of the "Turb-Al" wheel-brake units.

Additional contrast is gained in the crystal clear, aluminum vapor coated canopies with the strong *"Crater Red"* of the plastic molded interior striking a sharp note. The red is rhythmically repeated in glimpses as the drag brakes open.

Bright metal trim in all cases is the byproduct of the existing natural protective finishes on equipment and structural components. Other touches of color are provided by medallions on the tail fin and in the wheel centers, the name Firebird III in red letters on the rear body side, and the red of taillight lenses on trailing edge lights. Prominently located on the front hood is the multicolored Firebird emblem, capturing the spirit of the car as well as the Indian origin of the name.

Although not styling items in themselves, the mechanical components have a great influence on the final shape of the car.

1. *Nose Section*—Inside the tapered nose are the auxiliary engine and the accessories it powers. Fresh air is taken into the nose inlet and fed through the cockpit air conditioning unit which surrounds the accessory-drive engine.

Retractable guidance coils are positioned in the front of the stainless steel belly pan. Front hood access is provided by two power-operated panels. The main hood panel opens like an alligator's jaw. It pivots at the rear and is held in place by a smaller panel which is hinged at the nose and clamps down tightly. In sequence of operation, the small panel opens first, allowing the main panel to be raised.

2. Located directly behind the passengers, the *main power compartment* houses the Whirlfire regenerative gas turbine engine and transmission assembly.

One access panel immediately behind the passenger compartment opens rearward to reveal the gas turbine engine. It incorporates a polished aluminum underside to reflect engine heat. A pair of rectangular openings allows engine-mounted exhaust stacks to protrude. Another panel hinged on the same axis as the gas turbine panel folds forward to reveal batteries, rear suspension and turbine oil cooler. These two power-operated panels can be completely removed, leaving the entire upper rear portion of the car exposed for service.

3. *Electronic Nerve Center*—One of the highlights of Firebird III is the electronic nerve center, a compartment which brings together in a single spot nearly all of the electronic controls of the car. Located immediately forward of the left rear wheel, the color coded electronic components are easily serviceable through a hinged access panel. On the right a dual fuel tank fills the equivalent space.

TECHNICAL EXTERIOR BODY DESIGN

1. *Fins*—Besides adding a feeling of sweep and thrust to the aesthetic design of the car, the seven fins of Firebird III perform a true aerodynamic function—high-speed stabilization. The designers positioned the fins (which become more important with increased streamlining) by

utilizing information gained in wind tunnel tests on Firebird I conducted in 1954 at the California Institute of Technology.

Styling engineers explain that if a sudden crosswind would hit the Firebird and it did not have stabilizers, it would tend to push the nose off course. The fins, particularly the dorsal fin, on the rear of the car tend to counteract this force. They keep the vehicle from yawing. Below the dorsal fin are two lateral fins extending out on either side of the rear of the body at a very slight downward angle. These fins help control air flow around the bottom rear of the car. Farther forward a pair of fins directly above the wheels guide the air along the top of the body controlling lift and exhaust gas flow. Two fin-shaped deflectors directly forward of the rear wheels serve to guide air flow along the side of the body and into the Turb-AI brakes.

The effect of these fins on air flow around the body was checked on full size test in the General Motors Technical Center wind tunnel.

2. *Drag Brakes*—On either side of the dorsal fin two rear hinged drag brakes open upward and into the wind stream. A single drag brake drops downward across the bottom of the car. These brakes open automatically whenever the driver slows the car and is exceeding city speeds. (The vehicle speed below which they remain closed can be regulated.) Captured air passes out through a narrow slot across the rear of the car. The brakes provide cooling air for the built-in hill retarder as well as aerodynamically slowing the car.

3. *Lighting System*—The lighting system is automatically controlled by photo-electric cells molded into small body panels at each side of the bubbles. The cells are regulated to measure real daylight and will not be activated by momentary changes in light, such as shadows passing over the car. A cold cathode light tube extends across the inside of the car's nose (there is no front grille). A series of horizontal polished aluminum slats project an even path of low-beam light in front of the car. Small, high-beam spotlights at either end of the tube provide long distance lighting on the open highway. White parking lights are molded into the body at each side of the nose.

The trailing edges of the upper lateral fins incorporate directional signals and brake lights. Imbedded in the recessed air exhaust slot extending across the rear of the car are red taillights which grow brighter as the drag brakes open. There is also a red safety light at the rear which flashes to warn approaching traffic when the car is decelerated suddenly. The back-up lights are also located in this rear exhaust slot. As a safety feature, they are on at any time the other car lights are on. This both identifies the car's presence to a driver approaching from the rear and also gives the approaching driver a better night view of the road ahead of him.

4. *Doors*—One of the most striking features of Firebird III's design is the shape and motion of its doors. The absence of a steering wheel in Firebird III made possible a new freedom of door design which allows unparalleled ease of access for passengers of such a low car. The doors are gull-wing in design and open diagonally upward to within four inches of each other over the center of the passenger compartment.

The doors literally wrap around the passengers. Each begins at the center of the car by including a portion of the bubble canopy, continues down over the seat and extends partially under the bottom of the body.

Each door is mounted on a single power operated hinge located at the center of the car just forward of the passenger compartment. On cue from a special *sonic key* which is operated from outside the car or on signal from switches inside the passenger compartment, the hinge electrically raises the gull-wing door upward and forward in a single motion. The sonic key much resembles a fountain pen and operates the door at a distance of 10 to 15 feet by emitting a signal far beyond the range of the human ear. Once open, the door exposes the entire seat and allows the passenger to sit down comfortably as he would into a lawn chair with no worries about ducking his head to avoid hitting a stationary roof.

Because each door moves forward and upward when opening, the door when fully open extends only four inches outside the widest point of its side of the car. This minimizes the danger of the door being struck by another vehicle while open and also offers rain protection to the passenger compartment.

There are no metallic locks on Firebird III's doors. Instead, the entire door-canopy is locked and sealed with air inflated rubber seals. Thus the door is completely suspended in rubber, giving complete weather and dust seal, plus eliminating the possibility of rattles and squeaks.

5. *Canopies*—A separate laminated plastic bubble waps around each passenger's head, giving him a full panoramic view. A highly reflective surface of vacuum-applied aluminum turns back the sun's rays but allows occupants to see out. The aluminum is thickest just above the passenger's head and grows gradually thinner as it extends downward to the rear. There is no coating applied to the forward portion of the bubble.

The door cut travels over the passenger's head from the center of the car diagonally toward the rear of the seat. The aft portion of each canopy is fixed to the body, while the front half swings with the door.

THE PASSENGER COMPARTMENT

The passenger compartment of Firebird III was designed to take advantage of the unique control features incorporated in the car. Unicontrol, which eliminates the steering wheel, brake and accelerator pedals, is combined with automatic guidance and speed control. Electronically adjusted air conditioning compensates for the outside weather without requiring help from the driver.

Designed around human comfort, twin seats offer a new approach to passenger accommodation. Fully-contoured lounge-type seats support the body from toe to head and side to side. Medical evidence indicates that seating fatigue is primarily due to concentration of pressure points. The new contour of the Firebird III seat alleviates this condition, as well as minimizing body sway during

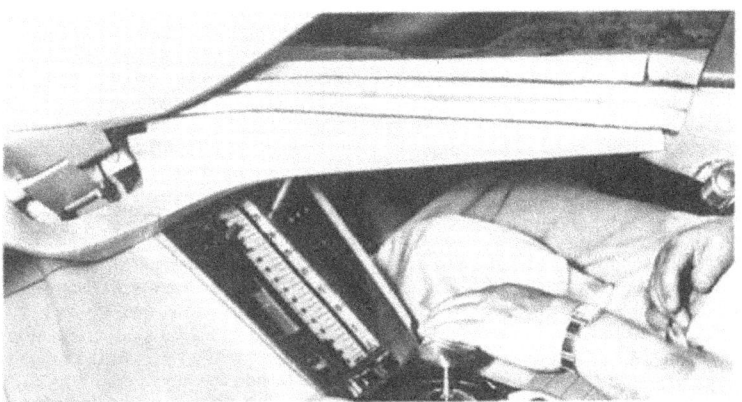

Unicontrol stick is located between the seats and operates at fingertip pressure from either passenger. There is no single driver as the center-mounted stick controls acceleration by moving it forward and pulling back to apply the brakes. Deflecting it to the right or left steers it in the desired direction. It's that simple.

The electronic nerve center of the Firebird III is located immediately forward of the left rear wheel. Color-coded electronic components are easily serviced through a hinged access panel. On the right side of the car a dual fuel tank fills the equivalent space.

cornering. Power-operated footrests and headrests complete the full length comfort of the seat. The headrest automatically retracts when the transmission is put into reverse. The seat itself is formed of vacuum molded plastic enclosing specially compounded foam rubber cushions supported by a molded fiber glass underform. The center section of the seat is pleated to allow comfortable deflections from the body and also to allow air to circulate. Circulation can be augmented by a built-in blower.

In keeping with the Firebird III's emphasis on driving ease, all essential controls are placed in between the seats so as to be at the fingertips of either passenger.

The Firebird is controlled manually by means of a wing-shaped handle which cradles the driver's fingertips. The shape of this handle allows maximum "feel" of the unique control system. The forearm of the driver is supported by an armrest. This handle is mounted on a four-inch stem which extends upward from a brightly polished metal globe set in a dark-grey metal panel. The handle is pushed forward to accelerate, drawn back to slow down, tilted left to turn left, and right to turn right. A 20-degree rotation of the handle puts the car in reverse, while a rotation of 80 degrees provides the park position. A small squeeze button at the front of the unit applies the retarder and drag brakes.

Gray in color and slanted for best visibility, the instrument panel presents necessary information in simplified form. A broad, orange tape moves up the middle of the panel in thermometer fushion as the speed of the car increases. A similar though narrower red indicator immediately to the right of the speedometer portrays the Whirlfire turbine speed. To the left of this central unit is a smaller gauge showing fuel level by means of a blue tape. As a precautionary feature, the small "fuel" indicator above the gauge alerts the driver by turning red when the fuel supply is dangerously low.

An electric *clock-timer* located at the upper left of the instrument panel can be set to automatically start the auxiliary power unit. This in turn preconditions the cockpit to the regulated temperature. If the driver has not inserted the key at the end of half an hour, the auxiliary power unit automatically shuts off.

An odometer set in the lower left of the panel can be used either to measure the miles traveled or miles left to go to a certain destination. (A counter which records the total mileage is located in the electronics area.) Complementing the fuel gauge, the right side of the panel holds a 13 element tell-tale warning light. When the complete warning panel is dark, the car is functioning perfectly and the driver is not bothered with reading a variety of instruments. (A button below the warning panel allows the driver to instantly check the circuits.)

Simplified starting is accomplished by inserting the sonic key at the upper right of the instrument panel. The first part of its travel starts all the electronics of the car; pushing it farther fires up both engines. Engines may be started and stopped independently by means of push-buttons beside the key.

Across the bottom of the instrument panel are three switches which take the car from manual to automatic control. Reading from left to right, they are: "Speed," "Manual" and "Direction."

Their functions are as follows:
a. *Manual* — When this switch is pushed in, the car is completely under the control of the driver through the Unicontrol stick.
b. *Speed* — When this button is pushed in, the car has *Cruisecontrol* and the speed of the car automatically is regulated at the position indicated by a pointer on the speedometer. (This pointer normally functions as a safety speed minder.) Now the stick merely steers the car.
c. *Direction* — When this button is pushed halfway down, the guidance coils are lowered. When a signal is being received from the wire in the center of the road, the "Direction" button lights up.

When the button lights up, it can be pushed to its second position, which completely engages the electronic guidance system of *Autoguide* and removes the steering function from the Unicontrol stick.

It is important to note the wide range of control Firebird III provides its driver. It employs three different systems and he can shift instantly with push-buttons back and forth between these different combinations:

a. He can manually control the entire car with one hand through Unicontrol.
b. He can give up speed regulation to Cruisecontrol and retain the steering.
c. He can give up steering to Autoguide and use the stick for throttle and brake.
d. He can put the car under completely electronic control through Autoguide and Cruisecontrol together, leaving his hands free, just as an airplane can be completely controlled by an automatic pilot.

Because Firebird III was designed as a show car as well as an experimental vehicle, special provisions were made for putting it through as many of its paces as possible while appearing at shows. A special remote control unit is placed in the rear of the car. It receives signals from a small radio transmitter carried by a lecturer. He may stand at a considerable distance from the car and each time he pushes a button in his control device the Firebird III will go through another of 16 different functions which are preset in any series he wishes. The panels which provide access for service also prove valuable for show purposes. A color scheme has been chosen which uses a variety of bright colors to identify the various units when the car's skins are opened or removed. This allows the general public to see a maximum number of the features that make Firebird III the most advanced automobile of its era.

1960

Cleaner styling highlights the '60 Pontiac Catalina and sales checked out at over 210,000. Top production option is 425-A tri-power 389. Super-Duty parts and pieces raise output to 363 hp.

THE CLEAN AND MEAN APPROACH

Pontiac cleans up its act with super-sano sheetmetal and engine options to keep everyone happy

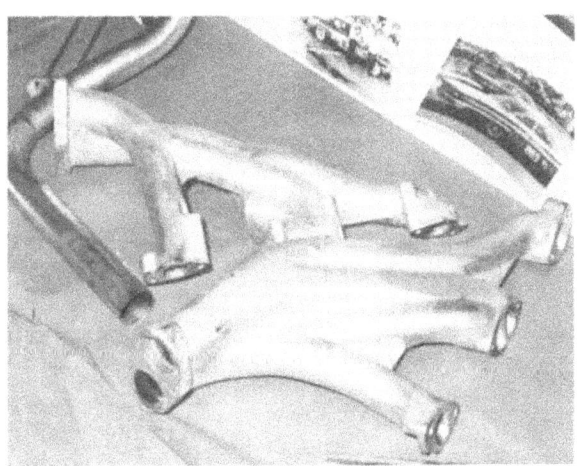

Pontiac offered cast tuned headers for use on Super-Duty 389 and later 421.

CAPSULE COMMENTS

WITH AMA's anti-racing hype behind them, Pontiac engineers concentrated on upgrading the performance options for 1960.

The top competition package for 1960 comes with special big-port heads, high-lift rockers, 11-to-1 forged aluminum pistons, header-style exhaust manifolds with split-flow and dual outlets, Malcom McKellar's Number 7 cam and a matching high-rev valve train. With a single four-barrel it's rated at 348 hp and, with Tri-Power, 363 hp.

For efficient use of the new engine goodies, the chassis/suspension options were beefed to include a wide selection of HD springs, shock absorbers, hubs, wheels, limited-slip rears plus truly off-road steering system parts. By checking the right order box in 1960, you can order any model with Borg-Warner's smooth-shifting T-10 four-speed complete with neat floor shifter.

Mix and match are the key words and you can have just about any combination of performance and road equipment, including super bucket seats and dynamite aluminum wheels with super brakes. Bunky Knudsen believes that Pontiac should offer a model and option for every possible taste. And, Pontiac did just that.

Fireball Roberts shocked the NASCAR boys with his over-150-mph '60 racer and Pontiacs all over the country are doing a lot of winning on the shorter tracks. And, at the NHRA Nationals Jim Wangers cleaned house with his four-speed Super/Stock eliminator from Royal Pontiac. It's a 363-hp stocker that ran 102.04 mph in 14.14 seconds. He took Class as well as Eliminator honors.

1960 PONTIAC HIGH-PERFORMANCE ENGINES

CUBIC INCHES	BORE	STROKE	HORSEPOWER	COMPRESSION	INDUCTION
389	4.06	3.75	283 @ 4400	10.25-to-1	Two-barrel
389	4.06	3.75	303 @ 4600	10.25-to-1	Four-barrel
389	4.06	3.75	318 @ 4600	10.75-to-1	Tri-power

Jim Wangers ran 102.04 mph in 14.14 seconds with the Royal S/S and cleaned house at the NHRA Nationals.

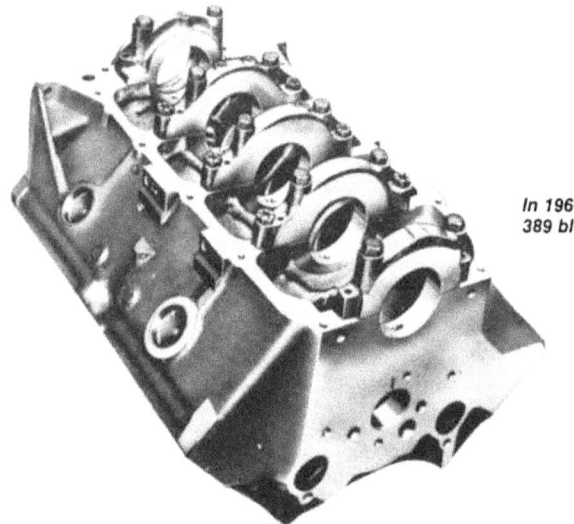

In 1960 you could order a four-bolt-main 389 block under the Super-Duty listing.

1961

WIDE-TRACKING TO THE TOP!

It's a milestone sales and styling year for Pontiac and the high-performance engine beat goes on

CAPSULE COMMENTS

THERE is little doubt that Pontiac has the most extensive performance development program in the industry today. Apparently it's selling cars; but the inevitable result is that there is a lot of special Pontiac performance equipment you cannot order on a new car coming off the assembly line. The low-production volume makes it impractical to stock the parts for assembly-line installation.

Right now the hottest Pontiac engine option that may be ordered on a new car is the Trophy 425A engine. One version has a single-four-barrel and rates 333 horsepower at 4,800 rpm, while the other has tri-power and 348 horsepower at the same speed. Both have 10.75-to-1 compression, long-duration hydraulic cam, tight valve springs and lifters, special ignition, free-flow exhaust headers, forged crank and four-bolt main bearing caps. And the Tri-Power has an aluminum intake manifold. Both of these engines can be readily tuned to put out their advertised horsepower at the clutch, so they're in good shape in the new NHRA stock-car drag strip classes—as the ratings are low enough so many models fall in the A and B/ Stock. Option prices are 134 dollars for the four-barrel engine and 168 dollars for the

Pontiac built more than 69,000 Bonnevilles in 1961. It's really hard to beat a 348-hp tri-power 389 convertible wih factory alloy wheels

1961 PONTIAC HIGH-PERFORMANCE ENGINES

CUBIC INCHES	BORE	STROKE	HORSEPOWER	COMPRESSION	INDUCTION
389	4.06	3.75	267 @ 4200	10.25-to-1	Two-barrel
389	4.06	3.75	287 @ 4400	10.25-to-1	Four-barrel
389	4.06	3.75	333 @ 4800	10.75-to-1	Four-barrel
389	4.06	3.75	348 @ 4800	10.75-to-1	Tri-power
421	4.09	4.00	405 @ 5600	11.0-to-1	Dual-quad

Carol Cox ran 105.63 mph in 13.80 seconds to take S/SA honors at 1961 Indy Nationals. Ventura is powered by a 389 Super-Duty engine.

Powered by a dual-quad 421 engine, this trick coupe lines up against a hot Ramcharger at Richmond, Virginia, drag strip.

The author's '61 Bonneville, powered by a 348-hp motor, was a Project Car for CARS Magazine during the early-Sixties.

New Tempest with flexible drive train boosted Pontiac's sales picture by over 100,000 units. This is the full-dressed LeMans model.

Tri-Power, and you can get the engines with three-speed, four-speed or Hydra-Matic transmissions and with a wide variety of ratios with/without limited-slip differentials.

But this is only the beginning of the Pontiac performance option story. Over the counter you can get special big-valve cylinder heads with high-lift rockers, several new camshaft grinds for mechanical lifters, special valve springs and keepers, forged pistons, heavy-duty oil pump and high-capacity pan, special aluminum intake manifold for a huge Carter four-barrel, special dual-outlet headers with alternate-firing cylinders paired on each side, special parts for pinning the rocker studs in the heads, etc. There are even "optional" parts in the books that we don't know the status of yet—like special aluminum exhaust headers, bumpers and radiator.

Smokey Yunick was prevented by NASCAR officials from using a new carburetor and radiator at Daytona because they weren't listed in the official spec sheets! So all this special stuff will be a headache for technical inspectors around the drag strips. Time will tell how it works out. It can be said with some certainty, though, that it would cost a miniumum of 1,200 dollars for parts alone to build up a real all-out '61 Pontiac racing engine with all the goodies. This is above the cost of the basic engine! But you will at least have a horsepower rating to call your own; factory engineers reached into the blue and pulled down the figure of 368 horsepower at 5,600 rpm . . . which is what you can claim for your all-out Pontiac engine that will put out close to 400 *horses* if you do a half-way decent job of setting it up!

1962

THE YEAR OF THE SUPER-DUTY

Pontiac's new Grand Prix steals the specialty car scene while Super-Duty 421 engines rule the racing roost. And General Motors builds its 75-millionth vehicle, a '62 Pontiac Bonneville convertible!

Classic Grand Prix started a whole new market segment and sold over 30,000 in first model year. Only 3,639 were manual transmission models. With 421-inch engine it was a luxury killer car.

CAPSULE COMMENTS

PONTIAC people are going to continue right into 1962 with the most extensive performance program in the industry. One continues to wonder how a relatively low-volume company can afford to spend this much on a limited segment of the market. But they show no signs of letting up. It's quite obvious that Pontiac's new performance "image" is selling a lot of cars in *all* segments of the market. Just as Pontiac manager Knudsen said: "You can't sell an old man's car to a young man; but you can sell a young man's car to an old man." The theory seems to be working.

Leading Pontiac's list of new '62 performance equipment is a new four-inch stroke forged crankshaft. This is used with a 1/32-inch overbore on the standard block to get a whopping 421 inches! (And you can legally bore this another .060 in., according to NHRA rules, to get 433 inches! This is what Hayden Proffitt had in the Thompson Pontiac.) Then they have a brand new aluminum manifold to mount two big Carter four-barrels—plus a new McKellar No. 11 cam with longer duration and more lift. Various other beef-up parts include stronger bearings, a heavy-duty oil pump and an eight-quart oil pan. Last year's big port heads, with 1.92-inch intakes and 1.66-inch exhaust valves, are continued unchanged. With all these changes

1962 PONTIAC HIGH-PERFORMANCE ENGINES

CUBIC INCHES	BORE	STROKE	HORSEPOWER	COMPRESSION	INDUCTION
389	4.06	3.75	305 @ 4600	10.25-to-1	Four-barrel
389	4.06	3.75	318 @ 4600	10.75-to-1	Tri-power
389	4.06	3.75	333 @ 4800	10.75-to-1	Four-barrel
389	4.06	3.75	348 @ 4800	10.75-to-1	Tri-power
389	4.06	3.75	385 @ 5200	10.75-to-1	Four-barrel
421	4.09	4.00	405 @ 5600	11.0-to-1	Dual-quad

Pontiac has only boosted the official horsepower rating from 368 to 373! The Pontiac people have always been very conservative on power ratings; they believe in letting performance speak for itself ... and it certainly has a foghorn voice in their case!

It should be pointed out right here that none of the new equipment listed above will be available on new Pontiacs coming off the assembly line. This is another area where the Ponchos play it cool. They realize that a true high-performance engine is bound to be a continual service headache. They would rather sell much cooler engines to the public—and then keep the hot parts on a shelf where the boy who is really interested can come and buy them, and install the stuff himself. This plan has worked real well for Pontiac. The special equipment still gets into the hands of the capable racers who know how to use it and maintain it—so Pontiacs continue to win on the race tracks and drag strips. The hottest engine you can buy on a '62 off the line is the Tri-Power 348 horsepower Trophy job with hydraulic lifters.

That's how Pontiac stacks up for 1962. Right now, in the light of Indy results, it looks like the car to beat.

Briggs Cunningham built a very special GP in 1962. Weber-carbed 421 engine is Latham-blown yet still surrounded by air conditioning and power steering hardware.

Super-nice street machine is powered by 405-hp dual-quad 421 and was a low-priced choice back in 1962.

Millie and Don Von campaigned this 405-hp Grand Prix sponsored by the late Les Ritchey's Performance Associates in Glendora, California.

THE SUPER-DUTY SAGA

By Roger Huntington

Our man in Motown was there when Pontiac Chief Bunkie Knudson and chief engineer (and now GM President) Pete Estes decided to blitz the youth market with the now-legendary 421-inch powerhouse. This is how it went

Talk about the good old days! That's Jim Wangers, left, and Frank Rediker and their Royal Pontiac Super-Duty car. This photo was taken just before Wangers left for the Winternationals. He won the B/FX class at the 1963 NHRA Nationals. The drag strip version of the SD engine used two Carter AFB pots on a big-port alloy manifold and developed over 500 hp after blueprinting.

MANY OF OUR younger readers who were weaned on 450-cubic-inch factory engines of the early Seventies would hardly remember that the Super-Duty 421 Pontiac was the biggest engine in the industry when it was introduced in 1962. In fact that period was the beginning of the "cubic inch race" that eventually led to those 454-455 cubic inch monsters of the Seventies.

But the Super-Duty 421 Pontiac was a lot more than just a big engine of its time. It was also one of the strongest-performing factory options of that time. It was successful on the NASCAR speedways as well as the drag strips. And, Mickey Thompson even used four supercharged Pontiacs to turn speeds up to 406 mph with a Bonneville streamliner in the early Sixties!

It's a fascinating story.

A little background first. We have to go back to 1957, when the Automobile Manufacturers Association (AMA) decided to ban factory participation in various forms of auto racing and performance advertising—(mostly because of government pressure). Things suddenly looked pretty dark for stock car racing in general, and for Detroit's growing thrust aimed at the youth market.

But Pontiac was one division that didn't take it lying down. Their newly-appointed general manager, Semon "Bunkie" Knudson, and chief engineer Pete Estes, were well aware of the importance of the youth market in Pontiac's future. They had to figure a *legal* way to squeeze around the AMA ban. And they did. It was very simple: Don't build the hottest stuff on the assembly line for sale to the public. Develop plenty of special performance goodies—but just offer them over the counter to serious racers. This would satisfy NASCAR, who were much more strict about "factory" equipment than they are today. And it shouldn't bring criticism from the government or AMA because the hot cars weren't going to the public. And, Pontiac wasn't actually sponsoring race cars and drivers.

The idea worked like magic. After the 389-cubic inch engine was brought out in 1959 Pontiac dominated the NASCAR tracks for the next three years! Especially the team of "Fireball" Roberts driving, and "Smokey" Yunick on the wrenches. Their black-and-gold Pontiac won more races in the three-year span from 1959 thru '61 than any previous team. And in 1961 three Pontiac drivers—Roberts, Marvin Panch and Bobby Johns—won 30 out of the 52 NASCAR Grand National races!

This isn't an article about the 389 engine. But these developments were leading up to the magnificent 421-cubic inch mill that was introduced for the 1962 season.

Most Pontiac enthusiasts don't realize it, but some of the special performance parts that were developed for the 389 in the 1960-'61 period were transferred directly to the 421 in 1962. The 421 was essentially an "over-the-counter" engine, hand-built in the factory tool room. It was an out-and-out racing combination. Not over 100 cars went out the door with this engine in 1962. And not just anybody could buy one. You had to be a legitimate racer or have connections. Factory cars were built for both track and drag racing. Supposedly this "off-road" designation took the sting off with the AMA and any Washington critics.

The most notable Super-Duty 389 part that was transferred to the 421 was the cylinder head. These heads

V8-421 Super Duty—1963 Model Year Production

Part No.	Carburetor	Code	Car Model	Number Produced
545012	1—4 Bbl.	12-5	Catalina and Grand Prix	13
545013	2—4 Bbl.	13-5	Catalina and Grand Prix	59
545024	2—4 Bbl.	24-5	Unspecified*	5
545075	2—4 Bbl.	75-9	Tempest	11
			Total	88

*Believed to be Catalina built with aluminum front end sheet metal.

Above volumes are engines built in production facilities and do not include component parts for retail sale or engines built experimentally for test and development programs.

The following parts were released in November and December, 1962, for use with 1963 V8-421 super duty engines:

Part No.	Description
9772389	Manifold-Intake
9772381	Spacer-Carburetor Assembly
9772389	Carburetor Assembly (Carter Model 36365)

Note: Part number 9772389 Carburetor Assembly (Carter Model 36365) is the unit with two (2) round primary throttle blades and a single rectangular secondary throttle blade. This model has been popularly referred to as "3-Barrel" or "Trap Door"

1963 Catalina & Ventura Aluminum Body Parts

Part No.	Part Name	Quantity Made	Quantity Shipped
9771818	Hood Panel Assembly	44	43
9771800	Right Front Fender Assembly	41	41
9771801	Left Front Fender Assembly	40	40
9771816	Right Front Fender Skirt	88	72
9771817	Left Front Fender Skirt	75	72
9771831	Radiator Support Assembly	30	30
9772470	Radiator Support Assembly (trans. ign.)	6	6
9771836	Radiator Grille Brace	347	347
9771844	Right Front Bumper Bar	162	162
9771845	Left Front Bumper Bar	157	157
9771846	Right Front Bumper Bar	158	158
9771847	Left Front Bumper Bar	151	151
9771843	Front Bumper Impact Bar	85	85
9771848	Rear Bumper Impact Bar	96	52
9771798	Front Fender Cross Brace	210	44

The difference between quantity made and quantity shipped reflects the number of parts that were either in need of repair or retained for R&D work.

Documented by Pontiac Engineering, the charts above tell the real story. The factory was very involved in those days. Below we see Wangers doing his thing at the Indy Nationals where he won class honors. Other B/FX car was campaigned by Stan Long Pontiac.

had considerably-larger ports and .100-inch larger valve diameters than standard 389 heads. And, there were no exhaust crossover passages for manifold heat. They definitely weren't street heards. Also they were fitted with 1.65-to-1 rocker arms—(rather than the standard 1.5 arms)—to give more valve lift with less acceleration of the lifters and pushrods on the other side of the rockers.

Another interesting thing about these early 421 heads is that combustion chamber volume was only 64 ccs, using a narrow bathtub-shaped cavity. Pontiac engineers didn't like to use pistons with weird-shaped domes to get high compression ratios. With the 64-cc chambers they could get over 12-to-1 with flat-top pistons. Of course this meant tight chamber walls and some "shrouding" around the valve edges. Breathing might have been hurt a little. It was a different idea that we didn't see much of on later Detroit performance engines. (Remember the open-chamber big-block Chevy had 120-cc volumes.)

The 421 cylinder block was essentially a bored-and-stroked 389—1/32-inch larger bore, ¼-longer stroke—with ¼-inch larger main bearings and four-bolt main bearing caps. No standard engine had used the four-bolt caps before. The 421 also was given new forged steel connecting rods, beefier than the untreated forged rods used in all 389 engines. This was a big step forward in high-rev durability—especially with the longer stroke—and these forged 421 rods were in great demand by Pontiac engine builders for many years after they went out of production. The 421 also used a forged crankshaft, of course; but these were used on some other Pontiac performance engines in the late Sixties and early Seventies. A high-volume oil pump, aluminum bearings and six-quart pan rounded out the bottom-end goodies.

Carburetion was always a problem in the early days of the factory

Super-Duty 421 engines came from the factory with elaborate Tri-Y cast-iron exhaust manifolds with dual outlets. Later drag cars got aluminum versions weighing 40 pounds less. Primary passages were paired to prevent overlapping of exhaust pulses. Photo at left was taken at Pontiac Engineering, showing special room full of single and multi-carb "special use" 421-cube engines.

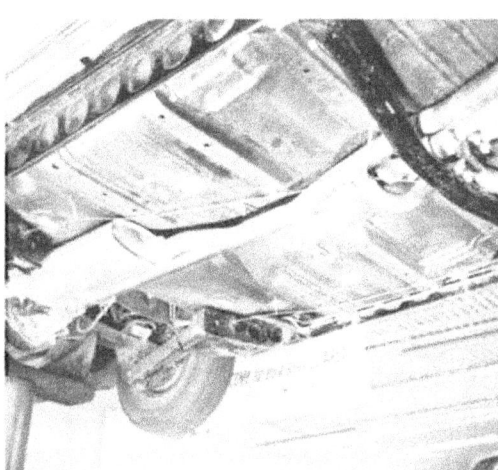

The factory saved the racers work by mounting the batteries in the trunks and leaving out sound deadener and matting on inner body panels. This was standard equipment on factory SD-421 performance models.

Factory SD-421 cars came through with a single exhaust system under the car tied into dual tuned headers. If you look really close you can see the Swiss Cheese lightening holes in the frame rails. The SD-421 engine used a special block, right, with four-bolt mains (3¼-inch) and a very stiff forged steel crankshaft.

There's a lot of enthusiasm around these days to preserve the great old factory race cars. Finding aluminum front ends and parts for a '63 Pontiac SD is like finding good gas! Pontiac offered an HO street version of the 421 engine in the mid-Sixties. The most popular performance combo, right, is the 370-hp job fitted with tri-power and a 288-degree cam.

Super/Stocks, simply because nobody made a really *big* four-barrel carburetor at that time. Holley wasn't in the performance business then. Carter brought out their famous AFB series in 1961—but only in air flow ratings up to 550-600 cfm. That wasn't big by today's standards. But these had to suffice for NASCAR racing, as NASCAR rules limited you to one four-barrel carb. Pontiac had used *three* two-barrel Rochesters for 389 drag strip packages, and these gave pretty good top-end power—though the total cfm capacity of the three was less than 800 cfm.

The answer for 421 drag strip engines was obvious: *Two* Carter AFBs, for a total of 1000 cfm flow. Pontiac engineers designed an excellent new two-plane aluminum dual-quad manifold to fit the big-port heads, with no exhaust crossover. This setup gave at least 25 hp more at 5500 rpm than the single-quad NASCAR system. (Pontiac rated that 1962 421 dual-quad package at 405 hp at 5600 rpm.) It did a great job on the strips.

How about the cam and valve gear? Pontiac had an engineer named Malcolm McKellar who was a real sharp camshaft designer. Since NASCAR and NHRA rules then required factory cams, this gave Pontiac an advantage over some other companies. McKellar came up with some beauties for both the 389 and 421 engines. He never used much valve lift—(.470-inch was considered a lot)—but he had the ability to design lobe profiles that would give a broad torque curve, good top-end power and stable valve train dynamics in the range of 5500-6000 rpm. He didn't believe in revving about 6000, so only single valve springs were used. The 421 engines were always very competitive on top-end power, though.

One of the more interesting new pieces for the 421 was a unique set of cast iron "Tri-Y" exhaust manifolds. You have to remember that NASCAR required factory exhaust manifolds in those days, so the engineers busted their heads to come up with new ideas. The new castings had the primary passages for each bank paired into dual outlets, in such a way that exhaust pulses were phased 180 degrees apart—(like the Tri-Y tubing headers that were on the market at that time). The new manifolds were good for an extra 20 horsepower. But, needless to say, the things were very big and heavy—over 70 pounds in cast iron! This prompted Pontiac engineers to try casting them in *aluminum* for the drag strip cars. You heard it right, guys—aluminum exhaust manifolds! They figured that the heat build-up on the drag strip wouldn't be enough to melt the thick casting walls. And they could save 40 pounds with the aluminum.

Well, it did work, believe it or not. Strip Pontiacs using the aluminum castings had noticeably better traction because of the reduced front end weight. And I never knew of one of the passages "burning out"—though I've seen more than one drop of melted aluminum on the strip after one of the cars took off! Those were the fun days, guys.

So far we've talked just about the 421 engine. Actually the special factory-built race cars that housed these engines had some neat gimmicks, too. Like the drag strip jobs had their weight cut over 200 pounds with aluminum bumpers, hood and front fenders. Pontiac was able to stamp the aluminum pieces on standard steel dies. The bodies also had sound-deadener and matting omitted. And of course the aluminum exhaust manifolds helped. The full-size Catalinas weighed less than 3600 pounds with five gallons of gas. Batteries were positioned in the trunks for better weight distribution.

Drive line? GM didn't supply automatic transmissions with race-type engines in those days—(like Chrysler did)—so you had the choice of a Borg-Warner T-85 floor-shift three-speed or the famous T-10 four-speed. Believe it or not, the three-speed was stronger. If you recall the T-10 four-speed was based on the T-85 three-speed gearcase, so the gear teeth had to be made narrower to squeeze them in. The T-10 was notoriously unreliable in the early Sixties. But many successful strip cars used them. With the 421 you could order either transmission with Hurst floor shifter and 4.30 or 4.88 rear end gears, with Positraction.

Did it go? Yes it did. I recall testing the strip 421 with four-speed belonging to the Royal Pontiac dealership in Royal Oak, Mich. On the Detroit Dragway strip driver Jim Wangers (remember him?) turned a best of 12.38 seconds at 116.23 mph! That was with all factory equipment, open exhaust, cheater street tires and 4.30

gears. I figure it would take over 500 honest horses to turn that with the car weight involved.

That was almost 20 years ago, guys!

The 1963 version of the 421 competition engine was improved considerably over the '62 model. The cylinder head castings were modified with higher intake ports, oval-shaped exhaust ports, and valve diameters were increased to 2.02 inch intakes and 1.76 exhausts. Compression was raised from 11 to 12.5-to-1 with new higher-deck forged pistons. A new McKellar "No. 12" cam was developed, and this was used with dual valve springs to allow shift points up to 6400 rpm without breaking things. Pontiac only raised the 421's official power rating from 405 to 410 hp to account for the new 1963 goodies. But mechanics knew the new heads, compression and cam were good for at least an extra 40 to 50 hp!

Plus they took almost another 100 pounds out of the strip cars with plexiglass side windows and aluminum deck lids. I know the Royal 421 with Jim Wangers driving could turn in the low 12's at 117-119 mph early in the 1963 season. Then he won the B/FX class at the NHRA Nationals in September with this same car. It was obviously much stronger and quicker than the '62 Catalina.

Unfortunately things were not quite so happy on the NASCAR tracks for the 421. At the start of the 1963 season you'll recall that Chevrolet surprised everybody with the new 427-cubic inch "mystery" engine with Junior Johnson driving and Ray Foxx on the wrenches. This was the prototype of the modern big-block stagger-valve engine that had such a successful racing career in the late Sixties and early Seventies. The ports and valves were bigger than anything that had been seen in 1963—and the thing put 50 to 75 horses more than any of the Fords or Chryslers or Pontiacs. The Johnson-Foxx team swept the NASCAR tracks early in the 1963 season. Then before anybody could come up with competitive hardware the GM front office unexpectedly put an anti-racing clamp on all the divisions.

And that put an end to *all* competition-type cars and engines from all the GM divisions. The 421 was among those that got the axe. The next step was the GTO-type car in 1964.

This story wouldn't be complete without mentioning the very excellent H-O *street* version of the 421-cubic inch engine that Pontiac offered in their full-size cars in the 1963-'66 period. In fact I recall testing several of those cars, and I believe it was one of the smoothest, most responsive high-performance street engines that was available in the musclecar era.

The most popular combination used the well-known Tri-Power carburetion system from the 389 engine—three Rochester two-barrels with progressive throttle linkage. They also used medium-port 389 cylinder heads, but with intake valve diameter increased to 1.92 inch, to give the best compromise between low-speed response and top-end power. The hydraulic camshaft was also a masterpiece: McKellar designed the famous HO cam at this time, with 288 degrees duration and .414-inch lift, which proved so excellent that it was used on 428 and 455-cubic inch high-performance street engines clear into the Seventies. Fairly mild valve spring pressures were used, though, and you couldn't turn the HO 421 much above 5600 rpm.

The HO 421 retained the four-bolt block and forged crank, but went back to the cast 389 rods and cast pistons. There was no need for too much exotica with peak revs under 6000. New cast iron exhaust manifolds were designed with very large passages and easy curves, but with the single outlet per side, to match a conventional undercar dual pipe/muffler system.

Pontiac gave this Tri-Power 421 HO a gross power rating of 370 hp at 5200 rpm. And I believe the *net* power was over 300 hp. I recall testing one in a '63 Grand Prix that weighed over 4000 pounds. With a wide-ratio four-speed and 3.23 axle gears, we could turn quarter-miles ets in the low 15's at 92 mph without winding above 5000 rpm! That was the easiest *belt-in-the-back* I can remember up to that time. And if you let it all hang out that baby would run up to 135 mph right now!

It seems like another century. Gas only cost 32¢ a gallon. Who cared if the 421 only gave you 10 or 12 mpg? It's just a memory now. Today we've got to learn to have even more fun with little cars that go 30 or 40 miles on a gallon.

53

"YOU DON'T HEAR THAT SOUND ANYMORE"

By Jim Kurzen

Jim Kurzen is currently on medical leave from Pontiac Motor Division where he has been employed for more than 25 years. He started with Pontiac in 1954 and has been drag racing Pontiacs ever since Pontiac started producing high-performance cars. Attached to the Pennsylvania Zone in the capacity of Manager of Zone Service Operations, he is considered one of the most knowledgeable Super-Duty historian/enthusiasts in the world. He's also one helluva nice guy. Ed.

MY SUPER/DUTY Catalina was assembly-line-produced the last week of January 1962 and is one of the 177 produced that model year. The 1962 Super-Duty production breakdown is as follows: Body Style #2239 (1), #2347 (156) and #2311 & 69 (20). Out of a total of 177 SD cars built, 20 came through with bucket seats. Total SD engine production that year included 15 389-cube and 225 421-cube motors, with 63 set aside for replacement applications.

After taking delivery in Canton, Ohio (Edwards Pontiac) on February 8, 1962, we hit the road and headed for Daytona Beach, Florida. The car was delivered in time to leave for the legendary Daytona Speed Week, with engine break-in on the road. There wasn't even enough time to install the optional valve springs that Pontiac put in each SD trunk to increase the redline by 1000 rpm!

Starting with the Daytona drags (on the back stretch of the 2½-mile oval) we won two races and three trophies running Super Stock/Stick (SS/S). Considering that the car was not lightened, chassis left stock, heater and heavy rubber floor mats in place and the steel front end, the results were fantastic. Because of my pride in the car's appearance (alloy front ends dent too easily when you race) I decided to stick with the steel front end.

During 1963 I swapped to a single four barrel carburetor, making it a 390-hp NASCAR model which ran in B/Stock. Not all tracks would accept this combination, but we managed to race a lot that year. I actually won half of the Top Stock runs that year. However, I carefully avoided many of the special meets in 1963 and confrontations with the Ramchargers, Mickey Thompson, Harold Ramsey and Arlan Vanke!

From January thru April 1963 I worked with Pontiac in Orlando, Florida and drove a Bonneville convertible. The 421 Super-Duty was stored in Canton, Ohio and I went "fun racing" with the Bonneville. Interesting enough, I won six out of seven nights at Daytona that year, turning in the 13's with my daily-transportation tri-power Bonneville!

After we officially retired the Super-Duty in 1964, it was driven on special occasions by myself, my wife Chris and our two sons Mark and Paul. We still manage a few times a month to slip it out of the garage and take it for a blast. And, of course, we drive it to East Coast Pontiac Club shows and meets. In 1970 I converted to variable ratio power steering to make life a little easier! It has been seriously shown since 1972 as a Special Interest category car and never fails to bring home a trophy.

Being a member of the Pontiac-Oakland Club International, plus the New York-New Jersey and Penna. chapters, I have enjoyed the shows and friendship of Pontiac club mem-

The author of this article and owner of this legendary race car is currently on medical leave from Pontiac due to cancer-related surgery. Whenever possible he takes his street-driven Super-Duty Catalina to Pontiac meets. You can literally eat off the dual-quad 421 engine which is stock and super-strong.

Photos by the ThunderAm Staff

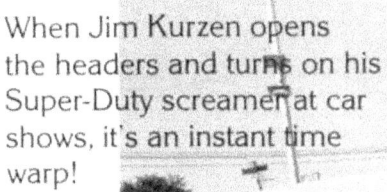

When Jim Kurzen opens the headers and turns on his Super-Duty screamer at car shows, it's an instant time warp!

These photos were taken at the POCI Penna. Chapter Meet in Lancaster which boasted a record turnout of cars. Jim walked off with a First in the Daytona & Specialty Class, beating out one other '62 Super-Duty car and some other unique vehicles. Because it is fitted with steel and not aluminum body panels, the car is as straight as a brand new stocker.

bers. A serious illness this year curtailed my participation. With assistance from some of the club members, my wife, and the people at Jones Pontiac in Lancaster, I was able to attend the Lancaster Mini-Meet.

Sometimes I open the headers at the meets and the sound is unbelievable. When the crowd comes around someone always says, "You don't hear that sound anymore". It really takes you back to the performance days which we all loved. Considering that the SD has never been restored and was seriously raced for two years, it represents quite an accomplishment. I am in the process of changing the original exhaust system which has held up for 17½ years.

Except for a few races and some show trips, the SD has been fed a steady diet of Unleaded fuel which wasn't even supposed to work in the good old days. That's probably why the exhaust system has lasted so long. The mufflers don't even have rust holes at this point. It's just that the outer skin is tearing from back-pressure!

The side striping on this car was my idea and was actually done before official delivery to brighten up a rather dull beige car. I chose beige so that the interior would be cooler during summer runs and it would be easy to spot during night racing.

By the way, the lowest gas mileage registered with the dual quad SD engine was 13.1 mpg on the 1000-mile break-in trip from Canton, Ohio to Daytona Beach, Florida. Not exactly bad for a race car!

A Pontiac experimental department engineer takes the topless Tempest for a spin around the Milford Proving Grounds. Note chopped plexi windows and windshield and the molded fiberglass top boot.

TEMPEST IN A TEAPOT!

Mini-size Monte Carlo is the quickest and fastest dream car on the show circuit or the street

The sporty interior featured blue leather buckets with special race car support panels, console-mounted-four-speed and a combination boost and vacuum pressure gauge. In typical GM show car fashion of the Sixties, the carpeting was inlaid with chrome stripes and an extensive amount of chrome plating was used.

Knock-off Halibrand slotted magnesium wheels added that genuine race car touch. Tires are Firestone Super Sports, a genuine high-performance tire in 1962.

Power for this low-rider came from a GMC-blown Tempest four-banger with wall-to-wall chrome and aluminum. Monster pop-off valve and flame arrestor proved that this was no show—only machine. Power was unreal for a car powered by half of an eight cylinder engine!

On February 11, 1962, Pontiac unveiled its Tempest-based supercharged sports car, the Monte Carlo. Finished in Pearl White lacquer with twin blue racing stripes, this topless terror with racing screen windshield was a mind-blower.

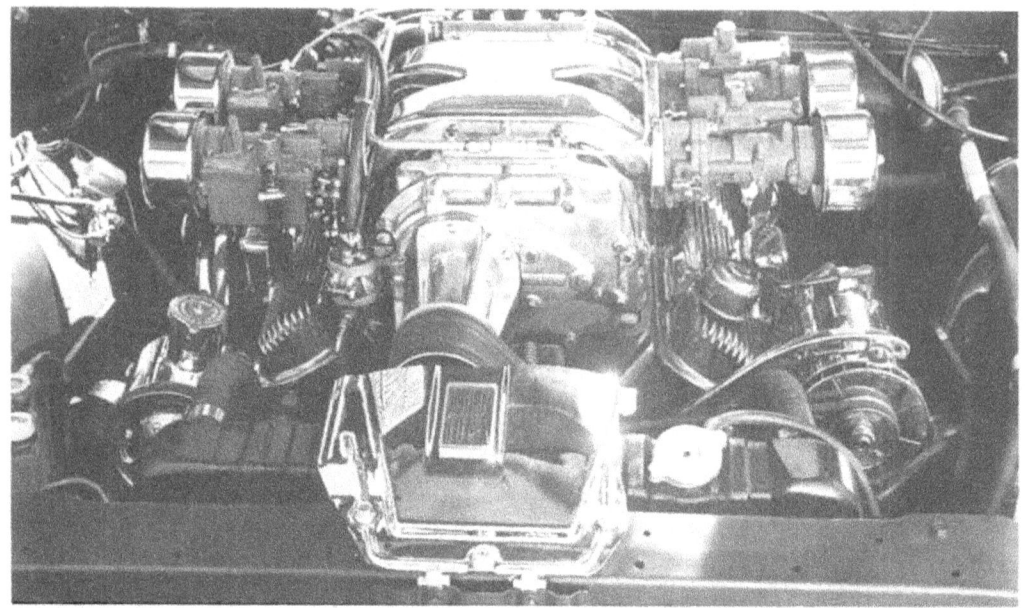

Pontiac's association with Mickey Thompson netted the Chief with a brace of GMC-6-71 blown V-8 engines, similar to the ones Thompson built for his stable of land speed record and drag-racing Pontiacs. Blowers featured Thompson speed equipment and seldom-seen sidedraft carbs.

GRAND PRIX X-400

Unique Grand Prix ragtop is a sunshine Supercar
thanks to a GMC-blown 389-inch V-8 and status trim to match

THE GRAND PRIX X-400, Pontiac's 1962 experimental show car is finished in a brilliant red with a white top. The distinctive Grand Prix grille is flanked by a pair of rectangular headlamps, protected by swing-up mesh stone guards. Twin grilled vents in the hood, and the accompanying designation "Supercharged," indicate that the X-400 gets extra power from positive-displacement supercharging.

Along the sides of this experimental convertible are brushed-chrome concave moldings. The outside rear-view mirrors are enclosed in chromed bullet-shaped housings, and twin exhaust pipes emerge from the sides of each rear fender. The radio's normal central location is occupied by three instruments angled toward the driver: an 8,000 rpm tachometer, a supercharger boost pressure gauge and a clock. The floor console houses a glove box, the four-speed shift lever, and an additional level to select three degrees of quietness in the dual exhaust system.

Closeup of the Mickey-Thompson-engineered sidedraft carburetion used with the GMC blower. A multi-V belt drive was used as this was before the ribbed Gilmer belt became the standard for blower drives.

In typical European sports car trim, the headlamps are rectangular and covered with chrome mesh grilles. Grille panels in the hood along with Supercharger lettering gives this GP that one-of-a-kind touch.

Twin exhaust pipes exit from each rear fender. The noise level of the exhaust system could be controlled by a lever mounted in the console.

The X-400 Grand Prix one-of-a-kind convertible was finished in red with a white top. The folding top was hidden from view by a molded fiberglass tonneau cover or boot. Wheels are stock eight-lug factory mags.

ROYAL ROUTE OF THE SILVER STREAK

Jim Wangers after taking a brand new GTO to the drag strip—he won!

If Jim Wangers had never darkened Pontiac's doorstep, it still would have built great cars. But without his promotional expertise and ability to communicate with the street set, Pontiac would have been just another player in the Supercar Sweepstakes instead of the winner!

Jim Wangers, left, and Frank Rediker pose with Royal's outrageous Super-Duty 421 Trophy-taker.

IF WE had to single out just one person who we felt was responsible for the Supercar/Musclecar cult marketplace of the Sixties, that person would have to be Jim Wangers. It would be impossible to write about this period of time and Pontiac's involvement without giving credit to this hyper-active creative marketeer who parlayed performance into respectability and gave Detroit a new sales approach which lasted for almost a decade.

Jim Wangers didn't really invent the GTO, Trans-Am or Judge, mainly because nothing that comes out of Motown is ever invented by a single person. However, he was the guiding force behind these projects and was highly-respected by the men who headed the Division. Pontiac was building fast cars and was actively involved in racing and winning in stock car circles and drag strips before Jim Wangers got involved. However, Wangers was the man who showed Pontiac how to really capitalize on the performance image and use it to sell cars for the street. He proved that it really didn't matter who won the races as long as you could sell the kind of products that the youth market could relate to. On a pure horsepower basis, Pontiac was badly overshadowed by Chevy, Ford and Chrysler. The sales charts told a different story!

Whether Jim Wangers actually did invent the GTO and the Supercar market or simply crowned himself King is irrelevant. What is important here is that he was one of the first to understand the car-crazy kids, communicated with them regularly and was able to get Pontiac to recognize a virtually-untapped market. He was the kind of executive who preferred lunch at a local Woodward Avenue street racer drive-in with some of the local talent (street racers and auto magazine writers and editors) than a three-martini *snow job* at one of the fashionable *upward mobility* hangouts. He did much of the decision work on the street, not behind a safe, secure desk in an Ivory Tower!

Unlike most of his contemporaries involved in automotive marketing, Wangers had an unfair advantage. He was a drag racer and street racer—he "talked the talk" and drove the cars. He did his market research at the drag strip, street racer drive-ins along Woodward Ave. and at Ace Wilson's Royal Pontiac in Royal Oak, Michigan. With lots of help from the factory, he helped turn a local Pontiac dealership into a living legend.

He did enough drag racing and winning to make a name for himself in the Pontiac camp, took Super/Stock and Top Stock Eliminator honors at the 1960 NHRA Nationals and B/Factory Experimental and Little Eliminator at the NHRA Indy Nationals in 1963. When he spoke, factory engineers listened—and so did top management.

Before the GTO materialized, Wangers had set up a "back door connection" between Pontiac Motor Division and Royal Pontiac. This connection resulted in a specialty car and tuning kit program which grew to become the hot setup from coast to coast. Some of the goodies included a '62 Pontiac Catalina Royal Bobcat coupe with SD-421 power and trick Bobcat emblems, rated at 370 dyno horsepower; a '62 Tempest Bobcat with a 185-hp four-banger and even a Bobcat Grand Prix loaded with a Paxton-blown 389 rated at 400 hp. And, a full line of Royal Bobcat performance kits for street as well as strip-driven Pontiac products.

Wangers used Royal Pontiac to market the specialty items as well as for the preparation of all the Pontiacs that were road-tested by the enthusiast automotive magazines. He personally supervised the preparation and, in more than one case, these road test cars ran quicker and faster than modified versions prepared by speed shops! He was a firm believer in detail tuning and not bolt-on horsepower for street performance.

A well-dressed Wangers, left, with New York dealer Council people at the Introduction of his "Americana" Grand Prix.

After the introduction of the GTO, Wangers designed Royal Bobcat models with 389, 400 and 428-inch engines that became the ultimate Pontiac status symbols of the time. They were followed by trend-setting promotion sof shoe, records, tiger tails, posters, books, etc.—all designed to help sell Pontiac GTO musclecars. And they did in record numbers. Wangers' GTO record proved to be a surprise hit. It seemed that Wangers and Pontiac could do no wrong.

During those years Jim Wangers was employed by Pontiac's advertising agency—MacManus, John and Adams (now D'Arcy, MacManus and Masius). Pontiac still has the same agency, but Wangers left when the Musclecar marketplace took a radical turn for the worse in the early Seventies. While at the agency he acted as liaison between the agency and factory in the areas of product marketing and spent more time at the factory than he did at the agency. When management changed from exciting and forward-thinking to dull and me-too, Wangers was not exactly welcome anymore. Today Wangers is a consultant to a number of auto manufacturers and advertising agencies on special model marketing and image cars. He did the *Americana* Grand Prix for Pontiac in 1981, followed by Dodge's Charger 2.2. He still maintains a stable of performance Pontiacs (GTO Judge, GTO, Trans-Am, Grand Prix plus assorted street racing cars). He no longer street races but his cars are still consistent winners and he still does his market research on the street—the ultimate proving grounds for the products.

I guess if Zora Arkus-Duntov is often credited as the Father of the Corvette, then Jim Wangers is certainly entitled to Father of the Supercar. He may just be the last great American hero!

Wangers, left, at the 1980 Pontiac-Oakland Club International convention.

ROYAL'S RACING LEGEND

Long before the Bobcat GTO was developed, Royal Pontiac was a major force in Super/Stock racing

ROYAL's first Super/Stock race car was a '59 Pontiac which first ran in competition at the NHRA Winternationals at Daytona in February, 1960. The engine was the 389-cubic-inch, 345-hp model with standard heads, Tri-Power ram-type exhausts, and the Isky E-2 cam kit. The new 1960 Super-Duty engine parts — big-valve heads, big-port aluminum manifolds, McKellar cams, split-flow exhaust headers — weren't available when this car was put together.

Royal's '59 was a success right from the start. Driver Bill Sidwell ran away with the S/S class at the Daytona Winternationals on its first outing. This was the last year that top speed trials were run on the beach, so the Royal crew had a crack at that too. They hit an unofficial 151 mph in one direction in practice runs, using 3.08 rear gears! A few weeks later the Detroit Dragway opened and Royal was there on opening day. Their '59 was the first stocker to go over 100 mph and get in the 13-second bracket on the new strip. Best times with this car were 13.91 and 102 mph. This was with 345 hp!

Pontiac's new Super-Duty engine package was becoming available, so Royal switched over to a '60 Pontiac model in mid-season. The new 363-hp hardtop first ran at the July 4th drags at Detroit, with Jim Wangers in the driver's seat. Frank Rediker and Winston Brown were on the wrenches at this point. It was during this period that Frank Rediker developed the Bobcat engine package that helped put Royal Pontiac in the Number One spot.

Royal's 1960 Super/Stock was a slow starter. At first it wasn't any quicker than the '59. A switch to the new Borg-Warner four-speed transmission helped chop .3 to .4 seconds off the et and the car began to drop into the 13-second bracket. The '60 was about 100 pounds heavier than the '59. Best times for this car were 13.81 seconds at 104 mph. But all hell broke loose at the NHRA Nationals at Detroit Dragway in September, 1960. Wangers copped not only the S/S class win, but managed to beat out Pete Seaton's 363-hp '60 Pontiac for Top Stock Eliminator. He was turning in the very low 14s and 100-102 mph consistently. Wangers' consistent starts made the difference. But the fact was that Royal's toughest competition in S/S at the Nationals was another Pontiac!

It should be mentioned that Royal also sponsored a Super/Stock Automatic with the 363-hp engine hooked to a four-speed Hydra-Matic. It could run consistently around 14.5 et at 98 mph.

The 1961 drag season saw another two-car team fielded by Royal — rating 368 hp with "Number 10" McKellar cams and running a close-ratio four-speed in one and the new three-speed Hydro in the other. The race cars were white, with red lettering. The tow cars were red, with white stripes going over the hoods and roof. Royal Pontiac took its drag racing very seriously!

Performance was considerably better than the '60 Pontiac racer. Weight was down to 3,870 pounds, mainly due to the new cast aluminum headers (nearly 50 pounds lighter than the cast-irons), aluminum bumpers, and the shorter rear overhang on the '61 bodies. Unfortunately, this shorter rear overhang also hurt the traction considerably. Wangers could never get off the line like he did with the '60 Pontiac. Mechanic Frank Rediker finally hit on the idea of going up from 4.55 to 4.88 gears and using wide-ratio gears in the four-speed, then starting in *Second* gear (1.92-to-1 ratio). This seemed to give the best starts on most strips, unless traction was unusually good. Best times for the '61 four-speed stick were 13.13 seconds at 107.12 mph. Royal won Stock Eliminator at the NHRA Regionals at Muncie, Ind., and Alton, Ill. Both cars were consistent class winners. The automatic was even more successful than the stick in 1961. With Dick Jesse at the wheel, it could run consistent 104-105 mph in 13.7s.

For the 1962 season Royal concentrated all its efforts on a red and gold hardtop with the 421-cubic-inch, dual four-barrel engine and four-speed. This, of course, was a factory racing car. New aluminum parts included front hood, outer and inner fender panels, radiator brackets, as well as the bumpers and exhaust headers. The '62 race car weighed only a shade over 3,600 pounds with five gallons of gas. The 4.30 rear end and new M&H tires gave excellent traction and Rediker could get well over 450 horses out of the engine. Wangers could wind 6,400 rpm with the new long-stroke setup before the valves gave up but he generally shifted at around 6,000.

And there is little doubt that Royal's was possibly the quickest Pontiac in the country at the end of the 1962 season. Just before the Detroit Dragway closed, Wangers got his best-ever run in — 116.23 mph in 12.38 seconds! The Royal team broke records at eight different Midwest and East Coast strips during the season. It was rarely beaten in its class.

The legend continued in 1963 with the aluminum car with "Swiss cheese" chassis and onto 421-inch Tempest. Royal kept on winning on Sunday and selling on Monday!

RACING IMPROVES THE BREED

Looking back at the good old days when Pontiac was in racing to win!

WHEN it came to racing Pontiac top brass decided to have at least a small piece of the pie. A factory hookup was made with veteran Indy 500 mechanic Lou Moore, and he was commissioned to prepare a couple of new Pontiacs for the Daytona Speed Weeks in February 1956. Factory engineers cooperated with heavy-duty suspension equipment and a power kit for the larger 317-cubic-inch engine. This included dual four-barrel carbs, 10-to-1 heads and a long-duration solid-lifter cam. They claimed 285 hp at 5,100 rpm. Cotton Owens and Ed Kretz were signed to drive.

That first outing was impressive, but not very rewarding. Kretz hit an *unofficial* 132 mph in practice runs on the beach but a combination of poor beach conditions and mechanical troubles prevented them from making an official record attempt before the runs were shut off. In the 160-mile Grand National race on the 4.1-mile beach-road course, Owens and Kretz pushed Tim Flock's Chrysler 300 for a few laps, until they both threw fan belts and overheated. The cars proved to have plenty of performance.

Meanwhile, performance development was speeding up. Displacement of the original V-8 block was upped to 347 cubic inches for 1957 and a new triple two-barrel carburetion system was developed, called "Tri-Power." The racing camshaft used lightened solid lifters and special valve springs to allow speeds over 5,500 rpm. Rating of the 1957 racing engine, using Tri-Power carburetion and 10-to-1 compression, was 317 hp at 5,200 rpm.

This competition engine was to be a dealer-installed package; the hottest thing you could order off the assembly line was the Tri-Power 290-hp engine with hudraulic cam. This was the start of Pontiac's policy of holding back their hottest equipment for over-the-counter sale to qualified racing people or private buyers.

'Fireball' Roberts and his '63 Pontiac Grand Prix street car. Roberts was Pontiac's main man on the NASCAR Grand National circuit and one of the all-time roundy-round greats.

Pontiac factory-connected racers shocked the troops with lightweight Tempests powered by 421-SD motors. This trick Tempest was sponsored by Hodges Pontiac in Florida and was lined up to run against a factory Ramcharger car.

This was the hot setup in 1962—Super-Duty 405 hp engine, four-speed, alloy body panels and eight-lug aluminum wheels. All goodies came right from the factory.

Pontiacs all but swept Daytona clean in February, 1957. John Zink, Jr., had the highest two-way average of any stock car at 136 mph. But on the engine tear-down one of his combustion chambers was found to be undersize, and the car was disqualified. But Joe Littlejohn's car still won its class at 131.7 mph and another '57 Pontiac took its class in the standing-start mile at 83.5 mph. And, Cotton Owens won the 160-mile Grand National race on the beach-road course.

Shortly after the Daytona race NASCAR officials announced a new ruling that all superchargers, fuel-injection and multiple carburetion systems would be banned in Grand National stock car racing. They said that, with the factories sponsoring full-time racing teams, the small private owners couldn't get the hottest special equipment for themselves, so factory cars had an unfair advantage. A few weeks later, in June 1957, the AMA anti-racing resolution was announced. This stopped all factory association with racing, advertising of racing, and promotion of performance.

These two developments had a major effect on Pontiac's future performance plans. The Rochester fuel-injection system was shelved. Pontiac engineers felt it had too limited a market at the $500 price to warrant development costs, especially since it could no longer be promoted via racing. Tri-Power carburetion was retained as a street option but the dual four-barrel setup was dropped. And much more attention was given to efficient carburetion with a large single four-barrel.

Pontiac wasn't quite as depressed by the AMA ruling as some of the other companies because they proceeded to sweep the Daytona Speed Weeks again. They started by winning the Pure Oil safety and performance trials. On the measured mile, Dr. L.P. Morris had top stock car speed of 137.69 mph (two way average) with his '58 Pontiac 330-hp Tri-Power. The next five fastest cars were '58 Pontiacs. Paul Goldsmith came back to win the important 160-mile Grand National with his 315-hp single four-barrel Pontiac. Bob Pemberton's Air-Lift Special '58 Pontiac, (330-hp), topped it with a one-way speed of *146 mph* on the beach, with Lee Petty at the wheel! Most of the winning Daytona Pontiacs were set up by Ray Nichels Engineering in Highland, Indiana.

For 1959, the V-8 was stroked to get 389 cubes, and top compression ratio was held at 10.5-to-1. The high-performance street options and competition engines had specially-beefed blocks with four-bolt mains. Ratings with the new solid-lifter Isky E-2 cam were 330 hp with single four-barrel for NASCAR and 345 hp at 4,800 rpm with Tri-Power for the drag strips. On the Daytona sand Bob Pemberton's Air-Lift Pontiac averaged 140.35 mph but was later disqualified for having oversize tires (15-inch wheels). In fact the top *six* Pontiacs were disqualified for one reason or another. But a '59 Pontiac did turn top speed in the accelerating mile at 87 mph.

This was the year that the new 2½-mile high-banked Daytona Speedway was opened. Pontiacs hadn't been doing too much on the Grand National circuit. Most of the tracks in those days were flat half-mile dirt and paved tracks. and the relatively high weight and long wheelbase of the Pontiacs was a great disadvantage in cornering. Where all-out horsepower and speed were key factors, they did great. And it was hoped that this new Daytona speedway would give them a chance to unwind.

And it did. A formidable new team showed up, with veteran mechanic Smokey Yunick handling the tuning and Fireball Roberts doing the driving. The pros didn't run on the beach that year but it soon became obvious that the Yunick-Roberts team had the fastest car on the speedway. Roberts practiced at lap speeds above 145 mph, substantially higher than the closest competition in the new 320-hp, 348-cubic-inch Chevys. Mechanical trouble put him back in the starting field in the 500-mile race but he quickly charged into the lead, averaging 144 mph for the first 125 miles. Then fuel pump trouble put him out.

The enthusiasts were noticing. Pontiac just nipped Plymouth for Third place in the 1959 sales race. From Sixth place to Third place in three short years, riding on styling, performance, racing, and a new youth image. Bunky Knudsen had the right formula.

At Daytona the new '60 Pontiacs were the hottest things running. Fireball Roberts turned top qualifying time of 151.56 mph (100 miles) but dropped out of the 500-mile race early with engine trouble. Most of the rest of the '60 Pontiacs dropped out and Bobby Johns' '59 Pontiac finished second behind Junior Johnson's Chevy. But the Pontiacs started winning more races on the shorter NASCAR tracks. And things were booming on the drag strips. At the NHRA Nationals in September, Jim Wangers drove the 363-hp Royal Pontiac four-speed car to win S/S class and then went on to take Top Stock Eliminator. His best times were 14.14 e.t. at 102.04 mph.

And 1961 was even better. Two new McKellar camshaft grinds from the factory put new power in the 389. Marvin Panch won the Daytona 500 at a record average speed. turning lap speeds up to 158 mph. New Pontiacs also took Second and Third. On the GN circuit. Pontiacs won 30 out of 52 races! They dominated the fast high-banked speedways. When the NHRA Nationals rolled around in September. Pontiacs were the favorites in the stock ranks. Hayden Proffitt drove Mickey Thompson's new 421-car to an OS/S class win at 12.55 seconds and 110.29 mph. (A '61 409 Chevy won Top Stock Eliminator, but was later disqualified.) Pontiacs also won the three classes in the automatic transmission division.

The Tempest compact was never designed as a high-performance car. But it had a rather checkered career in racing. NASCAR organized a 150-mile road race for compacts at Daytona in February. 1961, using part of the speedway with some turns in the infield. Smokey Yunick prepared a Tempest for Fireball Roberts with trick equipment. He claimed over 200 hp at 6,000 rpm. The car could hit 130 mph on the straights but transmission trouble slowed down Fireball, so he couldn't keep up with Lee Petty's hot Valiant. The car showed excellent handling, however. At the start of the 1962 model year Pontiac Engineering authorized use of the big engine in the Tempest as a "dealer-installed" option. This made the package eligible for the new NHRA Factory Experimental class. Mickey Thompson built up a Tempest with a V-8 engine and all the special equipment (using a standard Pontiac rear axle in place of the Corvair-based independent rear) and Hayden Proffitt proceeded to run away with the A/FX class at the '62 NHRA Winternationals with times of 12.27 seconds and 117 mph!

And there was more performance news for 1962. The high-erformance engine was bored and stroked to 421 cubic inches. The special heads were given slightly larger valves and ports, a new dual four-barrel carburetion package was developed and the factory came up with improved forged pistons and cams. The setup put out 405 hp at 5,600 rpm and a lot more with a little dyno tuning. A few weeks earlier, NHRA officials had announced a ruling that any car had to be produced on an assembly line to be eligible in the stock classes. This put Pontiac on the spot, since they had a policy of supplying their speed equipment only over the counter. But they had to go along to stay in the running.

Enter the 1962 Pontiac 421 racing package. It had everything—421 engine with either single or dual four-barrel carburetion, super-duty clutch and light flywheel, exhaust cutouts, four-speed transmission with the Hurst linkage, Heavy-Duty suspension, 4.30 rear end with Safe-T-Track limited-slip. And, Pontiac engineers had been quietly developing a method for stamping light aluminum body panels on production dies. The Super-Duty 421s came with aluminum hoods, front outer and inner fender panels, front bumpers, and radiator brackets. They weighed about 200 pounds less than all-steel Pontiacs and were considerably quicker on the drag strip. The weight saving in front not only reduced the total weight, but improved traction through better front-rear weight distribution. The SD 421s would run in the high 12s at 110-114 mph on the strip. They were the cars to beat on the NASCAR circuit. Fireball Roberts won the Daytona 500 at a record average of 152 mph, hitting over 170 mph on the back stretch, and Pontiacs again dominated the speedways through the summer. They were also highly successful on the drag strips. cleaning house at the NHRA Winternationals in Pomona in February.

Rare "bathtub" dual-quad Super-Duty intake manifold had big plenum chamber, lift-off four-barrel carb mounting plate and provision for Corvair Turbo center carb for idle circuit use on street. A block-off plate was supplied for center carb replacement.

1963

THE SUPER-DUTY BEAT GOES ON!

Total restyling, an even more fantastic Grand Prix plus a full-blown Super-Duty drag and NASCAR racing program steal the thunder

Grand Prix received all new sheet metal for 1963 and sales went to over 72,000 units including 5,157 with manual transmissions. Styling is ageless.

This is what the original Royal Pontiac "Swiss Cheese" SD-421 Catalina looks like today. It's being restored back to original by the Heck Brothers and they just happen to have one of the rare aluminum chassis made for this car.

CAPSULE COMMENTS

THE NEW Pontiac Grand Prix has been given the description "quiet elegance" by Pontiac Division General Manager E. M. Estes. The theme is set by a sweeping grille with vertically arranged headlights and sculptured side panels. The rear backlight is concave. Chrome has been used sparingly, and this car's tail lights have been integrated into the rear panel rather than located in the fenders as on the regular Pontiacs. They are not visible except when in use.

1963 PONTIAC HIGH-PERFORMANCE ENGINES

CUBIC INCHES	BORE	STROKE	HORSEPOWER	COMPRESSION	INDUCTION
389	4.06	3.75	303 @ 4600	10.25-to-1	Four-barrel
389	4.06	3.75	313 @ 4600	10.25-to-1	Tri-power
421	4.09	4.00	353 @ 5000	10.75-to-1	Four-barrel
421	4.09	4.00	370 @ 5200	10.75-to-1	Tri-power
421	4.09	4.00	390 @ 5800	12.0-to-1	Four-barrel
421	4.09	4.00	405 @ 5600	12.0-to-1	Dual quad
421	4.09	4.00	410 @ 5600	13.0-to-1	Dual quad
326	3.72	3.75	260 @ 4800	10.25-to-1	Two-barrel

There was no convertible model, but this GMC-blown 421-inch ragtop made the show circuit and caused quite a stir from coast to coast. Where is it now?

Grand Prix, a two-door coupe, is available in 15 solid colors. Bucket seats are standard as are such normally-optional extras as a console with shift lever, a rear courtesy light, a tach or vacuum gauge and a locker compartment. Standard engine for this car is the 303 hp, 389 inch V-8.

Pontiac's engine lineup is as versatile as ever. Standard in Catalina and Star Chief models is the 389 V-8 with two-barrel carb and 8.6-to-1 compression. Next comes a 318-hp version with a four-barrel. Most powerful of the 389 engines is the 348-hp, Tri-Power version having a 10.75-to-1 compression ratio.

Two versions of the famous 421-inch engine are rated at 405 hp with a large quad and 430 hp with dual quads. Of course, the number of speed parts available through Pontiac dealers for personal installation is almost endless.

New suspension features include front upper control arm shaft bushings made of rubber rather than steel to eliminate the need for lubrication and improve cushioning on uneven road surfaces, a 1.5-inch wider rear track with new, rubber lower control arm bushings, and self-adjusting brakes. The Delcotron alternator is standard equipment on all new Pontiacs, and a new air conditioner has been integrated with the heater to provide air conditioning or heat only, or a combination of both.

Optional is a tilting steering wheel adjustable to seven positions for maximum steering comfort and easy entry and exit. Also new, and standard, is a fully transistorized ignition system

For maximum power there's nothing like an SD-421 breathing through a pair of free-flowing quads. You could get SD and HO models.

designed for lifetime operation without parts wear.

Tempest bows in with a larger body on the same 112-inch wheelbase as last year, for an overall length of 194.3 inches. New in the suspension department are a new rear suspension lower control arm "L" shaped and formed to provide a bottom seat for the coil spring, a strengthened differential, increased rear axle diameters and self-adjusting brakes.

New in the engine department is the 326-inch V-8 available in the Tempest and Le Mans as an option. The engine uses many 389 V-8 components including valve train connecting rods and bearing caps.

MYSTERY MANIFOLD!

Aluminum dual-quad manifold is part of Pontiac's legendary Super-Duty 421 drag racing program and was designed to take a pair of Carter quads with a sidedraft one-barrel carb from a Corvair engine in the center for idle-circuit use only

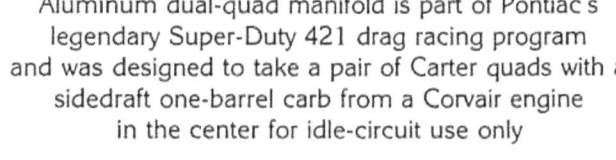

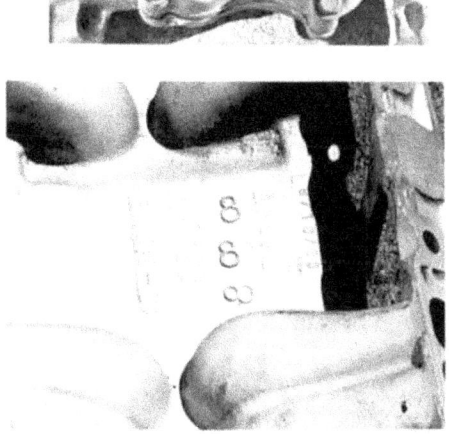

1963 SUPER-DUTY REFERENCE GUIDE

SUPER-DUTY PERFORMANCE EQUIPMENT (GROUP 35)

Pontiac for 1963 introduces TWO NEW SUPER DUTY CARS, the 421 Dual 4-BBL. and the 421 Single 4-BBL. These cars are designed only for all-out performance enthusiasts.

Both cars use the famous Pontiac 421 cubic inch engine, with special parts designed for extraordinary performance. Both have special chassis equipment suited for particular performance needs. Both are available only in the Catalina 2-door sedan (2311) and 2-door hardtop (2347).

The 421 Dual 4-BBL. Car is designed primarily for maximum ACCELERATION trials in organized competition. The 421 Single 4-BBL. Car is intended primarily for more SUSTAINED high speed performance in organized competition.

The following pages present engine characteristics which are shared by both cars. Then each car is described in more detail, including engine and chassis components, maintenance information and suggested optional equipment.

THE BASIC 421 SUPER DUTY ENGINE
(Applies to both cars)

SPECIAL REQUIREMENTS OF SUPER DUTY ENGINE OPERATION

The Super Duty cars are designed exclusively for extraordinary performance. If your prospect buys one of these cars, be sure that he is aware of the following engine characteristics which make them unsuitable for general passenger car use.

1. The engine should always be kept at a minimum idle speed of 1,000 RPM

or above. This is necessary to insure adequate lubrication of bearings and valve mechanism.

2. The standard ignition system of the Dual 4-BBL. engine is designed for high speed operation only. Consequently, sustained low speed operation can cause burning of the breaker points in the distributor. Provisions for low-speed operation are explained under COMPETITON PACKAGE INCLUDED.

3. As part of the maximum performance tuning of these engines, the exhaust heat is blocked out of the intake manifold. This results in extremely unpleasant operation during the extra long warm-up period. In fact, full warm-up is never obtained during cold weather operation.

4. The large capacity oil pan reduces ground clearance, and is subject to severe damage if driven over obstructions in the road.

5. Engine noise is objectionable due to the large clearances required for expansion under maximum engine speed. Valve train and piston noise, in particular, are most noticeable in normal driving conditions.

6. Winter starting and warm-up operations are particularly bothersome due to the thickness of the recommended heavy weight oil.

7. Finally, general operating expenses are higher than normal, due to the required use of "super premium" fuel, and an engine oil supplement. Not only are these items more costly to purchase, but in many cases they may not be readily available.

> CAUTION: Many states have rules or laws governing use of exhaust systems having muffler bypass devices. Therefore it is suggested that local regulations be checked before the Super-Duty exhaust system is used.

BASIC SPECIFICATIONS OF THE 421 SUPER DUTY ENGINE

The piston displacement is 421 cubic inches. Bore, 4.0849-4.1049. Stroke, 3.996 - 4.004.

CYLINDER HEADS AND VALVES

Special high compression ratio cylinder heads have streamlined ports and large valves for free breathing. The intake valves are a special alloy and have a head diameter of 2.02 inches. The exhaust valves are also a special alloy steel and have a head diameter of 1.76 inches. Both intake and exhaust valves are undercut and swirl polished under the heads to reduce the adhesion of deposits. Standard stem to guide clearance is used.

VALVE MECHANISM

Special dual valve springs are factory installed for general use up to 5500 RPM, but it is recommended that still higher load springs (Part Numbers 9772216 and 9772217) which are supplied in a package with the car, be installed for competition only. It should be kept in mind that very high cam loads result from the use of high load valve springs. To avoid cam scuffing during the initial wear-in period, it is recommended that whenever a camshaft is changed, new valve lifters should be installed and the cam contact surface should be lubricated with Type A-9 Hypoid lubricant at build-up.

The valve rocker arms are special to provide a 1.65 to 1 instead of 1.5 to 1 ratio of valve lift to cam lift. Lubrication for the rocker arms and valves is supplied through the solid lifters and tubular push rods. Intermittent spurts of oil are directed through small holes in the rocker arm push rod seats to spray the interior of the rocker chamber with oil.

The camshaft is the No. 10 grind which provides the following valve timing:

Intake Opens	42° BTC
Intake Closes	86° ABC
Intake Event Duration	308°
Exhaust Opens	95° BBC
Exhaust Closes	45° ATC
Exhaust Event Duration	320°

Refer to the valve spring discussion for recommended procedure with respect to valve lifters and their lubrication when installing a new camshaft. The recommended cold lash adjustment is .012" on the intake and .018" on the exhaust valves. Hot lash adjustment should be .010" on the intake and .015" on the exhaust. It is essential to maintain correct valve lash for optimum performance and for maximum durability.

CYLINDER BLOCK

The cylinder block features larger main bearing bores to accommodate a special crankshaft having larger (3.25" nominal) main journals. Special four bolt main bearing caps reinforce the cylinder block to provide extra strength to meet the special requirements. There is a machined relief at the top of each cylinder bore to achieve free breathing through the larger diameter intake valves.

PISTON AND CONNECTING ROD ASSEMBLY

Forged aluminum alloy pistons, having valve clearance notches machined in the head, are fitted with .009" to .013" clearance at the top of the skirt. Thick chrome faced piston rings are used in both compression ring grooves and are fitted with .025" to .035" gap in the 4.095" (nominal) diameter bores. The connecting rods have a special heat treatment for increased strength and are machined to provide .030" to .035" side clearance (for 2 rods) on the crankpins. Piston pins are fitted with .0009 to .0011 clearance in the pistons and are locked in the connecting rods with a pressed fit (the same as the standard engine). Connecting rod bearing liners are M-400 aluminum alloy and are fitted with .0020" to .0031" clearance.

OIL PAN AND OIL PUMP

The oil pan and oil pan baffle are revised to provide a 6-quart sump capacity. The oil pump is special to provide a higher regulated pressure and is equipped with an oil inlet tube and inlet screen assembly as required by the oil pan.

FLYWHEEL AND CLUTCH

The engine is equipped with a light weight flywheel for reduced inertia and it has special machining for attachment of the increased capacity clutch cover and pressure plate assembly. The clutch driven member carries special high-strength facing material which is thicker than standard. The clutch fork ball is a special length to accommodate the cover plate. The clutch lash adjustment procedure is the same as the standard car.

HARMONIC BALANCER AND ACCESSORY DRIVE

A special harmonic balancer (spring pack type) is used on the Super-Duty engine. It is tuned to meet the requirements of the crankshaft at high engine speed. The fan belt drive pulley groove is a special design to guard against belt throwing at high speed. Similar pulleys are used on the water pump and Delcotron alternator. The fan belt is .50" wide and is specially constructed for increased strength.

EXHAUST SYSTEM

Special dual outlet tuned type exhaust manifolds are designed to take advantage of the inertia effect of a moving column of exhaust gas to assist in scavenging the exhaust from the cylinders and minimizing exhaust back pressure.

Exhaust ports are provided on the exhaust pipe adapter attached to each exhaust manifold. Removal of a cover plate provides an unobstructed, 3-inch diameter outlet for the exhaust from each manifold. When the cover plates are in place, the exhaust is directed through 2.25 inch exhaust pipes to low restriction reverse flow mufflers on the 4-barrel car and to a single muffler on the dual 4-barrel car, then on rearward through a 2.0 inch diameter tail pipe.

> CAUTION: Many states have rules or laws governing use of exhaust systems having muffler bypass devices. Therefore, it is suggested that local regulations be checked before the Super-Duty exhaust system is used.

FUEL AND CRANKCASE OIL

The high compression ratio, and extreme operating conditions that this engine was designed for, makes the use of super premium fuel mandatory. Similarly the crankcase oil should be SAE-30 viscosity for service "MS" (most severe) plus one 16 oz. can of Engine Oil Supplement, (Part number 3755788) for each six quarts of oil used. The factory fill oil is suitable for transport operation only. The special oil and oil supplement that is shipped in the luggage compartment must be installed prior to placing the car in service.

FUEL PUMP

The car is factory equipped with a standard (5.25-6.5 p.s.i.) pressure fuel pump. A high pressure (12.5 to 15.0 p.s.i.) fuel pump (Parts Pkg. #5621680) is supplied with the car for maximum speed running. It is not installed in production and is not recommended for normal running because of the probability of carburetor flooding at low fuel flow.

ALTERNATOR AND STARTER

The Delcotron Alternator is equipped with a large (3.5 in. diameter) deep-groove drive pulley, making it especially suitable for high speed operation. The starting motor is equipped with a special mounting flange to avoid interference with the exhaust manifold. It is otherwise identical to the premium-fuel engine starter.

COMPETITION PACKAGE INCLUDED

A competition package shipped in the luggage compartment of all Super Duty cars contains the following items that must be installed before high speed operation.

- Six quarts of SAE 30 oil and one 16 oz. can of Engine Oil Supplement should replace the factory installed crankcase oil. The original oil is suitable for low speed "car in transit" running only.

- On the Dual 4-BBL. Engine equipped with standard ignition, the resistor block No. 1931385 (.3 ohm) should replace the factory installed 2.2 ohm resistor No. 1941604 which prevents burning the distributor points during low-speed operation.

- High load valve springs, #9772216 and #9772217, should be installed before exceeding an engine speed of 5500 RPM.

- High pressure fuel pump, #5621680, is required to insure sufficient fuel for maximum power operation.

SPARK PLUGS

The factory installed AC-44S spark plugs allow low speed operation without fouling. The owner should procure and install AC-42 (or equivalent) spark plugs prior to high speed operation, otherwise pre-ignition damage will occur.

THE 421 DUAL 4-BBL. CAR (Code 13)

(Primarily for maximum acceleration)

INDUCTION SYSTEM
(Two 4-Barrel Carburetor)

The intake manifold is designed for maximum engine output making use of two 4-barrel carburetors. The manifold is made of cast aluminum for light weight. Exhaust heat is not supplied to this manifold so that the mixture will remain as cool as possible for maximum volumetric efficiency.

Two special large bore 4-barrel carburetors are used. They are alike except for choke provisions on the rear unit and the throttle lever linkage attached to the throttle arms. The primary throttle bores are 1-9/16" diameter and the secondary bores are 1-11/16" diameter. Both carburetors are calibrated about 5 percent rich for maximum power. A manual choke is provided on the rear carburetor.

Two low restriction air inlet cleaners are used. They are made of buffed aluminum for minimum weight. The cleaning elements are made of flattened aluminum wire. Operating without air cleaners does not require a calibration change because the carburetors are balance vented.

Engine idle speed is to be maintained between 1000 and 1200 RPM.

SPECIAL EQUIPMENT INCLUDED, 421 DUAL 4-BBL. CAR

Engine

- Carburetors — two 4-barrel
- Intake Manifold — cast aluminum.
- Camshaft — No. 10.
- Cylinder Heads — new, larger exhaust ports. Washers under head bolts. 12.0 to 1 compression ratio.
- Pistons — Forged aluminum. See Performance Options.
- Cylinder Block — 421 cubic inch displacement.
- Exhaust Manifolds — new, to match heads. Cast aluminum, flanged ends.

> CAUTION: This engine is designed specifically for maximum <u>acceleration</u> trials. <u>Sustained</u> speeds above 70 M.P.H. cannot be maintained without risking severe damage to the aluminum exhaust manifolds.

Also see Performance Options.

- Valves — tuliped for light weight.
- Valve Springs — new, aircraft quality chrome-silicon steel.
- Push-rods — specially selected for straightness.
- Harmonic Balancer — 4 top center marks, cyanide hardened front plate.
- Drive Pulleys — deep groove.
- Fan Belt — premium cord.
- Ignition System — dual breaker distributor. See Performance Options.
- Secondary wires — copper.

Transmission and Clutch

- Clutch — 10.5 in. diam. Borg and Beck. Stamped cover, tested @ 11,000 RPM.
- Clutch Disc — high strength facings.
- Flywheel — malleable iron.
- Flywheel housing material — cast iron. See Performance Options.
- Clutch controls — new, for reduced deflection.
- Transmission — 3-speed manual, 2.10 first gear, 1.45 second gear. See Performance Options.
- Shift Control — Hurst-Campbell. See Performance Options.

Chassis

- Propeller Shaft — high speed.
- Rear Springs — low rate, for better traction on starts.
- Front Shock Absorbers — no rebound control, for better traction on starts.
- Rear Shock Absorbers — no compression control, for better traction on starts.
- Axle — phosphate coated gears. Special locking differential has increased clutch spring loads for maximum traction. 4.30 ratio.
- Exhaust System — Single, with competition exhaust ports, aluminum adapter. See Performance Options.
- Frame — sedan frame modified for left hand exhaust manifold.
- Wheels — Standard fronts and spare. 14 x 7L on rears.
- Tires — 8.00 x 14.

Body

- Battery and tray — in luggage compartment, to put added weight in rear for maximum traction on starts.
- Front fenders, hood, doors, deck lid — steel. See PERFORMANCE OPTIONS for maximum weight saving components.
- Front and rear bumpers — standard gauge steel. See Performance Options.

PERFORMANCE OPTIONS, 421 DUAL 4-BBL. CAR

- Exhaust manifolds — stamped and welded steel construction.
- Raised-Head pistons for 13.0 compression ratio.
- Tachometer with electrical or mechanical drive.
- Full transistor ignition system.
- Flywheel housing — aluminum, for weight saving.
- Transmission —
  (a) 3-speed manual, 2.28 first gear, 1.45 second gear.
  (b) 4-speed manual, 2.2 first gear, 1.66 second gear and 1.31 third gear, with aircraft quality steel gears in an aluminum case.
- Shift Control — 4-speed Hurst-Campbell
- Dual Exhaust System with competition exhaust ports.
- Differential Carrier — aluminum, for weight saving.
- Windshield, backlite and side glass areas — light weight.
- Front and rear bumpers — aluminum for reduced weight.
- Front fenders, hood — aluminum for reduced weight.
- Doors and rear deck lid — light weight material for reduced weight.

THE 421 SINGLE 4-BBL. CAR (Code 12)

(Primarily for SUSTAINED high speed)

INDUCTION SYSTEM
(Single 4-BBL. Carburetor)

The intake manifold is expressly designed for high speed operation. It is made of cast aluminum for light weight and features large headers with streamlined runners. There is no manifold heat provision so that the mixture will remain as cool as possible for maximum volumetric efficiency.

The engine is fitted with a special large bore (1-11/16" diameter primary) 4-barrel carburetor. It is calibrated about 5 percent rich for maximum power. A manual choke is provided.

An extra large paper element air cleaner is furnished for efficient engine protection with a minimum restriction of the intake air.

Engine idle speed is to be maintained between 1000 and 1200 RPM.

CRANKSHAFT

The crankshaft is a heat-treated alloy steel forging that is machined to special dimensions for high speed durability. The main bearing journals are a quarter inch larger in diameter than the standard engine journals and are ground to provide a bearing clearance of .0020 to .0031. All main journal and crankpin fillets are ground to a large (.100 - .120) radius for extended fatigue life. General Motors M-400 aluminum alloy bearing liners are specified.

SPECIAL EQUIPMENT INCLUDED, 421 4-BBL.

Engine:

- Carburetor — one 4-barrel, increased capacity.
- Intake manifold — cast aluminum.
- Camshaft — No. 10.
- Cylinder Heads — new, larger exhaust ports. Washers under head bolts. 12.0 to 1 compression ratio.
- Pistons — Super Duty (see description in "The Basic 421 Super Duty Engine").
- Cylinder Block — 421 cubic inch displacement.
- Exhaust Manifolds — new, to match heads. Stamped and welded steel construction for light weight.
- Valves — flat, thin heads.
- Valve Springs — new aircraft quality chrome-Silicon steel.
- Push Rods — selected for straightness.
- Balancer — 4 top center marks, cyanide hardened front plate.
- Drive Pulleys — deep groove.
- Fan Belt — premium cord.
- *[redacted]*
- Secondary Wires — copper.

Transmission and Clutch:

- Clutch — 10.5 in. diam. Borg and Beck. Stamped cover tested @ 11,000 RPM.
- Clutch Disc — high strength facings.
- Flywheel Housing — cast aluminum.
- Flywheel — steel.

- Transmission — 3 speed manual, 2.28 first gear, 1.45 second gear.
- Shift Control — 3 speed Hurst-Campbell.

Chassis

- Propeller Shaft — high speed.
- Axle — Phosphate coated gears, 3.42 to 1 ratio. Super Duty axle shafts.
- Exhaust System — Dual, with competition exhaust ports.
- Frame — sedan frame, modified for left hand exhaust manifold.
- Wheels — 15 x 6K.
- Tires — 7.10 x 15.
- Brakes — Heavy Duty.
- Brake Linings — metallic M-83.
- Steering Gear and Shaft — 20 to 1 ratio for quick response.
- Steering Knuckles and Linkage — Super Duty.

PERFORMANCE OPTIONS, 421 4-BBL.

- Tachometer with electrical or mechanical drive.
- Transmission — 4 speed manual, 2.2 first gear, 1.66 second gear and 1.31 third gear. Aircraft quality steel gears in an aluminum case.
- Shift Control — 4 speed Hurst-Campbell.
- Differential Carrier — aluminum.
- Radiator — heavy duty aluminum.
- Front fenders and hood — aluminum, for minimum weight.
- Doors and Rear Deck Lid — light weight material for reduced weight.
- Windshield, side glass and backlight —light weight.

LAST MINUTE CHANGE IN IGNITIONS!

* IGNITION SYSTEM (left-hand column) is now DUAL BREAKER, *not* "full transistor".

- PERFORMANCE OPTIONS, 241 4-BBL. (right-hand column), now include IGNITION SYSTEM — FULL TRANSISTOR.

Form 516CSD Engine Addenda

Attach 2 copies to
Wholesale Order _____

ORDER FORM ADDENDA
SUPER DUTY SYNCHROMESH ENGINES

Date _____
Dealer Code _____
Customer _____

The following Super Duty Engines are available on Models 2311 and 2347 only. Air Conditioning is not available with Super Duty Engines.

Check appropriate blanks (_____) below.

421 SD Engines	Synchro. Trans.		Axle Ratios	Equipment Included
No. 12 (____) 4-Bbl.	(Std.) Code 5 3 speed (2.28 1st)	(____) Code T 4 speed Option (2.20 1st)	(std.) 3.42	Super Duty 4-Bbl. Carb. Forged Pistons 4 Bolt Bearing Caps Forged Crankshaft Special Camshaft Super Duty Air Cleaner Super Duty Clutch Super Duty Connecting Rods Super Duty Cylinder Heads Transistor Ignition System Super Duty Fuel Pump, Flywheel and Harmonic Balancer Mechanical (Solid) Lifter Assy. Standard Throttle Linkage Aluminum Intake Manifold and Super Duty Stainless Steel Exhaust Manifolds Dual Exhaust System with Competition Ports Special Oil Pan and Pump High Speed Propeller Shaft 44S Spark Plugs Heavy Duty Valve Springs Heavy Duty Starter 20:1 Ratio Fast Steering Gear Special Frame Standard Radiator Heavy Duty Brakes Hurst-Campbell Shift Control
		(____) Code U	Opt. 3.90 (____) 4.30 (____)	
No. 13 (____) Dual 4-Bbl.	(Std.) Code 4 3 speed (2.1 1st)	(____) Code U 4 speed Option (2.20 1st) (____) Code T 3 speed opt. (____) Code 5 (2.28 1st)	(Std.) 4.30 Opt. 3.90 (____) 3.64 (____)	Super Duty Dual 4-Bbl. Carb. Forged Pistons 4 Bolt Bearing Caps Special Camshaft Super Duty Air Cleaner Super Duty Clutch Super Duty Connecting Rods Super Duty Cylinder Heads Dual Point Distributor Single Exhaust System - Competition Exhaust Ports Super Duty Fuel Pump, Flywheel and Harmonic Balancer Mechanical (Solid) Lifter Assy. Mechanical Throttle Linkage Aluminum Intake Manifold and Super Duty Cast Iron Exhaust Manifold Special Oil Pan and Pump High Speed Propeller Shaft 44S Spark Plugs Heavy Duty Valve Springs Heavy Duty Starter Special Frame Standard Radiator Special Shock Absorbers Hurst-Campbell Shift Control 7 x 14 Rear Wheels

SUPER DUTY SYNCHROMESH ENGINES CATALINA SERIES Models 2311 & 2347 ONLY

GRAND PRIX X-400

With the Fleur de Lis Tempest in the background, the X-400 was the featured attraction at the 1963 International Auto Show in New York City. Its exterior is Pearl Yellow.

Still supercharged and still a convertible, the latest in the GP series steals the show at the Great Western Exhibit Center in Los Angeles

PONTIAC Motor Divison's experimental car, the X-400, made its debut on February 7, 1963, at the Great Western Exhibit Center in Los Angeles. The sleek and stylish yellow convertible was one of the featured attractions of the 1963 Winternationals Rod & Custom Car Show. The new experimental car is the third in a series of X-400 automobiles engineered by Pontiac and styled by the General Motors styling staff at GM's Technical Center.

Powered by a supercharged 389-cubic-inch engine, the X-400 is equipped with four sidedraft carburetors. These breathe cool air through grilled scoops at the front of twin blisters in the new fiberglass hood panel.

The distinctive Pontiac split grille is flanked by single headlamps of an unique vertical rectangular pattern behind chromed mesh guards. Lettering along the fenders identifies the X-400 as "Supercharged."

From the front wheel well to the rear bumper, the rocker panel along each side is flush brushed aluminum. It is broken only by twin rectangular exhaust ports just ahead of each rear wheel. Above these ports two indentations in the surface—one above and one below the fender peak line—direct air to two small square openings with slim vertical grille bars.

At the rear of the X-400, the trim and taillight layout is much like that of the Pontiac Grand Prix, with concealed stop and running lights. The X-400 is painted a pearlescent yellow, with matching color accents on the cast aluminum eight-lug wheels. A narrow black stripe follows the body highlight lines and adds interest to the hood and deck lid areas.

The interior is executed entirely in black, from the four bucket seats to the crackle-finish instrument panel. The normal Pontiac speedometer is supplemented by an array of six dials in line to the right, each in a separate housing angled toward the driver for maximum legibility. A new console design is also incorporated in the X-400.

Construction of the X-400 was completed on February 2, 1963 and it was shipped air-freight to the West Coast.

Vertical headlamps are protected by chrome mesh grille guards. Last year they were horizontal.

Like its X-400 predecessor, the GP is powered by a 389-inch Mickey Thompson blown engine with side draft carburetion. In place of the hot rod air cleaners are marine flame arrestors for protection against backfiring.

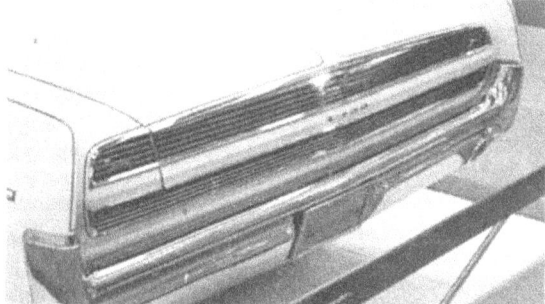

Scooped rear fenders have trick vertical grilles and are highlighted by dark pin striping.

Sleek bucket seats are highlighted by a full-length console with four-speed stick and chrome mesh carpet inserts for the driver and front seat passenger.

In typical Grand Prix fashion, the rear end is clean and trim. The grille treatment is unique with its X-400 emblem.

THE CAMMER CONSPIRACY

Overhead cam engines that 'almost were' from Malcom McKellar and the Special Engine Development Group

BETWEEN the years 1963 and 1968, engineers involved with the Advanced Design Section and the Special Engine Development Group and working with "Mac" McKellar and Bill Klinger came up with a brace of overhead camshaft Eight and Six-cylinder engines, proving that Pontiac didn't have to take a back seat to Ford, Chevy or Chrysler. Some engines were functioning, high-horsepower motors slated for installation in Firebirds and GTOs; others never even made it to the dyno rooms. All were outrageous and the pick of the crop is featured here.

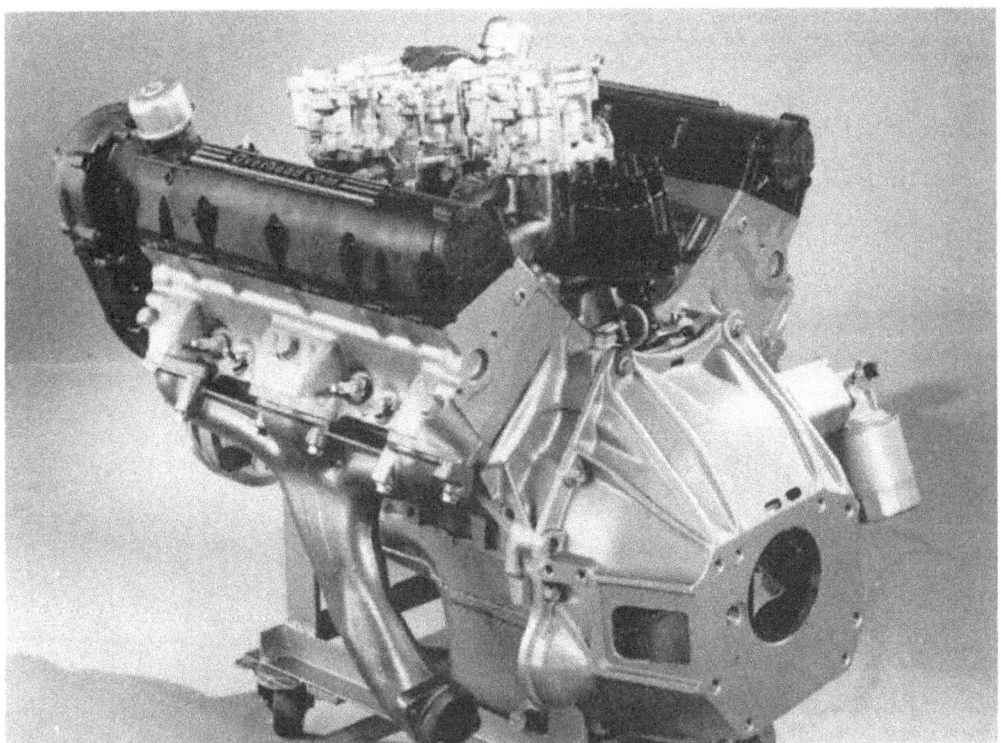

This SOHC (Single Overhead Cam) 421-inch engine put out over 630 hp at 6,800 rpm and weighed just 75 pounds more than a production 421 engine. The head layout is conventional with two-valves-per-cylinder and the overhead cams are belt-driven. This engine was debuted in 1963½!

This is the DOHC (Double Overhead Cam) 389 originally designed in 1963 around a stock HP-389 block. It boasts four-valves-per-cylinder, cross-ram aluminum induction tubes with eight butterflies and Pontiac's own speed-density fuel-injection system. Cams are mounted in alloy rocker box covers and feature hydraulic lifters.

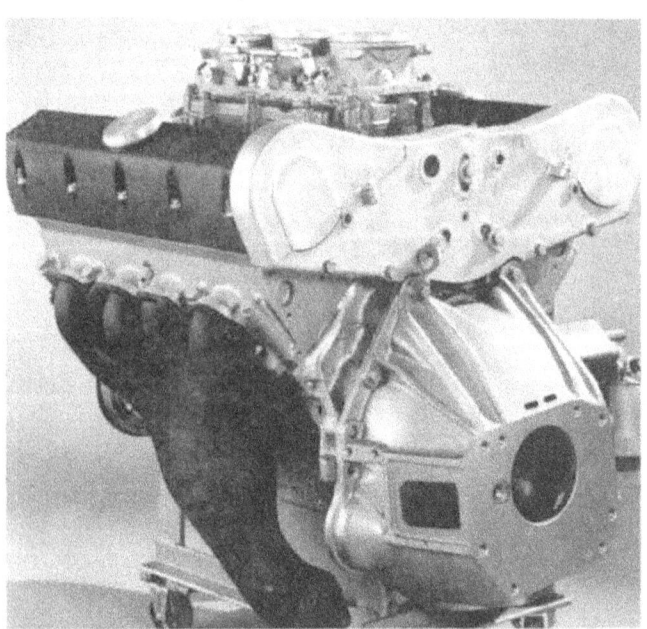

This is the SOHC (Single Overhead Cam) 421 with unique three-valve heads making use of one large 2.280-inch intake and two small 1.420-inch exhausts per cylinder. The drive for the cams is located under alloy covers at the rear of the engine, making accessory drive takeoffs for passenger car use a simple matter. The contoured headers were designed to fit into a passenger car engine compartment and hook up to a mufflered system. The induction system was made up from throttle-body carburetor parts. Special three-valve application piston is shown.

1964

THE YEAR OF THE SUPERCAR

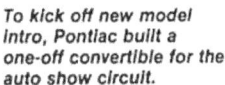

Royal Pontiac came into its own with Bobcat models and the factory sold a total of 8,245 tri-power GTOs.

To kick off new model intro, Pontiac built a one-off convertible for the auto show circuit.

This is what we call "telling it like it is."

Pontiac is responsible
for what will be described as
the start of the Supercar Revolution.
They spell it GTO!

1964 PONTIAC HIGH-PERFORMANCE ENGINES

CUBIC INCHES	BORE	STROKE	HORSEPOWER	COMPRESSION	INDUCTION
389	4.06	3.75	306 @ 4800	10.50-to-1	Four-barrel
389	4.06	3.75	303 @ 4600	10.50-to-1	Four-barrel
389	4.06	3.75	330 @ 4600	10.75-to-1	Tri-power
389	4.06	3.75	325 @ 4800	10.75-to-1	Four-barrel
389	4.06	3.75	348 @ 4900	10.75-to-1	Tri-power
421	4.09	4.00	320 @ 4200	10.50-to-1	Four-barrel
421	4.09	4.00	370 @ 5200	10.75-to-1	Tri-power
421	4.09	4.00	350 @ 4600	10.75-to-1	Tri-power
326	3.72	3.75	280 @ 4800	10.50-to-1	Four-barrel

The Grand Prix sold over 63,000 units in 1964, including 3,124 with manual transmissions. New 2+2 model stole some thunder and sold almost 8,000 units in first year.

The GTO started the Supercar Revolution and established Pontiac as the guru of the youth market.

Steidle Pontiac campaigned this B/S Goat squaring off against Golden Commando Taxi Cab!

A DEVICE FOR SHRINKING TIME & DISTANCE!

It was only an option but it started the Supercar Revolution and established the GTO cult movement that's as strong today as it was in 1964

"TO BE perfectly honest, the GTO is not everyone's cup of tea. Designed as a piece of performance machinery, its purpose in life is to permit you to make the most of your driving skill. Its suspension is firm, tuned more to the open road than to wafting gently over bumpy city streets. Its dual exhausts won't win any prizes for whispering. And, unless you order it with our lazy 3.08 low-ratio rear axle, its gas economy won't be anything to write home about. If all this dismays you, then you're almost certainly a candidate for one of our 27 other Pontiac Pontiacs and Pontiac Tempests. (Most people are.) But if you are tuned in to our particular wave length, if you start vibrating when you're at the controls of a sudden automobile, if you've driven enough different kinds of performance to know what it's all about, then you've got GTO written right across your forehead."

That's what Pontiac had to say about the Tempest GTO option in 1964. It was the option that became the moving force behind the Supercar Revolution of the Sixties and once again established Pontiac as the builder of super-performance cars. Essentially it started out as an engine swap option that grew to become a car and a performance image second to none in the automotive marketplace.

During 1962 and 1963, Pontiac was enjoying an incredible reputation as a builder of unstoppable race cars. They were, of course, the original Super-Duty cars powered by 421 cubic inch engines and available with all kinds of race engine parts, aluminum body parts, plexiglass windows and even a few swiss-cheesed chassis. Then the Ivory Tower guys at General Motors started slapping a few wrists. They demanded that the Divisions keep a lower profile as far as racing was concerned and stop building race-only cars. It was a grim day when the corporate message was distributed at Pontiac Motor Division.

It was especially hard for the top people at Pontiac for a couple of reasons. First off, they knew that racing and performance do sell cars and the racing image was giving Pontiac exposure that it couldn't get if they were out of the scene. And, the dealers loved it. Also, the heavies at Pontiac loved racing, understood the correlation between involvement in the sport and sales. They had an understanding of the youth market and the machinery they liked to drive. "Pete" Estes, now president of General Motors, was the Pontiac General Manager and John DeLorean was the Chief Engineer. And, there was an outsider by the name of Jim Wangers who possibly had the best understanding of the youth market of all the Pontiac people.

Jim Wangers at the time was an account executive on the Pontiac account at McManus, John & Adams and a nationally-known drag racer. He raced Pontiacs out of Royal Pontiac and eventually developed the legendary Royal Pontiac Bobcat cars and packages. He originally presented GTO concepts to Estes who in turn called in DeLorean. Together they came up with an engine swap, a

The tri-power induction package figured heavily in the creation of the GTO mystique. The setup above is a modified version for drag racing, while the Royal Bobcat '64 GTO, left, is just the way Royal Pontiac prepared it in 1964.

OPTIONS & ACCESSORIES

Comfort & Convenience: Power steering, power brakes, power tilt driver's seat, power windows. Custom air conditioner, tinted glass all around or just in the windshield, rear-window defogger (except Convert.). Washers, two-speed wipers. Seven-position tilting steering wheel, padded dash, console. Radios, electric antenna, regular or reverberating rear seat speakers (except Convert.). Luggage compartment light, ski racks, removable luggage carrier. Deluxe wheel discs, wire wheel discs, custom wheel discs. Black or white fabric top. Rayon cord whitewalls optional at no extra cost.

Performance: 4-speed all-synchro transmission with Hurst shifter, 2-speed automatic. Metallic brake linings, heavy-duty radiator, Safe-T-Track limited-slip differential. Custom sports steering wheel, handling kit (extra-stiff shocks and 20:1 quick steering) or extra-stiff shocks alone. Tachometer or rally clock, vacuum gauge. Exhaust splitters, mechanical 3-2BBL carburetor linkage. High-performance full transistor (breakerless) ignition.

ENGINES

	Standard	Optional
Type	ohv V-8	ohv V-8
Bore and stroke	4.06 x 3.75	4.06 x 3.75
Displacement, cu. in.	389	389
Compression ratio	10.75:1	10.75:1
Minimum allowable combustion chamber volume, cc	66.0	66.0
Carburetion	1-4BBL	3-2BBL
Total throttle bore area, sq. in.	7.62	12.19
Bhp @ rpm	325 @ 4800	348 @ 4900
Torque, lb-ft	428 @ 3200	428 @ 3600

Alloy cast iron block, five main bearings. High-compression flat-top pistons with valve indents. High-lift camshaft, high-performance hydraulic valve lifters. Large-diameter valves—1.92" intake, 1.66" exhaust. Dual exhausts. Clutch is 10.4" bent-finger Belleville with 2300-lb minimum load. Seven-blade, 18" fan, with declutching unit. Low-restriction air cleaners on 3-2BBL engine.

Dimensions & Capacities: Wheelbase is 115 inches. Overall length is 203 inches. Tread is 58 inches, front and rear. Overall width is 73.3 inches. Height is 53.5 inches for the Sports Coupe and Hardtop, 53.6 inches for the Convertible. Total trunk capacity is 32.1 cubic feet. The gas tank holds 21.5 gallons. Shipping weights: Coupe—3272; Hardtop—3292; Convertible—3422.

Transmissions: A 3-speed manual transmission is standard, with Hurst shifter curving up into your hand from between the seats. Ratios are 2.58:1, 1.48:1, 1.00:1, and 2.58:1 reverse.

Then there's an optional floor-mounted, aluminum-case, fully synchronized 4-speed. Ratios are 2.56:1, 1.91:1, 1.48:1, 1.00:1, and 2.64:1 reverse.

And, of course, there's a 2-speed torque converter automatic, its lever mounted on the steering column. Ratios are 1.76:1, 1.00:1, and 1.76:1 reverse, with a total torque multiplication off the line of 3.87:1. The governor is set for a maximum automatic upshift at 5200 rpm. The optional console accommodates the shift lever for all three transmissions.

AXLE RATIOS

Engine	Transmission	Standard axle		Special Order axle ratios		
325 bhp	3- or 4-speed	3.23	3.08#	3.36*•**	3.55*•**	3.90*‡§**
	automatic	3.23	3.08#	3.36*†**	3.55*†**	3.90*†‡§**
348 bhp	3- or 4-speed	3.23	3.08	3.23#	3.36**	3.90‡**
	automatic	3.23	3.08#	3.23	3.36	3.90†‡§**

Axle ratio	Mph per 1000 rpm in high gear
3.08	25.2
3.23	24.0
3.36	23.1
3.55	21.9
3.90	19.9

*Special radiator required at extra cost. §Metallic brake linings and Safe-T-Track required at extra cost.
†Speedo adapter required at extra cost. #Standard axle with air conditioning.
‡Heavy-duty fan required at extra cost. **Air conditioning not available.

Steering: Recirculating ball bearing steering gear. Standard ratio is 24:1. Optional quick steering is 20:1. Power steering is 17.5:1.

Suspension: Ball joint independent front, four-link rear. Shocks are valved specifically for firm ride and control. Heavy-duty coil springs have wheel rates of 90 and 110 pounds per inch, front and rear. Diameter of stabilizer bar is 0.938".

We'd suggest you try this already heavy-duty standard suspension before you make up your mind about the stiffer suspension components we have available.

Brakes: Hydraulic, duo-servo, self-adjusting. Diameter of finned drums is 9.5", with a swept area of 269.8 sq. in. Metallic brake linings are available as a separate option with all axle ratios except 3.08:1, but are recommended only for extreme duty service since they have the usual metallic brake ailments of squeaks, grunts, and high pedal pressure when cold.

NOTICE: All the options noted herein, including vinyl top, radio, wheel discs, custom sports steering wheel, and backup lights, illustrated on some models, are extra cost equipment unless otherwise specified. Ask your dealer for all price information on any model or special equipment you desire. Pontiac Motor Division of General Motors Corporation reserves the right to make changes at any time. Pontiac Motor Division, General Motors Corporation, 196 Oakland Avenue, Pontiac, Michigan.

new model name and some bolt-on trim all designed around the popular intermediate-wheelbase Tempest. The name GTO came from Ferrari and stands for *Grand Turissimo Omologato*.

Estes took a chance and estimated that production for the first year would run 5,000 and, if they were lucky, it would be around again in 1965. Well, by January 1964, Pontiac dealers already had orders for more than 10,000 cars, plus a wait list. When all was said and done, 1964 production ran 32,450 with 6,644 convertible models delivered. All parties concerned became heroes. Wangers became close friends with DeLorean and working together there, came a long string of performance Pontiacs that revolutionized the street scene. A few all-out racing efforts were also slipped in thanks to some of the factory engineers, Jim Wangers and the crew at Royal Pontiac. Other dealers throughout the country joined in, establishing Pontiac as the car to beat in many classes of competition.

The rest is history. With some help from Jim Wangers, Pontiac turned the GTO from an option into a car and on to a youth cult. There were GTO records, GTO shoes and a host of promotional goodies at both the factory and after-market levels. Of all the General Motors big-engined intermediates, the GTO was the most popular. Unfortunately, it became a victim of the times. The insurance companies didn't exactly help either! They tagged on all kinds of rate increases for cars such as the GTO which made ownership financially impractical for young enthusiasts. The last GTO in 1974 could hardly be considered more than a distant relative of the car that started the Supercar Revolution.

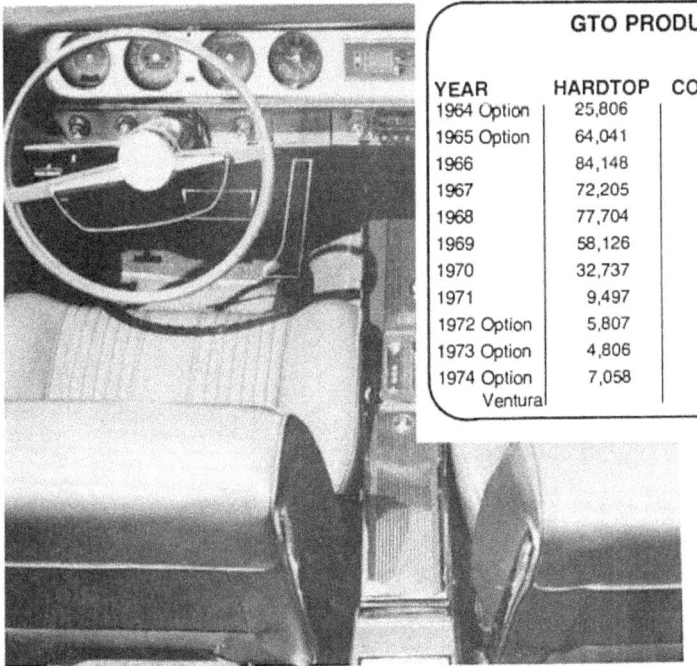

GTO PRODUCTION 1964 THROUGH 1974

YEAR	HARDTOP	CONVERTIBLE	JUDGE COUPE	JUDGE CONVERTIBLE	TOTAL
1964 Option	25,806	6,644	N/A	N/A	32,450
1965 Option	64,041	11,311	N/A	N/A	75,352
1966	84,148	12,798	N/A	N/A	96,946
1967	72,205	9,517	N/A	N/A	81,722
1968	77,704	9,980	N/A	N/A	87,684
1969	58,126	7,328	6,725	108	72,287
1970	32,737	3,615	3,629	168	40,149
1971	9,497	661	357	17	10,532
1972 Option	5,807	N/A	N/A	N/A	5,807
1973 Option	4,806	N/A	N/A	N/A	4,806
1974 Option Ventura	7,058	N/A	N/A	N/A	7,058

*N/A denotes not available

The total '64 GTO production run exceeded top brass estimates (six times more than estimated) for a grand total of 32,450 units. Convertible production ran just 6,644. All transmissions, even the stock three-speed stick and two-speed Automatic had console-mounted floor sticks. Interior appointments were targeted to the tastes of the youth market.

BIRTH OF THE SUPERCAR

There were quicker, faster and more powerful production cars in 1964, but it was the GTO that started the Supercar Revolution

PONTIAC's GTO is a perfect example of a car that is far more than the sum total of its parts and features. Simplistically speaking, the original 1964 GTO (first of a series of high-performance cars that lasted for a decade) is little more than an intermediate-sized Tempest with a big motor, beefier suspension and lots of exclusive ornamentation. In reality, the GTO started the Supercar Revolution in this country and established a cult movement that's as strong today as it was during the early-Sixties.

The GTO (actually an option on the Tempest and not an official model) came out of Pontiac at a time when living legends like Bunkie Knudsen, Pete Estes and John Z. DeLorean were involved in policy-making decisions at General Motors and Pontiac Motor Division. A drag racing account executive at Pontiac's ad agency (McManus, John & Adams) by the name of Jim Wangers pushed for the hot rod concept of putting a big engine in an intermediate car and that's what started the wheels turning.

At the time of the GTO, General Motors had two edicts in effect for its divisions. One involved racing and the other limited engine displacement for certain size cars. It was obvious to GM top brass that a car like the GTO would end up on the drag strips and race tracks and that Pontiac would eventually be involved in racing activities. They also frowned upon the use of the established 389-cubic-inch big-car engine (an engine that was available with three carburetors and high-compression) in the lighter-weight cars. What they did not realize was that Wangers and cohorts weren't really that interested in racing. They wanted to sell street cars and the street was exactly where the GTO excelled. That's what the Supercar Revolution was all about.

Even though enthusiasm ran high at Pontiac, the GTO got off to a rather inauspicious start. Wangers, a street racer and one of the very few people in his field who could communicate with the youth market, knew that the GTO concept had all the ingredients needed for success. It had styling, a very strong powerplant and matching driveline and enough exclusive ornamentation and status trim to turn on the drive-in set. He knew that market better than anyone at Pontiac.

However, Pontiac's General Sales Manager, Frank Bridges, didn't like it and had little faith in Wanger's gut feelings and understanding of a portion of the marketplace that had not exactly been Pontiac's turf. Since the GTO had been pre-sold to dealers around the country by DeLorean, Bridges went along for the ride and tagged production at 5,000. Needless to say he was surprised when the orders started pouring in and so were the tight-assed decision makers in GM's Ivory Tower. When all the smoke had cleared, Pontiac sold 32,450 GTO-optioned Tempests for the 1964 model year. In 1965 the sales figure more than doubled at 75,352 units and in 1965 the option became a car model and the sales figure tripled at 96,946 units. In the first year of production, convertible sales accounted for approximately 25 percent of

In keeping with the custom trends of the times, Pontiac lowered its prototype GTO all around, added chrome reverse rims, removed some of the body trim and even added race car Lakes-style exhaust cutouts behind the front fender wells.

This is the GTO used by Pontiac Motor Division to push the Supercar concept on the auto show circuit from coast-to-coast. Super-sano front end sports rectangular Cibie headlamps, cleaned-up grille and a macho functionally-scooped hood.

total sales (6,644 units).

Prior to the GTO effort in 1964, Pontiac had a reputation for building solid, good value cars for the masses. They also developed a name for themselves in racing with the legendary Super-Duty cars powered by both 389 and 421-cubic-inch V-8 engines on NASCAR stock car circuits, at Bonneville with a land speed record car and on drag strips. But the Super-Duty cars were not easy to buy, dealers were uninformed about performance and, even though the cars were great, they didn't amount to much in sales. The Wangers approach was to get the youth market into Pontiac dealers and give them a car with the kind of performance they had come to expect from Chevrolet and Ford. Wangers didn't want to build racing cars—he wanted cars that street people could relate to. And, that's exactly what the GTO was all about.

Being at Pontiac's agency, Wangers was able to back up the car with the kind of sales literature that would turn people

GTO PRODUCTION 1964 THROUGH 1974

YEAR	HARDTOP	CONVERTIBLE	JUDGE COUPE	JUDGE CONVERTIBLE	TOTAL
1964 Option	25,806	6,644	N/A	N/A	32,450
1965 Option	64,041	11,311	N/A	N/A	75,352
1966	84,148	12,798	N/A	N/A	96,946
1967	72,205	9,517	N/A	N/A	81,722
1968	77,704	9,980	N/A	N/A	87,684
1969	58,126	7,328	6,725	108	72,287
1970	32,737	3,615	3,629	168	40,149
1971	9,497	661	357	17	10,532
1972 Option	5,807	N/A	N/A	N/A	5,807
1973 Option	4,806	N/A	N/A	N/A	4,806
1974 Option Ventura	7,058	N/A	N/A	N/A	7,058

*N/A denotes not available

Convertible production in 1964 hit 6,644 units, approximately one-quarter of coupe/hardtop production. This pre-production ragtop appears to be lower than stock.

Pontiac played it fairly conservative with the prototype GTO's interior, staying away from excessive chrome trim and lots of extra gauges. They wanted something that the new breed of performance car could relate to.

on to performance cars. The classic 1964 GTO sales brochure titled "A DEVICE FOR SHRINKING TIME AND DISTANCE" said it all:

"To be perfectly honest, the GTO is not everyone's cup of tea. Designed as a piece of performance machinery, its purpose in life is to permit you to make the most of your driving skill. Its suspension is firm, tuned more to the open road than to wafting gently over bumpy city streets. Its dual exhausts won't win any prizes for whispering. And, unless you order it with our lazy 3.08-to-1 low-ratio rear axle, its gas economy won't be anything to write home about. If all this dismays you, then you are almost certainly a candidate for one of our 27 other Pontiac Pontiacs and Pontiac Tempests (Most people are). But if you are tuned in to our particular wavelength, if you start vibrating when you're at the controls of a sudden automobile, if you've driven enough different kinds of performance cars to know what it's all about, then you're got GTO written right across your forehead."

The GTO was the first of the real Supercars and led the way for the Olds 4-4-2, Buick Gran Sport, Mopar Street Hemis, Chevelle SS-396, Ford Fairlane 390 GT and others that boasted large-displacement engines in mid-sized cars. Since Pontiac was first with the GTO,

Pontiac is credited with the start of what later became the biggest combination performance and marketing concept ever to come out of Motown. It should be noted that GTO originally came from Ferrari and stands for *Gran Turismo Omolagato* which also means homologated or certified for Grand Touring Racing under FIA rules. Since Pontiac wasn't interested in FIA world class racing (for good reason) and Ferrari never built enough GTO models to qualify for FIA classification, the two great auto makers never really clashed heads over the GTO nameplate legality.

One area in which the original GTO excelled was in options. You could order either hardtop or soft-top configurations, full luxury appointments or spartan trim, Hurst-shifted four-speed or two-speed automatic transmissions, metallic brakes, special handling suspension with quick manual steering, extra gauges and either a single-four-barrel 389-inch V-8 rated at 325 horsepower or a tri-power version rated at 348 horsepower. If you were into saving money, you could even take a standard three-speed stick transmission. Gear ratios ran from a conservative economy 3.08-to-1 to what hard-core performance freaks ordered, 3.90-to-1. It was the kind of car that the kids who raced up and down the infamous Wood-

Pontiac General Manager, Pete Estes, left, front, and an assortment of Pontiac executives celebrate the breaking of a production record. A GTO convertible was the center of attraction.

The basic two-door pillar coupe represents the epitome of the Supercar concept. It was priced right for the performance enthusiast who was not interested in frills.

ward Ave. strip (major street racing "track" in the Royal Oak, Michigan area, often frequented by Jim Wangers and other performance-minded engineers who worked for the various carmakers) could understand and relate to. The ads, promotions, concept, and the car talked right to the marketplace.

Looking back at the first GTO and the overall concept, Jim Wangers while speaking at a meeting of the International Motor Press Association in New York City, said, "There was a need for some serious packaging. The Pontiac GTO was the first car to put it together and put a name on it. It had a lot of performance items, a lot of sophistication in styling, maybe not enough in tires, handling and brakes. But at least we put a package together that went out into the world with a name on it.

This was one of the biggest promotions that ever hit our town. The GTO became more than a car, it became an image. There were records about it. They named shoes after it. The promotion was a social

Tri-power GTO hardtop with Royal-Pontiac-framed status plate says it all about the Supercar era. This was the car that started the Revolution.

phenomenon.

The GTO started it all, and it was not very long before we had a ton of copiers. It created one of the most exciting and greatest growth periods in Detroit. All these cars did one thing. They beat somebody, and they looked good doing it."

Because of its history and the people involved in bringing the GTO to the marketplace, the car enjoys collectible status and, even though production was not that limited, the value of original and well-restored examples continues to rise each year. There are a number of GTO books on the market and many businesses have been built to service the needs of restorers and owners. The GTO was a very functional automobile right from the start and many enthusiasts still drive them on the street. It's the kind of car that drives as well as it shows and good examples can be bought for approximately one-half of the sticker price of some of Detroit's most mundane econoboxes. The GTO was a bargain in 1964 and a blue chip investment (especially convertibles) today.

You could get your GTO with automatic or stick, but the four-speed version was far superior as far as performance was concerned. The early automatics left something to be desired.

The seats of the prototype were reupholstered in a slightly different pattern, keeping the basic GTO look. The seats were more padded and genuine leather was used. Note the dressed-up door panel treatment and extra moldings.

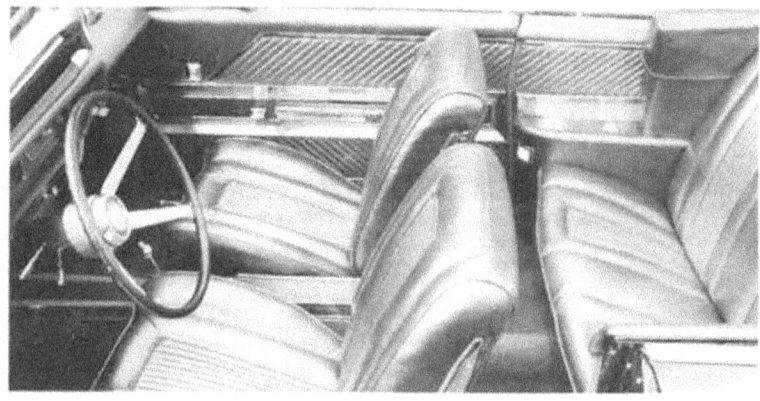

RARE GTO SUPERCARS

Year	Model	Engine	Transmission	Production
1968	Convertible	400 Ram Air	four-speed	92
1968	Convertible	400 Ram Air	turbo-hydro	22
1969	Convertible	Ram Air IV	four-speed	45
1969	Convertible	Ram Air IV	turbo-hydro	14
1970	Convertible	Ram Air IV	four-speed	20
1970	Convertible	Ram Air IV	turbo-hydro	13
1971	Convertible	455-HO	four-speed	21
1971	Convertible	455-HO	turbo-hydro	27
1972	Coupe	455-HO	four-speed	3
1972	Coupe	455-HO	turbo-hydro	7
1973	Coupe	455	turbo-hydro	25

*Source: The Gas Can, GTO Association of America, Billings, Montana 59104

THE ORIGINAL TIN INDIANS

'Win on Sunday and sell on Monday' was the motto at Knafel Pontiac during the Supercar Sixties!

The powers that made it all happen — Bill Knafel, center, Arlen Vanke, left and Bill Abraham. Team work paid off for this enterprising Pontiac dealer.

The famous 'Tin Indian' GTO and some of its impressive trophy collection. Knafel Pontiac did for the GTO what Royal Pontiac did for the full-size car.

IT WAS during Pontiac's golden performance years that a Pontiac dealer by the name of Bill Knafel helped establish the GTO as the car to beat on the drag strip as well as the street. With help from Pontiac's legendary "back door", driver Arlen Vanke and chief-wrench Bill Abraham, Knafel's "Tin Indian" Pontiacs became synonymous with winning. It was a professional operation and the detailed-to-perfection cars were backed up by advertising and both local and national tie-in promotions. Performance sold cars during the Sixties.

When Pontiac was selling performance during the Sixties, he promoted "Beat The Champion" events at drag strips, ran performance clinics at dealerships and even hosted a TV show called, "Knafel Pontiac at Dragway 42." Those were the days when you could count on selling on Monday, if you did a lot of winning on Sunday!

Bill Knafel is still very proud of his drag strip records and marketing accomplishments, including the elusive A/FX or

Vanke and Abraham finish off the blueprinted 360-hp GTO engine and get ready to fill the vacant spot in the Tin Indian's engine room. The old 389 really made some horsepower.

A/Modified NHRA record that he set at Alton, Illinois on 9/29/63 running 123.28 mph in 11.89 seconds. And, he'll never forget the day that the crew went out with their "Tin Indian" Judge and set three records in one day, swapping intake systems from single two-barrel and single four-barrel to tri-power. Those truly were the good old days!

Knafel's legendary Tin Indian Racing Team won more Regional, National and World Championships than any other Pontiac team in the history of the sport. Even though Knafel Pontiac raced at least three different Pontiacs on the tarmac every year from 1958 to 1970, the Tin Indian '66 GTO was the most outstanding of all the cars. It actually racked up 27 championships in one year thanks to the efforts of Bill Knafel, Arlen Vanke, Bill Abraham and Larry "Doc" Dixson.

Powered by a blueprinted tri-power 389/360 engine, this Goat was driven to the 1966 NHRA and NASCAR Championship titles by Doc Dixson. During the National Stock Eliminator Championships at Bristol, TN., Dixson made 39 runs with the car, popping the clutch at 5,000 each time to come off the line like a rocket sled. Pontiac built fast and durable cars.

To combat the low-cost Road Runner Supercar concept, Knafel came up with the Magnum 400, a GTO-powered Tempest with real Supercar performance at bargain-basement prices.

The good old days when Knafel Pontiac's used car lot was stocked with hot Goats, a couple of Super-Duty cars and even some hot Chevys.

If one is good, then two must be better! Knafel's 1966 NHRA and NASCAR Stock Eliminator Champion Goats ready to be trailered to another "Pontiac show."

STRICTLY FOR SHOW

Some of the best customizing
ideas of the Sixties came from the factory stylists.
Check out this '64 GTO ragtop

This GTO ragtop was part of Pontiac's "dog & pony show" in 1964. The factory stole the chrome reversed wheels from the Kalifornia Kustomizers, but those exhaust vents and rocker panel trim are strictly Motown Magic. The engine compartment was treated to the full chrome deal. This GTO was the highlight of the Pontiac Motor Division exhibit.

Neatly positioned inside the full-width grille are custom rectangular headlamps which look like dual conventional headlamps mounted inside wide frames.

Not that much was actually done to the stock GTO body. The lines were basically refined and re-trimmed to highlight certain style points. Those scoops are functional. If only Pontiac could mass-produce enthusiast cars with such quality trim and parts fit!

Convertibles were once taken for granted. Today, ragtops are in and the prices are going through the roof. The interior is basically stock GTO with plusher-than-stock upholstery, extra chrome trim and a lovely lady behind the wheel. In the mid-Sixties Pontiac offered the finest interior packages in Motown.

The latest in the X-400 line sports a swoopy front end with vertical rectangular Quartz lamps and a dual scooped hood with Supercharger trim.

GRAND PRIX X-400

The legend continues with yet another
Grand Prix convertible packing
Mickey Thompson
blown V-8 power

Carryover GMC-blown V-8 powers the X-400. Lots of chrome and aluminum highlight the GMC 6-71-blown 389-incher.

Models and the Grand Prix X-400 at the International Auto Show in New York City in 1964. It gave the radical Mustang I sports car, in the next exhibit, a run for the money.

Factory tach is built in at the left side of the dash. Wall-to-wall gauges with a one-off 160-mph speedometer, plus two radios, give the feeling of an aircraft cockpit.

Four bucket seats with a full-length console make for an eye-catching interior. Note chrome grille floor mats and plush upholstery.

Highly-detailed eight lug wheels with striped high-performance tires are in keeping with the X-400 motif.

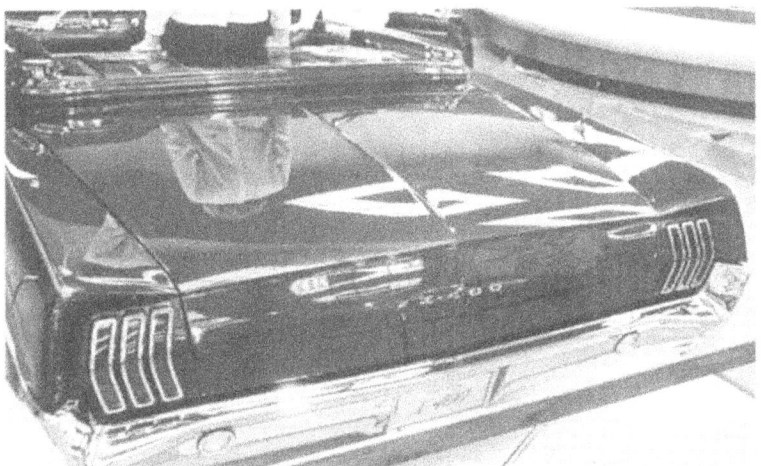
Except for X-400 ornementation, the back end of the Grand Prix showcar is pretty stock. A fiberglass boot is used to cover the folding top.

1965

PERFORMANCE SPOKEN HERE!

Pontiac's prime movers boast 'Coke bottle' styling plus performance in all sizes and shapes. The GTO becomes even quicker and faster

Dressed-up 2+2 with 421 power was popular choice or adult Supercar freaks who needed more space than GTO afforded. Pontiac sold over 11,000 units.

It was a good year for Pontiac and GTO, with 20,547 tri-power models sold.

In 1965, the GTO was the standard of supercar performance.

CAPSULE COMMENTS

WE DON'T know how they did it in the face of strong competition from other divisions, but Pontiac has succeeded in making the best handling cars with the most performance of any maker. Whether you take a hot GTO or a Catalina with the 421 optional engine, there is little doubt that Pontiac is equipped for quarter-mile hauls, fast corners or just all-around enjoyment. If you drive a Catalina aggressively, it's no great problem to keep it near its limit in any curve. If you are in trouble, apply a bit more power and the car heads back into the turn.

In terms of engines Pontiac has taken some significant moves forward. On the single four-barrel, manifold risers are higher and fuel distribution and top end performance improved. A three two-barrel version of the 421 is now available with an official rating of 376 hp at 5,000 rpm and 10.75-to-1. The more modest version of the 421 is rated at 338 horses and 4,800 rpm . . . same as a hot 3-2 389.

In terms of rear axle ratios the GTO, like all of the GM high-performance intermediate cars, is now blessed with a Salisbury rear. Mind you, this is a mixed blessing. On one hand it allows somewhat more noise control through improved gear alignment. On the other

The GTO fit nicely in NHRA stock classes (B/Stock) where it didn't have to compete against solid-lifter Chevys.

hand, changing gears is a pain compared to just changing them with an old-fashioned banjo housing. In fact, 3.42-to-1 is the highest gear ratio listed and it applies to the hottest 389 and 421 versions. Add absence of mechanical lifters and service department worries should be lessened.

There are some notable differences between the standard and optional 421 engines. for instance, Arma-Steel rods are replaced by forged ones in the optional engine, together with Morraine 400 bearings. Optional 421 pistons are forged. Morraine 400 aluminum on steel bearings is used in the lower half shells on the mains on all 421 engines. Valve spring rates are higher on the optional engine, but closing pressures are approximately the same. Cam timing is considerably more wild.

Body styling? Just look at that 2 plus 2 Catalina or at the vertical quad headlights on the GTO. Pontiac is where the action is!

1965 PONTIAC HIGH-PERFORMANCE ENGINES

CUBIC INCHES	BORE	STROKE	HORSEPOWER	COMPRESSION	INDUCTION
389	4.06	3.75	333 @ 5000	10.50-to-1	Four-barrel
389	4.06	3.75	325 @ 4800	10.50-to-1	Four-barrel
389	4.06	3.75	335 @ 5000	10.75-to-1	Four-barrel
389	4.06	3.75	338 @ 4800	10.75-to-1	Four-barrel
389	4.06	3.75	360 @ 5200	10.75-to-1	Tri-power
421	4.09	4.00	338 @ 4600	10.50-to-1	Four-barrel
421	4.09	4.00	356 @ 4800	10.75-to-1	Tri-power
421	4.09	4.00	376 @ 5000	10.75-to-1	Tri-power
326	3.72	3.75	285 @ 5000	10.50-to-1	Four-barrel

You could even get a cheaper–model Catalina with lots of performance goodies. The wheels are not stock.

Royal Pontiac (Bobcat GTO program), under the direction of Jim Wangers, grew to become the country's biggest specialty car merchandiser.

Pontiac dealer Don Gay competed in B/Fuel Dragster (early Funny Car class) with GMC-blown and injected 421 Pontiac supercar.

1966

THE CHOICE IS PONTIAC!

From mini (Sprint OHC Six) to maxi (Tri-Power 421) Pontiac continues to offer the most performance choices and options in the industry

CAPSULE COMMENTS

PONTIAC MOTOR DIVISION's 1966 models, from the Tempest to the Grand Prix offer extensive advancements in automotive styling, engineering, safety and model availability.

The entire Tempest line has been redesigned, expanded by the addition of five new models including a new GTO series, and for the first time in an American passenger car, an overhead camshaft six-cylinder engine is offered as standard equipment on all Tempest models except the GTO.

The GTO, a completely new 1966 series, has its own front end including grille, parking lamps, hood and ornamentation. The side view shows a

The GTO with tri-power was a super-hot street machine and the envy of every drive-in freak.

It was a hot year for Pontiac in the area of performance and styling. Factory built 11,311 GTO convertibles. Out of over 36,000 Grand Prix coupes, just 917 were delivered with manual transmissions.

full length rocker panel molding plus rocker extensions on the front and rear fenders. The GTO rear end has its own tail lamp design consisting of horizontal painted louvers on each side of the rear end panel. Each louver has a fine bright chrome edge and the red tail lamp lens is recessed in the slits between the louvers. Individual block letters are mounted on the central painted panel and a GTO initial ornament graces the deck lid. The new GTO series includes a sports coupe, hardtop coupe and convertible.

Pontiac's highly-rated V-8 engines, both the Tempest 326 cubic-inch option and the 389 and 421 cubic-inch engines available on Pontiac models, have been refined with the emphasis on smoother operation and greater economy.

Variations of the optional Tempest V-8 include a regular fuel two-barrel carburetor engine which delivers 250 horsepower up to a high-output engine with four-barrel carburetion and rated at 285 horsepower. The standard GTO engine is 389 cubic-inch, four-barrel carburetor and 335 horsepower. The GTO option is rated at 360 horsepower and has three two-barrel carburetors.

A slightly-modified version of the four-barrel OHC Sprint engine introduced as a Tempest option. Engine is resting in a later-model Firebird.

The author checks out one of 19,045 tri-power GTO supercars during a new car road test session while at CARS Magazine.

The Grand Prix was starting to become more of an adult supercar because of luxury appointments and overall size.

1966 PONTIAC HIGH-PERFORMANCE ENGINES

CUBIC INCHES	BORE	STROKE	HORSEPOWER	COMPRESSION	INDUCTION
389	4.06	3.75	333 @ 5000	10.50-to-1	Four-barrel
389	4.06	3.75	338 @ 4600	10.50-to-1	Four-barrel
389	4.06	3.75	335 @ 5000	10.75-to-1	Four-barrel
389	4.06	3.75	360 @ 5200	10.75-to-1	Tri-power
389	4.06	3.75	356 @ 4800	10.75-to-1	Tri-power
389	4.06	3.75	376 @ 5000	10.75-to-1	Tri-power
421	4.09	4.00	338 @ 4600	10.50-to-1	Four-barrel
421	4.09	4.00	356 @ 4800	10.75-to-1	Tri-power
421	4.09	4.00	376 @ 5000	10.75-to-1	Tri-power
326	3.72	3.75	285 @ 5000	10.50-to-1	Four-barrel
230	3.88	3.25	207 @ 5200	10.50-to-1	Four-barrel

1967

THE SUPERCAR AND PONYCAR SHOW!

The GTO gets a new 400-cube engine, tri-power becomes a piece of history and the Firebird rounds out Pontiac's assault on the enthusiast marketplace

Pontiac built only 1,768 models like this show beauty with a hood tach and hood locks. Engine is high-performance 428-incher.

New generation of GTO supercars was not availabe with tri-power. Top option 400-inch motor was Ram Air rated at 360 hp with single Quadrajet.

CAPSULE COMMENTS

Out of respect for the people who started it all we'll start with a rundown on the popular Tiger. The 1967 copy is far more of a supercar than its predecessors. It's more powerful (horsepower rating same as last year!), better handling, sharper looking and available with more performance and show items than ever before.

The big question when choosing a GTO this year is, "Which model do I buy?" For the first time the GTO can be had with an economy engine option (255 hp available only with automatic transmission), a good three-speed automatic transmission (Turbo-Hydra-Matic) and disc brakes (front wheels only).

Engine displacement is up this year from 389 cubic inches (since 1964) to 400 cubic inches and all GTO performance engines are fitted with big-

The big news was Pontiac's entry in the ponycar market which had been the property of Ford Motor Company. All-new car could be had with engines ranging from one-barrel 165-hp Six to 325-hp Ram Air 400.

It was the only year for a production Grand Prix convertible. This 428-inch ragtop was supplied via Royal Pontiac to the author for testing in 1967. They built a total of almost 43,000 Grand Prix units including 760 with manual transmissions.

valve, free-breathing heads as used on the biggest Pontiac 428 cubic-inch engine. There are no multiple carburetion options as General Motors ruled them out on all cars except the sporty Corvette Sting Ray. If you are looking for maximum image appeal and want to take advantage of the GTO's good looks without having to live with a *genuine* high-performance powerplant, then the optional single two-barrel-carbureted 255-hp V-8 with Turbo Hydra-Matic is for you. If you appreciate performance but don't want to go all the way, the standard 335-hp single-four-barrel-carbureted engine is just what the doctor ordered. Next up the power line is the Quadra-Power 360-hp engine which is also adorned with a single four-barrel carburetor and can be fitted with all the comforts of home, including air conditioning.

If it's super-performance you want then Pontiac has the answer in the form of a very conservatively rated (360 hp) 400 cubic-inch engine which comes with a high-rpm camshaft and valve train and can be ordered only with 4.33-to-1 rear end gearing. This gearing makes highway cruising uncomfortable (excessive engine rpm, noise, etc.) and naturally has an adverse effect on gas mileage. Because of a special Ram-Air induction system on this engine, the factory opens up the decorative hood scoop for fresh air intake.

All GTOs come equipped *stock* with heavy-duty suspension and handling components which should satisfy all but the drag and sports car buffs. For them there are even heavier-duty parts available including quick ratio manual steering and front disc brakes (highly recommended on all models). All engines, except the 255-hp-model, require premium fuel.

There is a wide variety of rear end gear ratios available on the GTO to cover all types of driving. Gearing ratios run from an ultra-economy 2.56-to-1 for high speed highway driving to 4.33-to-1 for maximum performance drag strip driving. Limited slip differentials are optional for maximum traction under adverse conditions on all models.

Air conditioning is optional on all but the Ram-Air 360-hp engine and there's a full list of convenience and performance options listed for Pontiac's "top cat." Available in hardtop or convertible trim, the GTO is the best optioned car on the 1967 supercar scene and still the one considered most likely to succeed!

1967 PONTIAC HIGH-PERFORMANCE ENGINES

CUBIC INCHES	BORE	STROKE	HORSEPOWER	COMPRESSION	INDUCTION
400	4.12	3.75	325 @ 5200	10.75-to-1	Four-barrel
400	4.12	3.75	350 @ 5000	10.50-to-1	Four-barrel
400	4.12	3.75	335 @ 5000	10.75-to-1	Four-barrel
400	4.12	3.75	360 @ 5100	10.75-to-1	Four-barrel
400	4.12	3.75	360 @ 5400	10.75-to-1	Four-barrel
428	4.12	4.00	360 @ 4600	10.50-to-1	Four-barrel
428	4.12	4.00	376 @ 5100	10.75-to-1	Four-barrel
326	3.72	3.75	285 @ 5000	10.50-to-1	Four-barrel
230	3.88	3.25	215 @ 5200	10.50-to-1	Four-barrel

Harry Wesch drove this trophy-taking Ram Air Firebird out of Myrtle Motors during the good old days. He was also in charge of the 428 Firebird program at Myrtle.

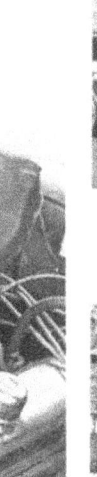

Prepared by Royal Pontiac and driven from Royal Oak, Michigan, to New York by the author, it was one of 751 GTOs built with Ram Air power. Author drove it on the street daily and won at the track on weekends!

THE FIRST-GENERATION FIREBIRD

Pontiac revolutionizes the long-hood/short-deck marketplace with a Ponycar which carries the name of GM's legendary rocket ship

PRIOR to Ford's Mustang blitz in mid-1964, there was no such thing as a "Ponycar"; nor was there recognition of the existance of a "youth market." The "General" was rolling right along with its blanket coverage of the marketplace until Ford discovered a whole new ballgame. Along came the Ford Mustang and, suddenly, long-hood short-deck fever spread through Motown like the plague. It was the right car for the right times.

The responsibility of meeting Ford's challenge was handed over to Chevrolet, with the net result being the new Camaro, first introduced to the market in 1967, after only a two-year development period. Pressured by Pontiac General Manager John Z. DeLorean for a two-seat sports car to compete against the Corvette, GM management ignored his request, instead choosing to develop more ammunition in its fight against Ford. This decision led to the creation of the Firebird.

Pre-production '67 Firebird convertible at the GM Tech Center during the summer of 1966. Pontiac built 15,528 ragtop models and 67,032 hardtops in the first model year. This car was lowered slightly for photography.

FIREBIRD ENGINE AVAILABILITY

1967

OPTION	ENGINE	DISPLACEMENT	HORSEPOWER	COMPRESSION	INDUCTION
Standard	Six	230 CID	165	9.0-to-1	One-Barrel
Sprint	Six	230 CID	215	10.5-to-1	Four-Barrel
326	V-8	326 CID	250	9.2-to-1	Two-Barrel
HO	V-8	326 CID	285	10.5-to-1	Four-Barrel
400	V-8	400 CID	325	10.75-to-1	Four-Barrel
Ram Air I	V-8	400 CID	325	10.75-to-1	Four-Barrel

1968

OPTION	ENGINE	DISPLACEMENT	HORSEPOWER	COMPRESSION	INDUCTION
Standard	Six	250 CID	175	9.0-to-1	One-Barrel
Sprint	Six	250 CID	215	10.5-to-1	Four-Barrel
350	V-8	350 CID	265	9.2-to-1	Two-Barrel
HO	V-8	350 CID	320	10.5-to-1	Four-Barrel
400	V-8	400 CID	330	10.75-to-1	Four-Barrel
Ram Air I	V-8	400 CID	335	10.75-to-1	Four-Barrel
Ram Air II	V-8	400 CID	340	10.75-to-1	Four-Barrel

1969

OPTION	ENGINE	DISPLACEMENT	HORSEPOWER	COMPRESSION	INDUCTION
Standard	Six	250 CID	175	9.0-to-1	One-Barrel
Sprint	Six	250 CID	230	10.5-to-1	Four-Barrel
350	V-8	350 CID	265	9.2-to-1	Two-Barrel
HO	V-8	350 CID	325	10.5-to-1	Four-Barrel
400	V-8	400 CID	330	10.75-to-1	Four-Barrel
Ram Air III	V-8	400 CID	335	10.75-to-1	Four-Barrel
Ram Air IV	V-8	400 CID	345	10.75-to-1	Four-Barrel

Since Chevrolet had been doing all the Camaro R&D work, it was a simple matter for Pontiac to jump on the bandwagon. Even though the project got a very late start, Pontiac was able to come up with a distinctively-styled Ponycar just six months after the introduction of the Camaro. With the Firebird, GM now had a double-barrelled shot at blowing away the car that started the whole thing.

The name Firebird came from the legendary Indian symbol which promised action, power, beauty and youth. It was first used by General Motors on its dramatic gas turbine car, the Firebird I, debuted in 1954.

The first Firebirds went on sale February 23, 1967, and were available in two body styles—hard-top-coupe and sporty-convertible. Five engines (plus one top performance Ram Air option) were available, including the overhead-camshaft Six as standard, up to the optional 400-cubic-inch performance Eights. Standard equipment included bucket seats, three-speed manual transmission (four-speed manual and two and three speed automatics were optional) and an all vinyl interior.

A number of performance and comfort features were made available so that the Firebird could be optioned for just about every segment of the marketplace. You could even get a hood-mounted tach-a

Well-detailed 400 Ram Air motor which made the First Generation Firebirds famous on the street racing scene. In a light Firebird body, the 400-inch Supercar motor really got the job done.

goodie which had been first introduced on the GTO. The first Firebird was built on an 108-inch wheelbase with an overall length of 188.8 inches.

The Firebird was an instant success, with over 82,000 units being produced the first year. Market studies showed that styling and performance were two key features in establishing youth appeal in the auto market—and these were the two main reasons cited by buyers for favoring the new Firebird.

In 1968, the Firebird's successful styling remained unchanged. There were, however, some engineering improvements in the suspension and ventilation systems, plus a high-output (HO) option on the newly-introduced 350-cubic-inch powerplant. There were actually two Ram Air options to choose from. The hottest, the Ram Air II, was released as a mid-year option (June 5, 1968). You could get this rare package by specifying Code WV or XT on the car order form. Pontiac pushed this option along with close-ratio, four-speed with a 2.20 First gear and either a 3.90 or 4.33-to-1 rear end.

By now, Pontiac was leading the way in effective merchandising of high-performance cars and they put out some outrageous advertising material to promote the new Firebirds. In 1967, they called the Firebird line the "Magnificent Five," included were the Firebird 400, Firebird HO, Firebird Sprint, Firebird 350 and Firebird. In 1968, they went one step beyond and hyped the "Magnificent Five" as the ultimate hip machines, flooding the market with brochures packed with technical engine and power train information. Highlights of this program included the Firebird 400—"The Boss;" Firebird HO—"Light Heavyweight;" and the Firebird Sprint—"Our European Thing."

Popularity of the Firebird continued in its second year, as production jumped to over 107,000 units. During 1968, Pontiac engineers were deeply involved in creating competition for Chevrolet's Z/28 Camaro. The result was the Trans-Am, introduced in the 1969 model-year.

The 1969 Firebirds took on added distinction with fresh styling and a lower appearance. Exterior styling was highlighted by front bumper extensions made of new, tough, body-color plastic. For the first time, a three-speed automatic transmission was available for all overhead camshaft Sixes and the 350-cubic-inch V-8s. Two Ram Air packages were continued for 1969, along with functional hood scoops that could be opened or closed by the driver.

The newest Firebird in the lineup was an impressive handling car with stagger-mounted shocks, a one-inch front anti-sway bar, quick steering and seven-inch steel wheels. Powered by the 335-hp Ram Air engine (and available in

The first run of '67 Firebirds on the way down the Lordstown, Ohio, assembly plant which was responsible for total Firebird and Camaro production in 1967. In 1968 the Van Nuys, California, plant shared the production load.

The '68 Firebird was essentially a carryover model with minor changes. Hardtop production jumped to 90,152 and ragtops hit 16,960 for the 1968 model year.

In 1969 the Firebird took on a heavier, more-macho look and sales started heading down. Ragtop production dropped to 11,649 units while hardtop sales slumped to 75,362. It was time for a change.

white with blue stripes and blue with white stripes) it soon became the car to beat on the street.

A Pontiac engineering group had been working on a special street-package Firebird and, in the Spring of 1969, the package was formally introduced as the ultimate Ponycar of the day—the Trans-Am. The prototype for the Trans-Am was the "PFST" Firebird, a cobbled up basic Firebird 400 with unique body trim and suspension components.

Not only was the Trans-Am unique in its performance approach, it was also unique in appearance. Exterior goodies included side scoops, functional scoops on the hood, special decals, and a rear spoiler which Pontiac engineers claimed kept a 100-pound, downward load on the car at 100 mph. Just 697 Firebird Trans-Ams were produced in the first year (eight convertibles), with total Firebird production dipping to 87,708 units.

By 1969, the handwriting was on the wall, and it was obvious that the public wanted more in the Ponycar field. They wanted more sex appeal, more performance options and more of the long-hood, short-deck styling; and, in 1970, Pontiac gave the public what has often been described as the ultimate expression of this styling theme. The Second Generation Firebirds were longer, lower, sexier; with better handling and performance than ever before. Regrettably, at the same time, convertibles were being dropped from the line-up, never to resurface under the Firebird nameplate. When's the last time you saw a Trans-Am convertible?

A rendering of the '67 Firebird convertible produced in 1965 by Pontiac stylists. This is one of the designs that got the nod from management. It's the raked and chopped windshield that really makes a difference.

Prior to the introduction of the '69 Trans-Am, Royal Pontiac offered Bobcat versions of Ram-Air 400 Firebirds. Promoted by Jim Wangers, the Bobcat Firebird did not enjoy the success of the Bobcat GTO. This was a CARS Magazine road test car prepared by Royal and driven by Marty Schorr and Joe Oldham.

One of the eight Trans-Am convertibles built in 1969. This is a coveted Pontiac collectible and is shown here in original, unrestored condition. It's a four-speed Ram-Air 400 model.

Pontiac also offered a OHC Six-cylinder engine and an optional Sprint version with four-barrel carb and free-flow exhausts. Special Sprint model Firebirds are highly-collectible. Performance is excellent for a Six. This one has been mildly-modified.

FIREBIRD PRODUCTION DATA

HARDTOP	CONVERTIBLE	TRANS-AM	TOTAL
1967			
67,032	15,528	N/A	82,560
1968			
90,152	16,960	N/A	107,112
1969			
75,362	11,649	697*	87,708

* Includes eight convertibles with L-74 engines, four with four-speed, four with automatic transmission.

FIREBIRD PRODUCTION LOCATIONS

In 1967, Firebirds were produced in Lordstown, Ohio. In 1968, Firebirds were produced at Lordstown, Ohio and Van Nuys, California. In 1969, an additional plant was devoted to Firebird production—Norwood, Ohio. Assembly lines at all three plants were programmed to build Camaros as well as Firebirds.

The Trans-Am was Pontiac's answer to the Z/28 Camaro and a good one. With its white body and blue racing stripes (or reverse colors), it was a patriotic answer to imported sports sedans. Pontiac produced a total of just 697 Trans-Ams in 1969 prior to the all-new '70½ Second Generation body style.

Pontiac stylist checks emblem size and fender dimensions on this pilot '67 Firebird. The Firebird was named after a legendary Indian symbol which promised action, power, beauty and youth.

Bringing up the rear of the new Trans-Am was a full-width wing similar to the one used on the GTO Judge.

THE SIX THAT ROARED!

In Sprint configuration the Overhead Cam Six gave V-8 engines a run for the money. This is one of the engines Pontiac should bring back

John DeLorean with the standard OHC Six. DeLorean headed a group which was responsible for the original OHC concept and design. It was refined for production by 'Mac' McKellar.

This text is part of a presentation on the OHC engine delivered by Malcom Mac McKellar to the Automotive Engineering Congress on January 12, 1966.

IN ITS standard regular fuel one-barrel version, the new engine produces 165 gross brake horsepower at 4,700 rpm as compared to 140 at 4,200 rpm for the previous pushrod-valve-operated engine. This is an increase of 18 percent in gross brake horsepower although displacement has been increased only 6.5 percent.

Low-speed torque has been increased by virtue of the slightly-increased displacement, but of significant note is the shape of the torque curve for the overhead cam engine. It remains relatively flat from 1,600 rpm to 4,000 rpm. A comparison of the brake mean effective pressure curves also emphasizes the extended duration of the specific torque output of the overhead cam engine.

Four-barrel high-compression engine output curves more accurately show the inherent power potential of the engine. This premium fuel 10.5-to-1 compression-ratio engine develops 207 gross brake horsepower at 5,200 rpm and peak torque of 228 foot pounds at 3,800 rpm. Note that torque at 5,000 rpm is the same as at 1,700 rpm—both values only slightly lower than peak torque. This extremely wide range of high torque output has been achieved while maintaining very good idle quality.

Idle speeds of both versions of the engine are 500 rpm, in Drive, for the automatic transmission engines, and 600 rpm for the manual transmission engines. The combination of good idle, broad range flat torque curve, and high engine rpm potential has been made possible by the overhead camshaft arrangement.

Increased engine performance results in equally impressive gains in the vehicle acceleration characteristics. Our tests indicate that with the one-barrel engine and equal axle ratios, acceleration time from zero to sixty miles-per-hour has been decreased by approximately 14 percent, as compared to the 1965 Tempest, while in the 60-75 mph range, acceleration time has been reduced by approximately 26 percent. All of this has been accomplished with a slight increase in level road fuel economy at most speeds.

The four-barrel premium fuel engine, available in the Sprint option, offers even more improvement in performance. Zero to sixty miles-per-hour time is approximately 18 percent less than the 1965 Six-cylinder one-barrel Tempest, while the 60-75 miles-per-hour acceleration time has been reduced appvximately 40 percent.

OVERHEAD CAM VALVE MECHANISM

Valve mechanism of the new engine is unique in a very significant respect. It combines for the first time the use of hydraulically-actuated zero-lash adjusters with an overhead-cam-type valve gear. Advantages of automatic hydraulically-actuated valve lash compensation are well known. Its application to this new engine was considered completely essential at the beginning of our design program. A number of initial studies were made to determine how hdraulic lash compensation could best be incorporated.

In the system released for production, a cam follower, located directly under the camshaft, is used to convert the rotary motion of the camshaft into reciprocating valve motion. Contact between the cam and the follower is on a ground surface having a .750-inch radius. Ratio of valve movement to actual camshaft lift is a nominal 1.5-to-1. At the valve stem tip, contact is in a milled groove so that the end of the cam follower is restrained from movement in a lateral direction. At the fulcrum end of the follower, a spring steel clip secures it to the lash adjuster plunger. Thus the follower is completely

HIGH-PERFORMANCE OVERHEAD CAM SIX SPECIFICATIONS

YEAR	HORSEPOWER	TORQUE	COMPRESSION	CARBURETION
1966	207 @ 5,200	228 @ 3,800	10.5-to-1	Four-Barrel
1967	215 @ 5,200	240 @ 3,800	10.5-to-1	Four-Barrel
1968	215 @ 5,200	255 @ 3,800	10.5-to-1	Four-Barrel
1969	230 @ 5,400	260 @ 3,600	10.5-to-1	Four-Barrel

NOTE: In 1966 the HP engine was optional in Tempest and LeMans models. In 1967 the engine was optional in the Tempest and standard in the Firebird Sprint. In 1968 and 1969 it was optional in the Tempest and LeMans and standard in the Firebird Sprint. In 1968 displacement grew to 250 cubic inches.

The optional four-barrel high-performance version of the OHC Six as installed in a Tempest Sprint. Note huge Quadrajet from V-8 engine.

stable, even without the camshaft in place.

CAMSHAFT DESIGN

Practical benefits derived from the increased rigidity of the valve train are graphically shown in a comparison of the lift curves of the 1965 pushrod valve operated engine and the standard 1966 overhead cam Six-cylinder engine. It has been possible to obtain a relatively high valve lift in a short duration, a prime consideration in the development of this engine. Maximum valve lift has been increased from .333 to .400-inch even though the total valve event has been shortened from 126 camshaft degrees to 114 degrees. Actual integral of lift has been increased by 14.5 percent. Because of the high rigidity of this valve train, opening ramp height at the valve is reduced from .00439-inch for the push rod operated camshaft to .00283-inch for the overhead cam, while the closing ramp of the overhead cam is approximately .001-inch less than that of the pushrod design.

Valve timing for the regular fuel one-barrel overhead cam engine valve train as developed is quite different from our previous 1965 Six-cylinder pushrod engine. Nominal total valve overlap is only 14 crankshaft degrees as compared to 38 degrees in 1965. Intake valve closing occurs 41 degrees after bottom center as compared to 54 degrees for the former pushrod engine.

The well recognized importance of the shape and timing of the intake closing event is illustrated in this engine. Relatively fast early closing of the intake valve is very helpful in maintaining good low-speed torque. At higher engine speeds, low-restriction characteristics obtained by the high-lift and large valve sizes maintain excellent volumetric efficiency. Exhaust valve opening point is 41 degrees before bottom center, or 11 degrees later than our former engine; yet when the piston has reached bottom center, the exhaust valve is already .021-inch farther open than its counterpart in the pushrod engine.

The premium fuel four-barrel car-

The hood tach thing started with the GTO and fit right into the scheme of things on the Firebird. With the OHC Six Sprint engine, a tach really came in handy.

buretor engine camshaft is similar in concept to the standard regular fuel one-barrel engine camshaft, except that it has been tailored to the freer breathing characteristics and to the compression

The author checking out a production Firebird Sprint complete with side stripes and hood tach. Front and rear spring rates with Sprint were the same as Firebird 400 with big V-8. With 180 pounds less weight up front than a 400-inch V-8 model, handling and braking were excellent. Engine responded best to four-speed application.

ratio of this option. Valve lift is .438-inch, while both intake and exhaust event are increased from 228 crankshaft degrees to 244 degrees. Overlap of 26 crankshaft degrees is 12 degrees more than the one-barrel engine. Peak valve opening and closing velocities are approximately the same. However, to attain even higher speed capabilities desired for the four-barrel engine, peak accelerations and rates of accelerations are slightly less than the one-barrel overhead camshaft. Combined with slightly-heavier dual valve springs, this option has a pump-up speed approximately 500 rpm higher than the standard engine.

TIMING BELT CAMSHAFT DRIVE

Successful application of a neoprene timing belt, utilizing a glass fiber tension member, has been the key factor in making the new engine feasible. Since no lubrication is necessary to prevent wear, the timing belt used to drive the camshaft and accessory sprockets is located outside the crankcase. Three surface hardened cast-iron sprockets are used; a 3.000-inch diameter crankshaft sprocket, a 6.000-inch diameter camshaft sprocket, and a 3.000-inch diameter sprocket used to operate the separate and externally-mounted accessory drive. Tensioning of the belt is accomplished by sliding the accessory housing on the inclined cylinder block pad and then locking in place by tightening six attaching bolts.

CYLINDER HEAD

The cylinder head of the new overhead camshaft engine features fully-contoured machined wedge-type combustion chambers. Compression ratio of the regular fuel standard engine is 9.0-to-1, compared to 8.6-to-1 of the 1965 engine. More accurate control of combustion chamber volume with fully-machined combustion chambers has made this compression ratio increase possible without an increase in fuel octane requirement. Twelve individual ports are used to provide complete flexibility in the choice of both intake and exhaust manifolding.

Valves are inclined at an angle of 15 degrees toward the manifold side of the engine. Cylinder block construction is greatly simplified since provisions for camshaft, valve lifters and pushrod covers are not required.

INDUCTION SYSTEMS

A conventional common runner manifold of simple configuration is used on the one-barrel engine. This design differs from the 1965 Six-cylinder intake manifold in several respects. Its cross sectional area is 10 percent larger and the riser height has been increased .875-inch. While this extra height was necessary in order to permit installation of an air cleaner which would provide clearance to the camshaft housing, it proved to be advantageous from a mixture distribution standpoint. Our tests indicate that cylinder-to-cylinder mixture distribution was markedly-improved, particularly at lower engine speeds and under medium acceleration conditions. This permitted leaner one-barrel carburetor calibration in the off-idle and part throttle range. The ability of the new engine to burn these leaner mixtures has been helpful in attaining our original goal of increased efficiency.

Our standard one-barrel carburetor has a venturi size of 1.50-inch diameter, while the throttle body diameter is 1.75-inch. It was found in the development program that torque output was increased, even at speeds as low as 2,000 rpm, by this larger venturi size.

A cross-section through the cylinder head and four-barrel intake manifold shows the adaptability of the individual intake porting to additional types of manifolding. The four-barrel power package utilizes the Quadra-Jet carburetor and an individual runner-type intake manifold. All runner lengths are relatively short and provide as direct a path as possible to each cylinder. Conventional 1-5-3-6-2-4 firing order of the Six-cylinder engine is very adaptable to this induction system. Firing sequence is such that alternate induction impulses occur through the front and rear half of the carburetor. A .75-inch balance hole cast into the separating web between the front and rear half of the manifold proved to be optimum for attainment of the best overall torque curve.

Small 1.00-inch diameter primary venturi size of the Quadra-Jet has made it possible to attain low-speed part-throttle driving flexibility even with relatively large intake manifold runners. Ample air capacity is provided by the 2.25-inch diameter secondary bores. This carburetor, with its centrally-located fuel bowl, proved insensitive to being mounted 90 degrees to the position normally employed on V-8 engines.

EXHAUST SYSTEM

The exhaust manifold of the standard one-barrel engine is simple in design. It utilizes a conventional thermostatically-controlled heat valve to direct exhaust gas to the floor of the intake manifold during engine warm-up. Exhaust gas is then directed around the riser through cast passages in the intake manifold and exhausts through the manifold's single outlet. After warm-up with the heat valve open, exhaust gas emits directly through the outlet.

A highly-efficient dual-outlet exhaust manifold with individual streamlined runners is a part of the four-barrel package. Here, as with the four-barrel intake manifold, the Six-cylinder engine lends itself well to an efficient flow system. Equal-interval flow impulses, separated by 240 crankshaft degrees, virtually eliminate flow interferences between the individual cylinders. During engine warm-up, exhaust gas from the front three cylinders is diverted to the intake manifold floor by the thermostatically-controlled valve in the front outlet to provide heat to warm the air/fuel mixture. After warm-up, with the heat valve open, exhaust gases emit directly through both outlets. The dual-outlet exhaust manifold provides a power increase of approximately 3 percent on this four-barrel engine, as compared to a single outlet manifold.

A well-dressed '66 Tempest Sprint. The OHC Six was installed in 24 percent of all '66 Tempests and 21.4 percent of all '67 Tempests.

This Firebird Sprint was used at the Proving Grounds to gather data and for special auto magazine road tests. With four-speed it was a great performer and handler.

STANDARD OVERHEAD CAM ENGINE

Bore 3.875
Stroke 3.25
Stroke — Bore Ratio .... .8387
Displacement .... 230 cu. in.
Firing Order 1-5-3-6-2-4
Compression Ratio 9.0:1
Carburetor Type .... One Barrel
Gross Brake Horsepower .... 165 at 4700 RPM
Gross Torque, Lb. Ft. .... 216 at 2600 RPM
Crankshaft:
   Material .... Nodular Iron
   Number of Main Bearings 7
   Main Bearing Journal Diameters
   & Bearing Lengths
      No. 1, 2, 3, 4, 5, 6, ... 2.30 x .80
      No. 7 .... 2.30 x 1.01
   Bearing Taking Thrust .... No. 7
   Projected Crankshaft Bearing
   Area .... 13.363 sq. in.
Connecting Rod:
   Length (Center to Center) 5.700
   Crankpin Bearing Diameter 2.000
   Crankpin Bearing Length .... .837
Pistons, Rings and Pins
   Piston:
      Material .... Al. Alloy (Tin Plated)
      Type .... Cam Ground Slipper
   Compression Rings:
      Number 2
      Type & Material
         No. 1 .... Barrel Face
         No. 2 .... Reverse Twist, Taper Face
      Finish:
         No. 1 .... Channel Moly Filled
         No. 2 .... Lubrite
      Width .... .078
   Oil Control Ring:
      Type & Material ..... Segmented Spring Steel
      Finish .... Chrome Face on Rails
      Width .... .186
   Piston Pin:
      Diameter and Length .... .927 x 3.00
      Type .... Locked in Rod
   Mean Piston Speed at
   5000 RPM .... 2708 Ft./Min.

STANDARD OVERHEAD CAM ENGINE (cont.)

Camshaft:
   Material .... Hardened Alloy Cast Iron
   Type of Drive .... Belt (.500 Pitch x 1.00 Wide)
Valve Train:
   Valve Head Diameters:
      Intake 1.92
      Exhaust 1.60
   Valve Seat Angles:
      Intake .... 30°
      Exhaust .... 45°
   Valve Stem Diameter .... .34
   Rocker Arm Ratio (Mean) .... 1.5 to 1
   Valve Lift .... .400
   Valve Spring Load-Pounds
      Valve Closed 97
      Valve Open 192
   Valve Timing:
      Intake Opens, °BTC 7
      Intake Closes, °ABC 41
      Exhaust Opens, °BBC 41
      Exhaust Closes, °ATC 7

HIGH COMPRESSION 4 BARREL CARBURETOR OVERHEAD CAM ENGINE

Gross Brake Horsepower ..... 207 at 5200 RPM
Gross Torque, Lb. Ft. .... 228 at 3800 RPM
Carburetor Type .... Four Barrel
Compression Ratio 10.5:1
Compression Rings:
   Finish:
      No. 1 & 2 .... Channel Moly Filled
Valve Lift .... .438
Valve Timing:
   Intake Opens, °BTC 15
   Intake Closes, °ABC 49
   Exhaust Opens, °BBC 53
   Exhaust Closes, °ATC 11
Valve Spring Load — Pounds:
   Valve Closed — Outer 62
            — Inner 31
   Valve Open — Outer 137
            — Inner 100
Balance of Specifications ..... Same as Standard
      Overhead Cam Engine

1968

CAR OF THE YEAR!

The GTO gets Motor Trend's award,
pioneers the Endura front end
and gets a shot of Ram Air adrenalin

They built 757 four-speed and 183 automatic Ram Air hardtops and 92 Ram Air four-speed and just 22 Ram Air automatic convertibles in 1968 model run.

The author blasts off the line in a GTO prepared by Royal Pontiac for a CARS Magazine road test. Car ran in D/S yet should have been classified in C/S because of use of '68½ Ram Air IV goodies.

CAPSULE COMMENTS

PONTIAC has made only minor changes in their 1968 engine line-up. The overhead-cam Six has been stroked from 230 to 250 cubes, raising the standard rating to 175 hp. But the four-barrel power pack version still rates 215 hp, for better classing on the drag strip.

The 326-cube V-8 has been bored to 350 cubes, and the four-barrel H.O. version of this engine has been up-rated from 285 to 320 hp. This one makes a neat performance-economy compromise in the Tempest LeMans.

The big 400 and 428-cubic inch Pontiac engines all use the new big-valve heads now—and for 1968, the exhaust ports are enlarged and the combustion chambers re-contoured. This has justified an increase in some horsepower ratings.

The big 428 H.O. engine is up from 376 to 390 hp at 5,200 rpm, and is now one of the strongest engines in the industry.

The standard GTO engine is up from 335 to 350 hp, and we again have the popular Ram Air option for the GTO and Firebird, still rated 360 hp at 5400. The setup is identical to 1967, with hood scoop feed to the Quadrajet carb and a 301-degree hydro cam with stiff valve springs; but the system is now incorporated with hot air feed to the carb at part throttle—for emission control. All Pontiac engines use the hot air emission system for 1968.

This is how the GTO could have looked if they hadn't decided to go the Endura route.

Arnie Beswick kept Pontiacs in front of drag racing fans for years thanks to the Farmer's fuel-burning Funny Cars.

The Grand Prix convertible and 2+2 went the route of tri-power and other goodies. Over 31,000 Grand Prix coupes were sold, including 306 with manual transmissions.

It was a fantastic sales year for Pontiac and they sold over 104,000 Bonnevilles. Those eight-lug alloy wheels look dynamite.

The Firebird was available with a wide choice of powerplants, ranging from one-barrel 175-hp 250-inch Six to 340-hp Ram Air II 400. Almost 20,000 convertibles were sold, compared with 90,152 coupes.

The Firebird had enough power choices to take on any ponycar on the market. The long hood/short deck styling concept really caught on.

This is one of Myrtle Motors' limited-production 428 Ram Air Firebirds, complete with hood tach, spoiler, mags and stripes.

1968 PONTIAC HIGH-PERFORMANCE ENGINES

CUBIC INDUCTION	INCHES	BORE	STROKE	HORSEPOWER	COMPRESSION
400	4.12	3.75	330 @ 4800	10.75-to-1	Four-barrel
400	4.12	3.75	340 @ 4800	10.50-to-1	Four-barrel
400	4.12	3.75	350 @ 5000	10.50-to-1	Four-barrel
400	4.12	3.75	335 @ 5000	10.75-to-1	Four-barrel
400	4.12	3.75	350 @ 5000	10.75-to-1	Four-barrel
400	4.12	3.75	360 @ 5100	10.75-to-1	Four-barrel
400	4.12	3.75	366 @ 5400	10.75-to-1	Four-barrel
428	4.12	4.00	375 @ 4800	10.50-to-1	Four-barrel
428	4.12	4.00	390 @ 5200	10.75-to-1	Four-barrel
350	3.88	3.75	320 @ 5100	10.50-to-1	Four-barrel
250	3.88	3.53	215 @ 5200	10.50-to-1	Four-barrel

BIRTH OF THE

TRANS AM

By Martyn L. Schorr

The year was 1968 and the guys who came up with the GTO Judge were asked to come up with a similar treatment for the Firebird. What started out as customizing exercise to keep the Firebird image alive until the new car was ready, ended up being the Midas touch. Today the Trans Am is one of the world's most recognized image cars

IN ONE respect the first Firebird Trans Am was no different than any other new model from the major automakers. It too was what is affectionately known as a committee car, a car which represents the design, engineering and production talents of a group of people. Contrary to popular belief, the first Trans Am was not DeLorean's car, Herb Adams' car or Jim Wangers' car. And, it wasn't patterned after a race car or designed to be homologated as a race car. Nothing could be further from the truth!

The Trans Am was actually an outgrowth of the very successful GTO Judge program and was a product of the very same group, a group comprised of some of the finest engineering, product planning and marketing and merchandising talent in Motown history. Also unique to this group of radical upstarts was the fact that one key member didn't *officially* work for Pontiac. An outsider had privy to the hallowed halls of dream machines at Pontiac. More about him later.

It has been written that the first Trans Am was actually an outgrowth of the Chevy-powered Firebird road racer driven by the late, great Jerry Titus. Actually the group that came up with the Trans Am concept (except for Herb Adams) was rather detached from road racing. They were into street performance, street image and selling street cars. They felt that they could sell more cars based on solid street performance and image than by racing on Sunday and selling on Monday!

The official-unofficial committee that came up with the Trans Am was fresh from the GTO Judge project which, to everyone's surprise, was a huge success. At that time John Z. DeLorean was at the peak of his power trip. He was in his young forties, General Manager of Pontiac, a Vice-President of General Motors and a hard-core performance enthusiast. When GTO sales started softening he had this committee formed to save the GTO image. The original group consisted of Herb Adams, Bill Collins, Ben Harrison and the illustrious Jim Wangers. Wangers, the non-employee and marketing genius, was known throughout the world as the man who single-handedly created the GTO cult. He street raced with the kids on Woodward Ave., created the Royal Pontiac Bobcat line, won national acclaim as a drag racer, wrote GTO copy for Pontiac's advertising agency (McManus, John & Adams), wrote the hit single "Li'l GTO" record, created a line of GTO shoes for Thom McAnn and he did a little work on the side for Pontiac. He also was a close personal friend of John DeLorean.

This group joined by Jeff Young simply took a Firebird 400, gave it the Judge image-style treatment and came up with the Trans Am. The car already had a good engine, driveline and suspension, so it was a relatively easy job.

With the Judge/GTO under their belt, the official-unofficial committee applied a similar styling exercise to the Firebird. What they came up with was the Trans Am which eventually became the country's leading youth image sports machine. With 400 Ram Air inches under its scooped hood, the Trans Am earned its stripes. The new Trans Am is a far more sophisticated handling car, but can't touch the original as far as straight line performance is concerned. It was a screamer!

Then came the naming process. After much deliberation three names were chosen for this new car. The first and most popular was Sebring, followed by Trans Am and Formula. Surveys were sent out to Pontiac owners to determine which name would be most closely associated with Pontiac. Sebring came back as Number One and Trans Am as the least desirable! However, since Plymouth had prior claim to Sebring and Formula seem to work best for some models they had on the plans board, Trans Am got the nod.

DeLorean gave the go ahead on the Trans Am name, giving very little thought to the fact that the Sports Car Club of America (founder of the Trans Am Series) had prior claim to the name and also had it tied up. General Motors legal checked the name out as far as car manufacturing was concerned and gave DeLorean the green light. SCCA stepped right in as soon as the car was announced and the rest is history. After negotiations General Motors agreed to pay SCCA $5 per car which, at the time, didn't amount to much. No one really thought the Trans Am thing would last much longer than the Judge, so the tariff was taken very lightly. Total Trans Am production in 1969 was only 697. However, by 1975 Trans Am production had reached 27,274 and today we are talking about

T/A production in excess of 100,000 units. For the amount of money GM has paid SCCA, they could have bought the whole organization instead of just the use of a single name! General Motors also licenses the Can-Am name from SCCA which has been used on limited-production intermediate Pontiac performance models.

The first Firebird Trans Am was introduced to the public at the Chicago Automobile Show in the Spring of 1969. The standard powerplant was the 400-cube Ram Air HO (L-74) with Quadrajet and dual exhausts. This engine was rated very honestly at 335 hp. Optional was the Ram Air IV engine (L-67) rated at 10 more horsepower. While three-speed stick was standard with the base engine and four-speed or automatic optional, the Ram Air IV engine was available *only* with four-speed or Turbo-Hydro automatic.

Out of the total production run in 1969, there were 55 Ram Air IV cars (9 automatics, 46 sticks), 634 base engine models (114 automatic and 520 sticks) and 8 convertibles with the base engine (4 automatic and 4 stick). To this date only three or four of the convertibles built have been documented. One of them is featured in this issue.

The 1969 Trans Am was an impressive road car, one which could hit 125-130 mph with good tuning. It was not as sophisticated or as quick and fast as some of the later versions, but it was a classic that was ready to take on all that Detroit could dish out in those days. The road racers were also happy as production allowed homologation of the scoops, spoilers and other aerodynamic parts. It was the car that started a cult, a cult which has become the largest of its kind in the world.

And where are the people who are responsible for the Trans Am. Well, DeLorean is now President of his own car company which is tooling up for production of the long-awaited DMC-10. Bill Collins went with DeLorean, designed the DMC-10 and is now chief engineer at American Motors. Tom Nell (a key T/A engineer) left Pontiac a few years back along with Herb Adams and is now running a sporting goods store in Michigan. Adams is in California, doing some road racing and building Fire Am parts and pieces. Ben Harrison is a top product planning engineer at Pontiac and is currently working on finalizing the 1982 presentation books for management. And Jim Wangers is still street racing on Woodward Ave and doing marketing and merchandising presentations for some of the major automakers. He drives a super-quick Trans Am and still owns choice GTO and Judge models. He's still a Pontiac freak and a good friend of mine.

PONTIAC FIREBIRD SPRINT TURISMO

The brainchild of John DeLorean, Herb Adams and
Jim Wangers, the PFST was the forerunner of the Trans-Am

One of seven built to test a Trans-Am concept, this model was powered by a Ram-Air 400 engine. All were painted white with offset blue racing stripes and simulated rear brake cooling scoops. The first car was powered by an OHC Sprint Six with three Webers and a "ventilated" hood for carb clearance. It had adjustable traction bars, roll cage, headers and full instrumentation.

PRIOR to the Trans-Am's introduction, Pontiac engineers working on the project came up with an R&D or Prototype Firebird that could have been introduced as a Firebird model or option in case the Trans-Am project was aborted. It was dubbed the PFST which stood for Pontiac Firebird Sprint Turismo and was essentially a Firebird with Trans-Am handling.

The main force behind the 1968½ PFST Project was Bill Collins, a super-bright suspension engineer and performance freak. His group built the car, Jim Wangers was brought in to publicize it.

The second prototype was powered by a short-deck 303-inch race motor, but the "production" car we drove packed a Ram Air 400 motor which had obviously been "breathed-on." Bill Collins' concept was to build an eye-catching ponycar that would handle like a road racer and offer enough straight line performance to keep the street freaks happy. The 400 engine was more than adequate to get the job done.

Collins started with a white 400 Firebird, opened up the hood scoops for functional ram induction, bolted on some air cooling scoops in front of the rear fender wells and applied an offset *patiotic* blue racing stripe. He added a one-inch sway bar, increased the spring rate from 92 lb./in. to 345 lb./in. and bolted on seven-inch optional rims. Unfortunately tire technology in 1968 left a lot to be desired and the car's handling qualities were severely hampered by his tire choice.

The PFST Project was well received by the Press which further encouraged Pontiac to go ahead with the Trans-Am. Pontiac could have saved a lot of money by going with the PFST designation since they are still paying the SCCA for permission to use the T/A nameplate!

The car featured here was one of the legal prototypes with Ram-Air 400 power and full suspension modifications. It was extremely quick. This was in 1968.

1969

Judy Frantini owns this immaculate, full-option Judge coupe, one of 6,725 built that year.

HERE COMES THE JUDGE!

Pontiac offers something for everyone— from a new Grand Prix and 370-hp Ram Air GTO & Judge to the Trans-Am Firebird which was to become America's favorite cult car

CAPSULE COMMENTS

Pontiac is well ahead of the pack for 1969. There is a 428 with a late style head and heavy-duty valve springs, that punches right out on the line. Many 428 goodies filtered down to the 350 four-barrel. Cylinder head castings are the same for both engines and the only difference is in the height of the full-machined combustion chambers.

Cold air packages with functional hood scoops have put in an appearance on all GM lines, including Pontiac. However, not to be outdone by an Olds 442, Pontiac also brings in a pair of large hoses from the front of the car. The two inlets are concealed behind a parking light but they are nonetheless supposed to be in high pressure areas.

Next comes a hot air supply from the manifold, plus the vacuum valves to switch from hot to cold. The new 350 engines receive a cold air supply by way of a small hood scoop that is similar to the tach housing on the GTO and matches it—this weights 10 pounds less than a GTO and does the same job.

Styling on the GTO and the Firebird are much changed. Last year, the GTO had a special bumper grille section made out of Endura and you could hammer on the stuff with lead pipes without damaging it. Unfortunately production problems arose with color matching and the Endura has not spread to the other lines. On the other hand, other plastic materials have put in an appearance on the Firebird and the other Pontiac machinery which allows shapes that could not have been produced in steel.

One of the legendary eight Trans-Am convertibles built during 1969 model run. Total Trans-Am production was just 689. Trans-Am could be had with top Ram Air IV option.

This Judge was an NHRA National record holder and in the early-Seventies competed in E/Stock.

Dash control on Judge is for fresh air ram induction for the 400-inch four-barrel motor.

Rare Judge convertible, one of 108 ragtops built, is owned by Barry Zwilling, Prime Pontiac. Only 59 were built like this one with Ram Air IV and four-speed.

The car of the year at Pontiac is the new Grand Prix. This is not a face lift of the old Grand Prix, but a brand new Super Car. It has a hood longer than a Continental Mark III—longer than most funny cars! The parking lights are more like aircraft landing units. Push a button at the side of the door and the recessed handle flips out. You'll look in vain for an aerial. It happens to be concealed within the windshield. If the sun is shining at the right angle, you might spot the glimmer of two tiny copper wires of .005-inch diameter. Similar wiring is embedded in the rear glass for a built-in electric heating system that defrosts and defogs the rear window.

Tear yourself away from the gadgetry and crank up the engine. It

HERE COMES THE JUDGE

comes to life with a 428 cubic-inch purr. Now take it for a quick spin around the test track on the set of G78 tires mounted on the 7-inch wide rims. The ride is plush and soft as you expect from the Grand Prix. You can't resist a few tricks, start rounding the corners faster and faster. Pretty soon you realize that all the stories you have heard about a buckboard ride being an essential part of handling are not really true. This thing gets around like greased lightning in complete quiet and comfort. In fact it's an amazing combination of smoothness, handling and power that is going to give the Riviera, the T-Bird and the Toronado something to think about—would you believe a few sleepless nights?

The GTO in years past always had good handling, but an exceptionally choppy ride, that was either an oversight or part of its tough performance image. The 1969 handling is improved and yet the ride is much smoothed out, the car sticks better in the corners and gets out of the hole as well as ever. The Firebird tops the GTO in handling.

They only built one Firebird Fiero convertible. Aerodynamic two-seater with 400-inch motor and 108-inch wheelbase could have put the Corvette out of business!

1969 PONTIAC HIGH-PERFORMANCE ENGINES

CUBIC INCHES	BORE	STROKE	HORSEPOWER	COMPRESSION	INDUCTION
400	4.12	3.75	330 @ 4800	10.75-to-1	Four-barrel
400	4.12	3.75	335 @ 5000	10.75-to-1	Four-barrel
400	4.12	3.75	345 @ 5400	10.75-to-1	Four-barrel
400	4.12	3.75	350 @ 5000	10.50-to-1	Four-barrel
400	4.12	3.75	350 @ 5000	10.75-to-1	Four-barrel
400	4.12	3.75	366 @ 5100	10.75-to-1	Four-barrel
400	4.12	3.75	370 @ 5500	10.75-to-1	Four-barrel
428	4.12	4.00	370 @ 4800	10.50-to-1	Four-barrel
428	4.12	4.00	390 @ 5200	10.75-to-1	Four-barrel
350	3.88	3.75	325 @ 5100	10.50-to-1	Four-barrel
350	3.88	3.75	330 @ 5100	10.50-to-1	Four-barrel
250	3.88	3.53	230 @ 5400	10.50-to-1	Four-barrel

The Grand Prix got a major restyling, complete with long hood/short deck treatment. Plus engines to 370-hp 428-incher. This one was special built by Royal Pontiac (Bobcat Grand Prix) and used by author for comparison road tests against other supercars in 1969.

Ram Air IV option established the GTO as the real King of the Street. Production was 549 four-speed and 151 automatic hardtops and 45 four-speed and 14 automatic convertibles.

Royal Pontiac also built this '69 Firebird Bobcat which the author and Joe Oldham street raced in New York City while Joe was doing an expose on the sport. It came from Royal Pontiac with one slick in the trunk and the other in the back seat!

GRAND PRIX, THE DRIVER'S CAR

Pontiac redefines the 'personal luxury car' concept with its long-hood/short-deck Grand Prix

SIGNALING a major shift in its model lineup, Pontiac Motor Division unveiled a revolutionary, new-generation Grand Prix in 1969.

The attainment of new goals in safety; a concealed radio antenna—a first in the industry; and Pontiac's precision engineering coupled with trend-setting styling established the Grand Prix as America's most distinguished automobile.

Called the Model J, the GP takes on classic proportions with a one-of-a-kind body that rides on an exclusive 118-inch wheelbase. The Model J was available in one body style—a hardtop coupe. It went on sale for the first time on September 26, 1968.

Among the Grand Prix's host of innovations in addition to the concealed radio antenna are an electrically-heated rear window defogger, a driver's command seat completely enclosed in energy-absorbing material for optimum protection and the longest hood in the industry.

A special custom option, called the Grand Prix Model SJ was also introduced. It features the 428 cubic-inch large valve V-8 engine, automatic level control, power disc front brakes, special instrument panel gauges, lamp group, Polyglas tires and special high-performance suspension.

"The '69 Grand Prix is totally new in image, concept and level of luxury," said John Z. DeLorean, a General Motors vice president and Pontiac's general manager at the car's introduction. "It is the blue chip in the specific body sports car field."

The Grand Prix front end styling is distinguished by a wrap-around bumper, individually-mounted headlamps and new large parking lamps at the front of the fenders which also serve as side marker lamps. A unique recessed fineline grille adds to the overall bold appearance.

From the side view, the Grand Prix roof line is as evident and attractive as the long hood. Large sail areas provide limousine-type privacy for rear seat passengers.

As was done with the hidden windshield wipers, Pontiac has concealed the radio antenna, marking another first in the industry. The hidden antenna is exclusive and standard to the Grand Prix in 1969. Fabricated with the windshield is a barely visible wire, .005 inches in diameter, which extends up the center of the windshield and across the full width at the top. A wire at the lower

Quad headlamps flank the pseudo-grille front end giving this newly-restyled '69 Grand Prix a luxury-macho look. New car outsold its predecessor almost 3½-to-1. Total production for the 1969 model year hit 112,486 units including 1,014 cars fitted with stick shifts.

Driving the '69 Grand Prix gave the feel of flying an airplane. The enclosed driver's seat, surrounded by energy-absorbing materials, and the driver-oriented gauges and controls, put the Grand Prix in a class by itself.

Renderings for the rear end styling of the new Grand Prix, presented by Pontiac's Styling Studio in May of 1967.

In May of 1967, a Pontiac stylist presented this rendering of the final version of the '69 Grand Prix. It was the first successful application of the Firebird long-hood/short-deck styling to a large car.

center of the windshield connects the antenna to the radio.

Another side feature is the exclusive door handle of an all-new flush design. It is operated by pushing the botton shaped end of the handle and pulling the handle as it comes out of its recessed position.

Side markers in the rear contain a new reflective technique as well as being a styling plus. Located above the wraparound portion of the rear bumper, three vertical openings are filled with a single-formed three-lens reflector assembly. Rear lighting is achieved with each set of tail lamps in a single, five-compartment section deeply recessed in the bumper.

Another Grand Prix feature is an electrically-heated backlight defogger. This new option which provides quick clearing of the rear glass, gives better visibility for winter driving and is one of the Grand Prix's many safety features. Current flows through small flat conductors which are molded on the inside of the glass and spaced approximately one inch apart horizontally across the rear window.

On its 118-inch wheelbase, the Grand Prix Model J has an overall length of 210.2 inches. It is 75.7 inches wide, 52.1 inches high and the wide track is 62 inches in the front and 60 inches in the rear.

The standard power train consists of a 350 horsepower, 400 cubic-inch large valve V-8 engine and floor-shift manual transmission with the Turbo Hydramatic transmission optional. Three other V-8 engines are also available.

The heart of the interior styling story for the '69 Grand Prix is the curving instrument panel which gives the effect of surrounding the driver as it flows into an integrated floor console. Both the instrument panel and console are fully-padded with energy-absorbing padding vinyl.

To complete this wide scope of protection, the passenger side of the instrument panel has the same gentle arc, giving the front passenger an unusual degree of roominess. This design was achieved by moving the glove compartment to the console for easy reach of the driver and passenger. Because of this new approach to interior styling, only bucket seats are available as is the console which also houses the shift controls and ash tray.

Three round, deepset, instrument clusters house the engine instruments, speedometer and clock. Heater and radio controls are directed toward the driver, and the windshield wiper switch and all accessory switches are of flush rocker design and clearly labeled.

Of special interest is the Grand

Prix recessed, squeeze-to-release door handle which discourages inadvertent opening and is an exclusive feature. Located deep in the energy-absorbing molded, padded, vinyl door trim panel, the door handle is operated by squeezing the release handle against the padded trim panel. Also, the remote controlled door-locking knobs have been moved forward approximately nine inches for easier convenience to front seat occupants and as an added deterrent to theft.

Among the safety features of the Grand Prix is a reinforcement barrier for added protection from side impact. A boxed, section steel member integrated in the doors and rear quarter forms a solid section for greatly improved strength.

Grand Prix wheels have new seven-inch rims on which are mounted wide G78-14 tires as standard equipment for increased steering response and excellent ride capabilities. Front suspension is of all-new ball joint design with upper and lower control arms mounted in rubber bushings. The steering knuckle is designed with the precise king pin inclinations which result in a scrub radius that is non-sensitive to brake pull. The optional front disc brakes with power assist have a new single-piston, floating-caliper design. The significant feature of the single-piston operation is that it is free to slide on the two mounting bolts which thread into the support bracket.

One of the secret's of the GP's styling is the clean lines with minimal geegaws. Bumper-mounted tail blinkers helped achieve this overall effect.

A new Grand Prix rolls down the Pontiac, Michigan, facility. Pontiac estimated production of the all-new Grand Prix to hit 120,000 units, but the new car fell slightly short of the mark.

Photo of one of the very-limited-production Royal Bobcat Grand Prix models created by Jim Wangers and marketed by Royal Pontiac. Exterior changes include hood tach, contrasting paint treatment, and status emblems. Under the hood is a Bobcat-ized 370-hp 428-inch motor hooked to a four-speed.

GRAND PRIX STEAMER

Pontiac's all-new GP is used by General Motors
in 1969 as a rolling test lab or evaluating a radical
vapor-cycle steam engine

Interest is high in low emission automotive powerplants, and steam power is being re-examined in the light of today's advanced engineering materials and technology.

The GM SE-101 steam car, developed by GM Research Laboratories, was designed to evaluate a vapor cycle engine in an automobile with a reasonable degree of passenger comfort, reliability, performance, and economy. It is the world's first steam car with complete power accessories, including air conditioning.

The entire steam powerplant -- including the expander, combustion chamber, steam generator, and condenser -- is housed under the hood of a 1969 Pontiac Grand Prix. Starting functions are automatic. The operator turns the key, waits 30 to 45 seconds for a light signaling adequate steam pressure, and drives away.

Starting Sequence

Several automatic operations are underway while the driver waits for a full head of steam. First, an electric pump fills the steam generator (boiler) with water. When the proper level is reached, a sensor energizes an electric motor which powers the combustion blower and fuel pump during startup. Fuel is sprayed into the combustion chamber, where it is ignited by a spark plug. When the steam generator reaches operating temperature and pressure a conventional automobile starter engages the expander; steam is introduced and the expander accelerates to idle. Further acceleration is

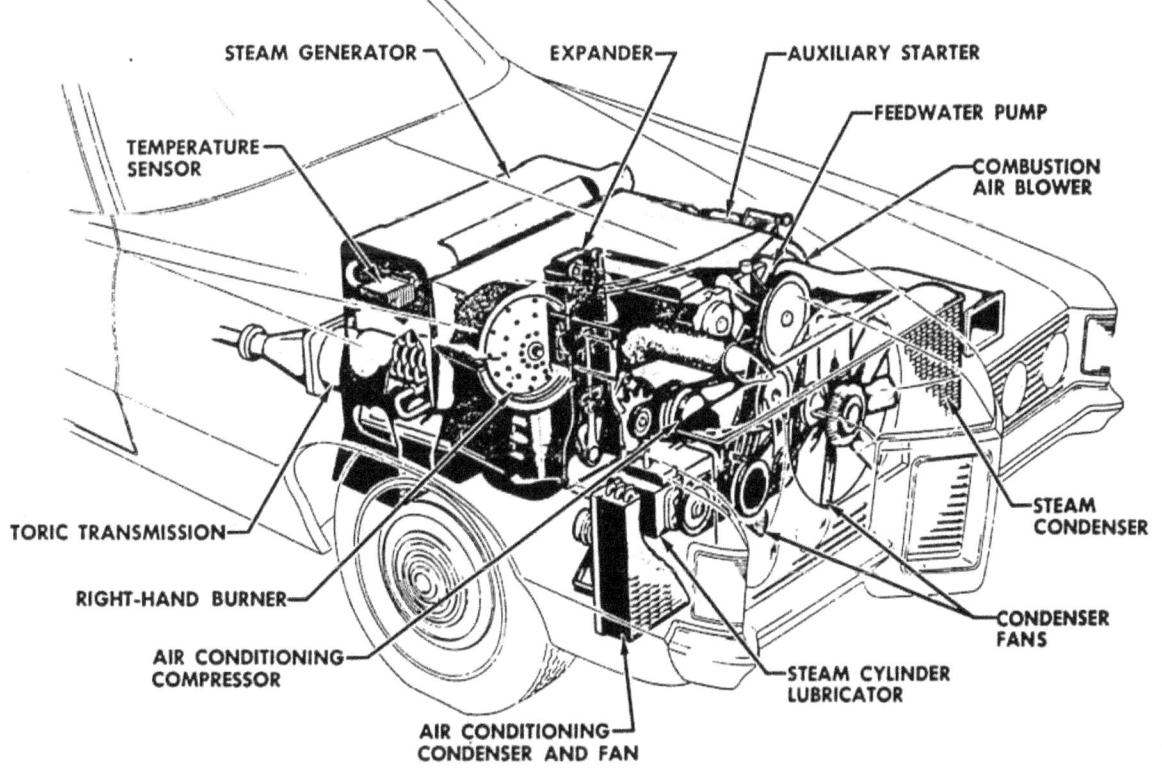

accomplished by the foot pedal in the usual way; the pedal operates a throttle valve which controls the amount of steam admitted to the expander.

Basically, here's what happens during steam engine operation. Heat from the burner converts the boiler water to a high pressure vapor. The expansion of this high pressure vapor, or steam, drives the pistons in the expander. Steam exhausted from the expander is piped to a condenser for water recovery.

Components

Expander. The four-cylinder expander is similar to an in-line internal combustion engine. It has a 101-cubic-inch displacement and develops about 160 maximum horsepower. Steam enters through poppet valves at the top of each cylinder, forces the piston downward, then exits through cylinder ports at the bottom and is piped to the condenser.

Steam Generator. The steam generator consists of several sets of small carbon steel and stainless steel tubes (total tube length is about 430 feet) arranged in a staggered array. This increases the turbulence of the combustion gases flowing over the tubes. Wherever possible, the tubes are finned to increase the heat transfer from the gases. These factors, plus the low water inventory (a few pints), facilitate rapid start-up from a cold boiler to a full head of steam -- 800 psi and 700°F.

Combustion System. A continuous spray of atomized fuel (diesel fuel, kerosine, gasoline, etc.) is supplied to two turbine-type combustion chambers. In the chambers, fuel is mixed with air from an engine-driven blower and ignited by a spark plug. Blower and fuel pump output vary directly with expander speed.

Preliminary tests with the combustion system indicate very low exhaust concentrations of hydrocarbons, carbon monoxide, and oxides of nitrogen.

Condenser. The condenser uses a plate-fin arrangement and is externally similar to a standard car radiator. However, it is about three times as large (22 x 40 x 5 inches) and its special brazed aluminum construction, with extended heat transfer surfaces on both the inside and outside of the tubes, will withstand both vacuum and pressure. The condenser will handle all of the steam required for normal highway operation. Extended operation at higher loads will result in some water loss in the form of steam vented from the system.

Controls. Operation is controlled automatically by sensors for steam temperature and pressure, boiler water level, expander speed, and blower airflow. These sensors send electrical pulses to a logic circuit which operates the appropriate solenoids. The accelerator pedal and the throttle valve which controls expander speed are linked mechanically.

Transmission. An experimental toric transmission developed at GM Research, the 250-TT, is used with the SE-101. Its advantages include automatic transmission performance without step shifts and operation of all accessories, including air conditioning, when the vehicle is stationary.

The 250-TT provides a wide torque range to cover all operating conditions. Without the transmission, an additional expander would be needed to drive the accessories.

Problem Areas

Problems with the experimental SE-101 are much the same as for any steam powered automobile at today's state of the art. They include:

Powerplant Size and Weight. Added components (combustion system, steam generator, larger condenser) make a steam powerplant bigger and heavier than a comparable internal combustion engine. The SE-101 system is 450 pounds heavier than the powerplant it replaced in the Grand Prix -- at less than half the horsepower. Installation required a seven-inch extension of the engine compartment.

Cost. No cost data is yet available for steam powerplants.

Water Consumption. The engine compartment poses severe restrictions on condenser size. In the SE-101, full water recovery cannot be achieved under adverse operating conditions, such as full-load operation or hot weather.

Freezing. Water has the best overall combination of properties of any vapor engine working fluid known. However, freezing is a serious problem. An automatic startup control, designed to prevent freezing when the car is parked, is being investigated for the SE-101. It would activate the combus-

Photo taken at the GM Tech Center in 1969 shows two steam-powered cars, the SE-124 Chevelle with a Besler Developments engine and the SE-101 steam-powered Grand Prix.

Researchers lower the expander and transmission (top photo) into the engine compartment of GM's SE-101 Steam Car. The next step is installing the combustion system – steam generator, which fits snugly over the expander and transmission.

tion system whenever temperatures approach the freezing point.

Lubrication. Adequate steam engine lubrication is difficult, since the lubricant must be mixed with steam at high temperatures and pressures. In addition, the oil must be removed before the condensed water is returned to the boiler; otherwise, carbon deposits would reduce boiler efficiency.

Acknowledgement

In addition to GM Research, several GM divisions and staffs cooperated on the SE-101 project. Included were:

● Harrison Radiator Division - steam generator, condenser and air conditioning systems.

● Delco-Remy Division - special electric system components.

● Engineering Staff - vehicle modifications.

● Pontiac Motor Division - test vehicle.

● Diesel Equipment Division - fuel system components.

● Packard Electric Division - wiring harnesses and fiber optics.

Future Uncertain

Whether a practical steam engine vehicle is in the motorist's future is still a widely debated and unanswered question. The experimental SE-101 points to some of the problems which must be solved and is serving as a test bed for further steam power research.

CIRRUS!

Part airplane, part car, this futuristic experimental Pontiac introduced in 1969 was years ahead of its time

THE CIRRUS, an experimental Pontiac featuring aerodynamic design and a two-passenger cockpit with jet aircraft atmosphere, was displayed for the first time at the Texas State Fair in Dallas on October 4-19, 1969. Sharing the spotlight with the futuristic Cirrus, whose name is derived from a stratospheric cloud formed of ice crystals, was a complete range of '70 Pontiacs.

The aerodynamic shape of the Cirrus is inspired by aircraft design and its entire body, including the undersurface, is enclosed for aerodynamic efficiency. Passengers enter from the rear, moving between the two seats as in an airplane cockpit.

Its instrument panel and an overhead roof console are filled with 21 instruments, 31 indicator lights, 29 toggle switches and four control levers. It has an aircraft-type steering control consisting of hand grips. Thumb buttons on each hand grip activate the horn and turn signals.

The Cirrus is painted a special silver with its interior finished in black. The top surface of the hood and instrument panel have a non-reflecting black surface to eliminate glare.

It has wide-tread tires for better handling. For air braking, flaps about two-feet square can be flipped out from each rear side quarter.

New lighting concepts are seen in the rear turn signal and stop lights are housed in a narrow, horseshoe-shaped strip. It shines blue as a taillight and changes to red when the brakes are applied. In a separate warning system for emergency stops, two large flipper panels open across the rear to expose intense flashing red lights.

1970

THE FUN OF DRIVING

Pontiac introduces a whole new generation
of Firebirds, GTO, Judge and Grand Prix models
plus a dynamite 455-inch engine for those
who take the fun of driving seriously!

The Judge came back in 1970 as a winged and scalloped supercar and the factory merchandised 3,629 hardtops and 168 convertibles. They probably could have sold a lot more.

You could still get a Ram Air IV engine in a GTO and that was the way to fly!

CAPSULE COMMENTS

PONTIAC's engine lineup is going to be considerably different for 1970. At the bottom end of the scale, the little six-cylinder overhead cam Pontiac engine is out, replaced by the 250-cubic-inch Chevy-style mill.

Somewhat stranger changes took place in the V8 lineup. For instance, the 350, which was a pretty neat class engine, is now available only with a two-barrel and you have to get into the 400-cubic-inch bracket to receive a four-barrel in either 330 or 350 horsepower. A new engine has been added, 455 cubic inches, designed as an answer to the other new GM big engines. The 455 is essentially a low rpm torquer, designed to give good street feel in spite of emissions control. It has more weight in the doors due to the new "safety" bars built into them. It's a bored and stroked version of the 428 with a 360 horsepower official rating.

For performance, you still turn to 400 cubic inches. We'll begin with a Ram Air III which is the standard Judge engine and the optional GTO engine, and has now beefed up four bolt main bearing caps. Ram Air IV pieces are still scarcer than hen's teeth on the open market, but the story is that for 1970 they will be a stock staple. Here you wind up with bigger ports, better heads, swirl-polished valves and an aluminum intake manifold.

The tunnel port Ram Air V is missing from the lineup for 1970. The story is that it is slated for later mid-year introduction, victim of a last moment delaying action. The cars are there, the engines are there, but the moment that Pontiac pulls the rabbit out of the hat will be one of the first decisions that new Manager, F.J. McDonald, will have to make.

The new '70 Ram Air IV in a GTO, coupled with the suspension and handling improvements, proved to be a tough package designed for both the drag strip and road. The low restriction exhaust system not only got rid of

It was a bad sales year for Pontiac and the new Firebird line was held up for a late intro. There were lots of new options and engine packages and it looked as though the Firebird was being primed for a long run. They only sold 3,196 Trans-Ams, but did manage to market 18,874 base Firebirds, 18,961 Esprit models and 7,708 Formulas.

The Trans-Am was launched during the height of Trans-Am race competition and Pontiac was represented by the legendary BFG Radial Tire-Birds. BFG built dupes for promotional shows around the country.

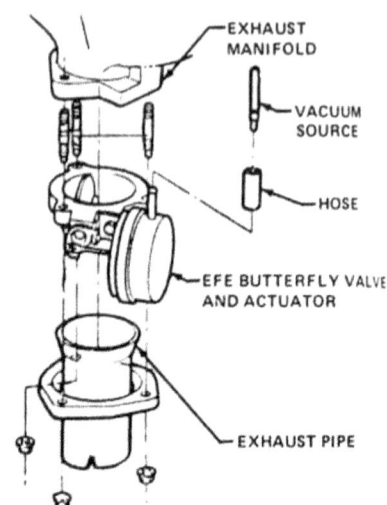

Schematic was supplied by Padgett Petersen and is of what was to be a vacuum-controlled exhaust cutout for the GTO and Judge. It was to be called "Tiger Button." Petersen drives one of the rare GTO station wagons from this era.

some of the bends and kinks but also provides a neat sound which deepens as you bypass the muffler. Ram Air IV's are available with any gear up to 4.33 which contributes in no small way in performance.

One intriguing package is a Trans-Am type Firebird with white and blue stripes. Standard power is a Ram Air III, and a Ram Air IV is optional. Climb into it and you are faced with a small black leather covered steering wheel. Handling, just like the wheel, feels tight and snug. Add to this a front spoiler, a wing over the trunk and some F60 rubber.

The new Firebird, which has semi-fastback styling, is built on a 108-inch wheelbase. The four-seat Firebird is available in one body style, a two-door hardtop.

It is offered in four models—standard, the luxury Esprit, the high-performance Formula 400 and the Trans Am. The base Firebird includes as standard a 250 cubic-inch, six-cylinder engine and a three-speed manual transmission. Standard on the Esprit is a 350 cubic-inch V-8 developing 255 horsepower, a three-speed manual floor shift, a custom interior and exterior decor moldings. For the performance-minded, the Formula 400 is equipped with a specially-molded fiberglass hood scoops. A 400 cubic-inch engine with a dual snorkle air cleaner and dual exhausts are standard equipment on the Formula 400. The high-performance Trans-Am includes a Ram Air engine, four-speed wide-ratio floor shift transmission, variable-ratio power steering, Formula steering wheel, power front disc brakes and rally gauge package with instrument panel tachometer and clock.

All Firebirds have a new suspension system for improved ride and better handling. For the Formula 400, the system includes a front stabilizer bar, higher-rate rear springs, firmer control shocks, and a rear stabilizer bar. For the ultimate in handling, the Trans-Am uses even larger front and rear stabilizer bars, and 60-series tires.

All 1970 Firebirds feature the long-hood, short-deck theme. Overall length has been increased 1.2 inches to 192.3 inches while the overall width is 73.4 inches.

1970 PONTIAC HIGH-PERFORMANCE ENGINES

CUBIC INCHES	BORE	STROKE	HORSEPOWER	COMPRESSION	INDUCTION
400	4.12	3.75	330 @ 4800	10.0-to-1	Four-barrel
400	4.12	3.75	330 @ 4800	10.25-to-1	Four-barrel
400	4.12	3.75	345 @ 5000	10.50-to-1	Four-barrel
400	4.12	3.75	350 @ 5000	10.25-to-1	Four-barrel
400	4.12	3.75	366 @ 5100	10.50-to-1	Four-barrel
400	4.12	3.75	370 @ 5500	10.50-to-1	Four-barrel
455	4.15	4.21	360 @ 4600	10.25-to-1	Four-barrel
455	4.15	4.21	370 @ 4600	10.25-to-1	Four-barrel

The Grand Prix beat continued with over 65,000 units sold, including 500 with manual transmissions. The long hood/short deck theme obviously worked even in a bad year.

New GTO can be had with 455-inch four-barrel, but hot setup is still 400-inch Ram Air IV with stick. Production of Ram Air IV cars includes 627 four-speed, 140 automatic hardtops and 20 four-speed and 13 automatic convertibles.

PONTIAC'S MAGNIFICENT FIVE!

At the height of the supercar sweepstakes Pontiac engineers slipped in the engine that could have positioned the Division as King of the Hill

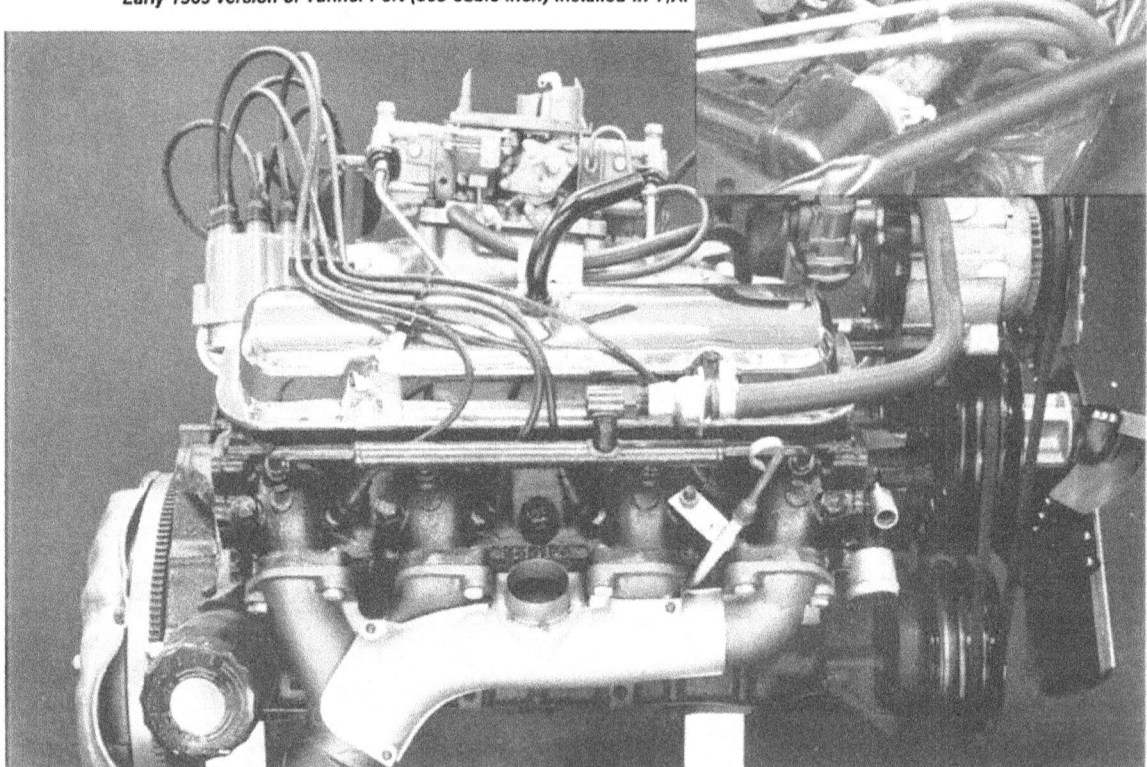

Early 1969 version of Tunnel-Port (303-cubic-inch) installed in T/A.

Complete 400-cubic-inch Tunnel-Port Ram-Air V drag racing engine.

THE RAM-AIR V was the first Pontiac engine since the 1963 421-SD to be developed around the concept of performance and durability outside the realm of normal usage. Although it looks like any other Pontiac V-8 Engine, almost every part in the engine is new and different.

CYLINDER BLOCK

The Ram-Air V cylinder block (#545686) is a grey iron casting with four-bolt malleable iron bearing caps. Lateral strength has been increased by the cross-ribbing at the lifter bosses; and all bulkheads have been strengthened with added material. The cylinders are honed for proper piston clearance and surface finish and the distributor hole is bored out from 1.373/1.374-inch to 1.636/1.637-inch for installation of the special distributor and distributor gear.

The two oil gallery holes at the front of the block, which normally receive a press-in plug, are tapped for the installation of ⅜-inch pipe plugs. This prevents the plugs from blowing out under high pressure and allows the plugs to be removed for cleaning the galleries. The ⅜-inch pipe plug at the rear of the oil gallery ending at the distributor hole has a .030-inch hole drilled through its center to provide metered oiling to the distributor gear.

CRANKSHAFT

The crankshaft used in the Ram-Air V (#545671) is a forged steel piece with five main bearings that are cross drilled. The main bearing journals are 3.0-inch diameter, the rod journals are 2.25-inch diameter, and the stroke is 3.75-inch. Polishing of the main and rod bearing journals on the crankshaft is done in order to obtain the optimum surface finish and journal sizing for bearing fits. The crankshaft is inspected thoroughly prior to assembly to ensure that all oil passage drillings are chamfered smoothly, and the crank is Magnafluxed to be sure that no cracks exist.

BEARINGS

The main and rod bearing inserts used in the Ram-Air V are Delco Moraine M-400 bearings, which have excellent wear and fatigue characteristics. No attempt should be made to use bearings with lower fatigue resistance, as serious engine durability problems are likely to result.

The main bearing inserts are plain lower and grooved upper for maximum load carrying capability and optimum oil flow to the connecting rod bearings at high engine speed. A selection of bearing sizes is used to establish proper clearances during assembly for both main and rod bearings.

CONNECTING RODS

The forged steel connecting rods (#545855) are checked for balance and thoroughly inspected, including Magnaflux, prior to assembly. The nominal weight of the complete rod is 900 grams, with 265 grams on the small end and 635 grams on the big end. The rod uses cap screws instead of bolts and nuts for added strength and reduced weight. Torque specification for these cap screws is 60-65 lb/ft with 20W motor oil used to lubricate the threads.

PISTONS AND RINGS

The Ram-Air V uses a TRW forged piston (#545856) with a slight dome to increase the nominal compression ratio to 10.5-to-1. The top compression ring is a barrel-face, moly-filled cast-iron ring. The second compression ring is the same as the top except taper face. The oil ring is a standard low-tension 3/16-inch unit.

Round-port aluminum intake manifold used on drag racing engine.

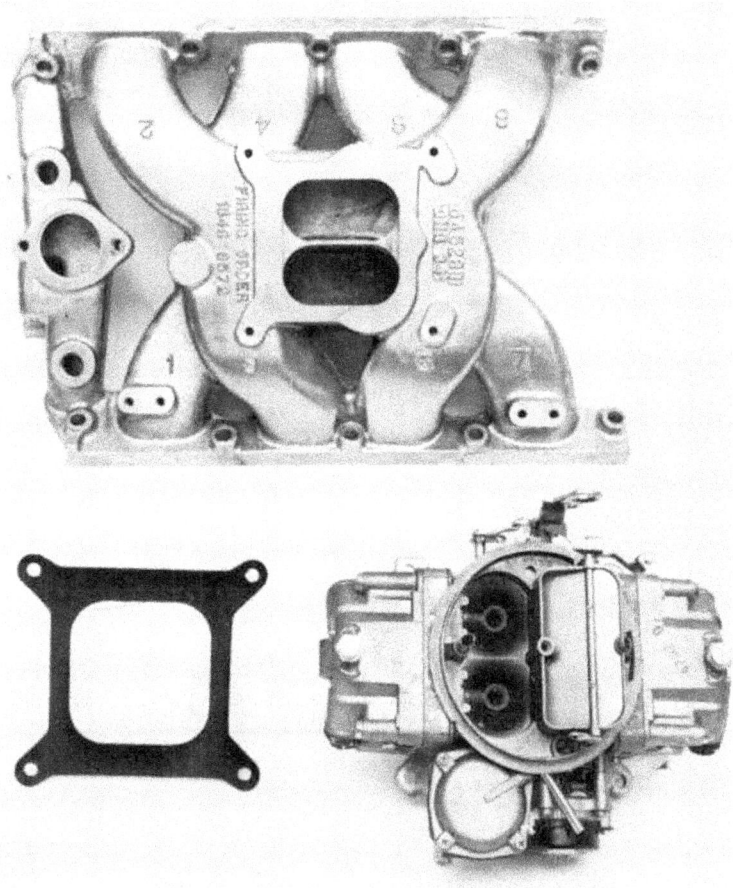

Holley induction system used by Pontiac only on Ram-Air V.

CYLINDER HEADS

The cylinder heads for the Ram-Air V (#546534) are the most unique part of the engine. They are a total departure from past Pontiac cylinder heads and feature large intake and exhaust ports with pushrods running through tubes sealed in the intake ports. The intake valves are lightweight, hollow-stem units that seal on fully radiused seats in the head. The exhaust valves are also lightweight but have the additional feature of being sodium-filled for better cooling. The exhaust valve seats in the head are stainless steel inserts which eliminate seat wear. Valve springs are single spring and damper units that allow engine speed in excess of 7,000 rpm without valve float.

CAMSHAFT

The Ram-Air V camshaft is a solid-lifter unit with 308 degrees of intake event and 320 degrees of exhaust event. Valve lash is .018-inch on the intake and .024-inch on the exhaust with the engine at room temperature (cold).

INTAKE MANIFOLD AND CARBURETOR

The intake manifold used on the Ram-Air V engine is an aluminum single four-barrel unit. This manifold yields fairly good mid-range torque with good peak power. The carburetor recommended for use on the Ram-Air V is the Holley 800-cfm four-barrel.

IGNITION SYSTEM

The distributor for the Ram-Air V Tunnel Port engine (#1111972) is a breakerless, "Mag-Pulse" assembly with the proper base pilot diameter and drive gear installed, and can be used with either transistor or capacitor-discharge amplifiers and coils. These units are capable of handling *any* obtainable engine speed.

Heavy-duty four-bolt-main block designed to handle racing loads.

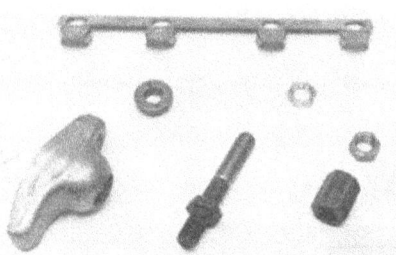

Tunnel-Port oil deflector, 1.65 rocker arm and component parts.

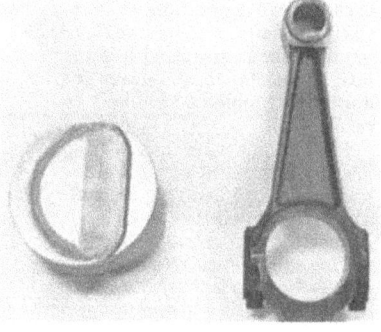

Unique Tunnel-Port head designed for high-rpm applications.

TRW made the forged piston used with lightweight forged steel rods for Tunnel-Port applications.

RAM-AIR IV VS RAM-AIR V

The Tunnel Port 400 (Ram-Air V) was released for *service parts only* and available only to Pontiac dealers in limited quantities. This engine differs from the Ram Air IV engine in the following major respects:

1. A revised cylinder head featuring round intake ports, 50 percent larger in cross-sectional area is used. Valve centers have been repositioned to allow for the larger intake valve and to permit use of a valve seat insert for the exhaust valve.

2. Intake valve diameter has been increased from 2.11-inch to 2.19-inch and valve stems are hollow. Sodium-cooled exhaust valves are used.

3. A new aluminum intake manifold having larger, round runners to match the cylinder head is employed. As in the Ram-Air IV engine, no exhaust heat is applied to the intake manifold.

4. The separate exhaust cross-over has been eliminated. Heated air to the carburetor is supplied during warm-up from two shrouds or stoves, one on each exhaust manifold.

5. Solid valve lifters replace the hydraulic lifters used in the Ram-Air IV. The camshaft is revised for use with these lifters.

6. The cylinder block has been revised to include heavier bulkheads for reduced deflection and increased durability. Cast ribs have been added, connecting the two banks of cylinders in the lifter base area for increased block rigidity. The distributor pilot hole is enlarged to accept a larger distributor and oil pump drive gear to increase durability of this gear.

7. New lightweight forged rods are used.

8. A forged crankshaft replaces the cast crankshaft. Cross-drilling is employed in the main bearing journals.

9. A high-inertia harmonic balancer is used.

10. The Holley four-barrel carburetor having an electric choke replaces the Quadrajet.

THE SECOND-GENERATION FIREBIRD

Pontiac gave new meaning to the word Ponycar with its long-hood, short-deck Firebird and Trans-Am

THERE is little doubt that the all-new line of Firebirds introduced in 1970 revolutionized the enthusiast car marketplace and created a whole new (almost-European) image for the long-hood, short-deck concept. Introduced to the public on February 26, 1970, the radical line of ponycars came to be known simply as the "'70½ Fantastic Four." Interestingly enough, the Second Generation project design was started just a couple of months after the first Firebirds were unveiled. The project officially started late in 1966.

Unlike many Motown projects, the F-Car program was headed up by a number of enthusiasts at a time when guys like DeLorean were in charge. It was viewed as a fun project—and it showed. Prior to his retirement General Motors Styling Chief William Mitchell reflected on the Second Generation F-Car, calling it a "designer's design" and rating it as the best and most successful design in his GM career. Those are pretty strong words from one of the world's top automotive designers who's known for his rather caustic appraisals of car design.

The Second Generation F-car was truly the Driver's Car of its time. In fact, dash design on the Trans-Am was heavily influenced by comments made by Chevrolet's Mr. Corvette, Zora Arkus-Duntov to the head of Pontiac's interior design studio.

Before getting into the top-performance Trans-Am, let's take a look at the well-rounded Second-Generation lineup—consisting of a base Firebird, luxurious Esprit, high-performance Formula and top-performance Trans-Am. The base car came stock with the lackluster OHV Six and three-speed stick transmission, while the higher-dollar Esprit was 350-inch V-8 equipped (also with three-speed stick). Performance-minded buyers could chose between the Formula with its 400-inch V-8 with dual exhausts and twin air scoop hood and the ultimate Ponycar—the Trans-Am with its Ram Air 400 engine, four-speed wide-ratio box, variable-ratio power steering, power front disc brakes and fully-instrumented Rally gauge package.

For '70½ the Trans-Am had its own image thanks to a host of styling treatments—some of which actually offered performance benefits. The Second-Generation Trans-Am was adorned with air dams up front and on each of the wheel openings, engine compartment air-outlets on the front fenders and a full-width rear deck spoiler. The front air dam and engine compartment air outlets actually reduced air pressure buildup under the front of the car to keep the wheels firmly planted on the ground at higher speeds. The all-new rear spoiler was designed manily for looks, but it also helped create a downforce at high speeds which can have a positive effect on understeer and actually improve high-speed stability.

The main idea behind the styling of the Second-Generation Firebird was to com-

Here's the Ponycar that set the standard for styling, performance and handling for many years. Even with standard engine it offered super-performance at a reasonable price tag.

1970½ FIREBIRD PERFORMANCE COMPARATOR

Performance comparisons of three different models, dyno-tuned to stock specifications and tested by a national magazine in 1970.

Firebird Esprit with 350 CID two-barrel engine rated at 255 hp and fitted with Turbo-Hydro and 2.73-to-1 rear end.

0 to 40 mph	0 to 60 mph	Quarter-Mile
4.5 seconds	9.8 seconds	79.4 mph in 17.2 seconds

Firebird Formula 400 with 400 CID four-barrel engine rated at 330 hp and fitted with Turbo-Hydro and 3.07-to-1 rear end

0 to 40 mph	0 to 60 mph	Quarter-Mile
3.4 seconds	6.4 seconds	98 mph in 14.7 seconds

Firebird Trans-Am with 400 CID engine rated at 345 hp and fitted with four-speed and 3.73-to-1 rear end

0 to 40 mph	0 to 60 mph	Quarter-Mile
3.1 seconds	5.7 seconds	103.02 mph in 14.1 seconds

*Note—thsse cars were delivered thru Royal Pontiac to the magazine.

1970½ FIREBIRD ENGINE AVAILABILITY

Code	Displacement	Type	Horsepower	Torque	Compression	Carb
L-22	250 CID	OHV-6	155 @ 4,200	235 @ 1,600	8.5-to-1	One-barrel
L-30	350 CID	V-8	255 @ 4,600	355 @ 2,800	8.8-to-1	Two-barrel
L-65	400 CID	V-8	265 @ 4,600	397 @ 2,400	8.8 to 1	Two-barrel
L-78	400 CID	V-8	330 @ 4,800	430 @ 3,000	10.25-to-1	Four-barrel
L-74	400 CID	V-8	335 @ 5,000	430 @ 3,400	10.50-to-1	Four-barrel
LS-1	400 CID Ram IV	V-8	345 @ 5,400	430 @ 3,700	10.75-to-1	Four-barrel

'70½ TRANS-AM PRODUCTION

MODEL	TURBO-HYDRO	STICK	TOTAL
Ram Air 400 LS-1	59	29	88
Ram Air 400 L-74	1,339	1,769	3,108
		Total	3,196

PRODUCTION

Base Firebird	18,874
Esprit	18,961
Formula	7,708
Trans-Am	3,196
Total	48,739

Photo taken on F-car assembly line of the first Trans-Am produced. If you look really close, you can see the Camaro to the left. Firebirds and Camaros are still produced on the same assembly lines.

bine American ingenuity and performance with European sports car design. To get this effect the styling people gave us large single headlamps, scoop-type, split grille openings, semi-fastback styling and an overall smoothness. The extended hood conceals the windshield wipers from view and the longer doors, which eliminate the quarter-windows, contribute to this sleek styling concept. Even the flush-mounted, lift-type outside door handles help achieve this European look.

However, Pontiac did not resort to styling to develop a driver's car. Even in box-stock Formula or Trans-Am trim, the new F-car truly earned high-performance nameplates. The engineers did their homework—the cars handled and accelerated like real high-performance cars. This was not a case of cosmetic surgery. The new car got new steering linkage, front and rear sway bars (Formula and Trans-Am) and in the case of the Trans-Am, a very serious injection of youth market goodies. It was the first Firebird to be available with a rear sway bar. The base Firebird has a .940-inch front sway bar; Esprit has the same; Formula has a 1.125-inch job and the Trans-Am came stock with a 1.250-inch bar. At the rear the Formula got a .625-inch unit and the Trans-Am a .875-inch piece. The wheelbase remained the same, but the overall length grew 1.2 inches to 192.3 inches and the width to 73.4 inches. The truck and rear seat area suffered slightly. And, of course, the new cars received Pontiac's exclusive Endura front bumper.

Even though the Trans-Am was loaded in stock shape, there were some options available so that the individual could tailor a car to his or her specifications. It is almost impossible to do this today. You could have your Trans-Am with either a Ram-Air 400 or Ram Air-IV motor, both factory-equipped with chrome dress-up goodies and flex fan and hooked to a functional Ram-Air "shaker" hood scoop. An electric solonoid switch would open the scoop for cold air induction to the Rochester Q-Jet when the pedal was floored. In later years the shaker scoop became a cosmetic piece which had to be converted by the owner to functional operation.

There were also gear-changing options with the Trans-Am. Standard equipment included an M-20 wide-ratio four-speed with Hurst shifter with options listed for an M-21 close-ratio box or M-40 Turbo-Hydro (one of the best ever offered by any manufacturer). Saginaw's high-effort, variable-ratio power steering with 2.5 turns lock-to-lock, offered the best of both worlds. Pontiac's excellent Y-96 handling package was carried over with the new sway bars and the 1.7-inch-increased front track width helped give the new Trans-Am a real *hugger* feeling. Standard was 7-inch Rally II wheels with Polyglas white-lettered bias-ply tires (F60-15)—a decent tire by 1970 standards yet obsolete by today's high-technology tire standards.

When ordering a '70½ Trans-Am you had a wide choice of colors—Cameo White with a blue/black stripe or Lucerne Blue with a white/black stripe. Interior color choices were also extensive—black or red!

If Pontiac top management could have pulled it off, the Trans-Am would not have been a Trans-Am. They wanted to call it Sebring, with Formula and Trans-Am as Second and Third choices. Since Chrysler already owned the Sebring name, Pontiac used both Formula and Trans-Am nameplates for its top performance Ponycars.

The '70½ Trans-Am is a very collectible car and one that should appreciate greatly in years to come. Its design was with us from 1970 to the end of the 1981 model year and there are few cars on the road today which can match its macho look and performance and handling. Not that many come up for sale, but the car has never really enjoyed the status and pricing of far inferior cars which cannot match the T/A's mystique or reality. It's the kind of car that rates as a legend—a legend that you can afford to own and drive.

The Formula 400 Firebird had a lot going for itself with good suspension, potent 400 engine and dynamite twin-scoop hood. You might say it was tastefully macho!

One of many race car renderings turned out by Pontiac stylists prior to the introduction of the Second-Generation Firebirds.

Pontiac experimented with 303-cubic-inch Tunnel-Port engines for Trans-Am racing and 400-inch for drag racing in 1970-'71. This is one of the factory-built 303-inch motors ready for installation in a Proving Grounds Trans-Am.

1971

THE WRITING'S ON THE WALL!

The Grand Prix gets a facelift, the GTO gets more luxurious, Firebirds can be had with 350, 400 or 455 engines and compression ratios come down in preparation of the future

With a wing on the back and 455 inches under the hood, the GTO was still a big threat on the street. Production of 455-inch HO models included 476 four-speed and 412 automatic hardtops and 21 four-speed and 27 automatic convertibles.

The Trans-Am was the standard of ponycar performance by which all others were judged. Trans-Am production was just 2,116 units, but 23,021 base Firebirds, 20,185 Esprit models and 7,802 Formulas were sold. That's Herb Adams (a Pontiac engineer at the time) behind the wheel of this test car.

CAPSULE COMMENTS

PONTIAC is fighting a great battle, but they are not necessarily getting the best end of it. Here is the world's most performance-oriented car maker and the highest performance engine they have has an 8.4-to-1 compression ratio. We are talking of the 455 HO, which is *standard* on the Trans-Am Firebird and on the Judge, and has been made optional in just about all other lines. As it's released, it comes through with a No. 068 cam featuring a .414-inch lift, a 288-degree intake duration and a 302-degree exhaust duration. The overlap is a modest 63 degrees to trap the compression that is there. What do you do with this engine when you get it?

Apparently, the best thing will be to head for the parts department. There you can pick up some Ram Air IV valve train pieces, such as a No. 041 cam, with a .527-inch lift, different springs and retainers, all of which stem from the Ram Air IV. Next step would be to mill the heads a good .060-inch to wind up in the 9.5-to-1 compression ratio.

In ordering Ram Air, you can either head for the Judge which has air scoops at the front of the hood, or for the Trans-Am that has a rearward facing *shaker* hood scoop. The Ram Air V engines that are left over from previous programs (only a hundred or so) are now available for substantial money and the purchasers of those

Optional wing with engine displacement decals was top head-turning treatment of the year. It was just the right size. Only 357 Judge model hardtops were produced in 1971 model year.

Budget GT-37 offered GTO performance at stripper-model prices. This model has become very collectible. Photos were taken during 1971 CARS Magazine road test session. Almost 45,000 T-37 models were built.

Grand Prix boasted restyling plus standard variable-ratio power steering, power front disc brakes and a 400-inch engine. The SJ package includes a 455-inch motor. Total production was 58,325.

START

Convertible production dropped to a super-low mark with only 661 GTO models and 17 Judge units being produced. The handwriting was on the wall.

Top performance engine in Trans-Am is 455-HO with functional Ram Air and enough torque to pull tree stumps!

One-off Trans-Am with louvered hood instead of shaker treatment did not get the nod from top management. Rear end has conventional spoiler treatment.

engines will be entitled to buy back-up parts.

Next step down from the 455 HO is a straight 455 that has an even lower 8.2-to-1 compression ratio and from there it's an even longer step to the 350 (which happens to be a pretty good engine that has suffered from long standing inattention to its performance potential).

The LeMans name now extends to all of the small sized Pontiac lines, and the Tempest name is dropped altogether. The price leader in the group is a T-37, powered by a Six. However, for a modest price increase, you get a GT-37 with a small 350 V8 and a three-speed stick shift—a Hurst at that. This, plus some extra trim, and a set of neat looking wheels, adds up to a car that handles well and moves right out, sort of a "poor man's GTO."

Next in line you'll find a LeMans and a LeMans Sport, followed by the GTO and the Judge. All of the Le-Mans series except for the GTO get a blade bumper instead of the one that loops around the grille, while the GTO benefits from a revamped Endura bumper and separate fiberglass rims for the headlights (last year they were all Endura).

The Firebirds are virutally un-

1971 PONTIAC HIGH-PERFORMANCE ENGINES

CUBIC INCHES	BORE	STROKE	HORSEPOWER	COMPRESSION	INDUCTION
400	4.12	3.75	300 @ 4800	8.20-to-1	Four-barrel
455	4.15	4.21	325 @ 4400	8.20-to-1	Four-barrel
455	4.15	4.21	335 @ 4800	8.40-to-1	Four-barrel

Pontiac produced over 48,000 Ventura II Nova-takeoffs to give the dealers a better shot at the marketplace. Unfortunately, only a handful received the treatment featured here. They were powered by 455-HO Trans-Am style engines, hood tachs, honeycomb mag wheels and F-60 Goodyear Polyglas GT tires. These were R&D cars and the project never reached production. As would be expected, these cars were screamers.

changed, except for small, functional engine compartment air extractors at the sides of the fenders. This innovation, directly from the Trans-Am, helps vent the air trapped under the hood and cuts down on front end lift, apart from lowering engine compartment temperatures.

Powered by a 455 four-barrel HO engine, the Trans-Am has a long list of standard equipment including: Four-speed floor shift transmission, variable ratio power steering, power front disc brakes and a firm ride and handling package consisting of high-rate rear springs, a 1¼-inch front sta-bilizer bar and ⅞-inch rear bar.

Also standard are a through-the-hood rearward facing Ram Air inlet with throttle operated valve, F60-15 white lettered tires, Honeycomb wheels, front and rear spoilers, wheel opening spoilers, rally gauges and clock set in an instrument panel trimmed with engine turned (swirl-finished bright metal), dual exhausts, engine compartment extractors on the front fenders, stripes and special identification.

All 400 and 455 engines have a compression ratio of 8.2-to-1, except the 455 HO which is 8.4-to-1. To maintain or improve engine performance, Pontiac engineers have taken the following steps: New camshafts have been put into the 350 and 400 two-barrel engines for increased low end torque and peak torque. On all four-barrel engines the secondary air valve opening time has been reduced to one second (from 2½ seconds) for faster response. For improved starting and acceleration, the air capacity has been increased on all four-barrel manual transmissions and 455 HO engines.

FIREBIRD CAFE RACER, STAGE I

Prototype Trans-Am with a louvered instead of Shaker hood was presented to Pontiac management in 1971 for possible marketing in 1972. It failed the test!

When they took the Shaker scoop away and replaced the special hood with a twin louvered affair, the Trans-Am lost a lot of its macho. Overall look, however, is super-clean.

One of the problems with the louvered hood was keeping the rain out. Rear facing louvers act as extractors, pulling the hot air out of the compartment as the car moves along. An outside vendor, with a louver press and dies, made the one-off hood for Pontiac Product Planning.

The interior is pure Trans-Am right down to the engine-turned dash with full instrumentation and padded racing wheel.

Without the Shaker hood, the side view makes the T/A look like half Firebird and half Trans-Am. Prototype was finished in black lacquer. Photo was taken at the GM Milford Proving Grounds.

The dual fender scoops shown here were totally functional, supplying venting for both the engine compartment and the front disc brakes. Open area inside the scoops is covered with wire mesh.

From the rear this prototype looks like any other Trans-Am. The car was "plated" with standard Michigan tags and was street driven for almost one year to test the louvered hood and side vents under all weather conditions.

THE ULTIMATE GRAND PRIX

Hurst Performance took Pontiac's new luxury personal car concept one step beyond and came up with this unique Grand Prix

THE SSJ HURST, a custom conversion of the Pontiac Grand Prix, was debuted by Hurst Performance Research, the Detroit subsidiary of Hurst Performance, in 1970.

Starting with a '71 Grand Prix, Hurst converted the car for Pontiac dealers by adding an electric sunroof, a padded Landau-style half-top and Hurst Fire Frost gold metallic paint areas accented with classic pin striping. Die cast SSJ HURST emblems and special Hurst gold accented Rally II wheels added the final touches to a car that was described by Hurst as "The Ultimate Grand Prix."

The 1971 SSJ HURST was distinguished by being the first automobile to offer the following optional Hurst factory installed equipment:

The new Hurst Auto/Stick Shifter, combines the rugged good looks and precision of the famous Hurst Competition/Plus shifter with the convenience of a Turbo Hydra-Matic transmission.

The SSJ Hurst Digital Computer, custom crafted for the SSJ by Harmon Electronics, provides a unique and highly-accurate digital readout of vehicle speed. Using over 2,300 transisters, 700 diodes and 2,185 resistors, it enables the driver to accurately measure the efficiency of his car.

The New B.F. Goodrich Radial ply Trans/Am GR 60 x 15 Tires provide a unique combination of superior road holding, traction and cornering ability, together with outstanding wear and luxury ride characteristics.

The Hurst Gold Accented American Aluminum Wheels further improve the ride and handling of the classic SSJ Hurst, due to their light weight.

Commenting on the '71 SSJ HURST Grand Prix conversion, Hurst Performance President, Bob Draper, stated that, "We believe that the SSJ offers a new dimension of motoring pleasure to the automotive connoisseur. It provides a combination of classic styling, luxury and sports car characteristics never before combined into one automobile."

The SSJ HURST was available through any authorized Pontiac dealer in two exterior color choices: Cameo White and Starlight Black, with contrasting black or white pin striping. All cars were manufactured at regular Pontiac assembly plants, then shipped to the Hurst conversion center in Detroit for installation of special components.

Linda Vaughn, Miss Hurst Golden Shifter, and the gold-trimmed white Hurst SSJ Grand Prix.

1972

THE END IS NEAR!

Confusion reigns supreme as the GTO is reduced to an 'option,' an announced GTO rear spoiler is never produced and what could have been the ultimate street supercar ('71 1/2 455-HO Ventura II) never makes the assembly line

Engineer whips a pre-production GTO through the tight pylon course at the General Motors Proving Grounds. Note pilot car spoiler which never officially reached production.

The Trans-Am was as hairy as ever, but sales showed only 1,286 units, approximately 10 percent of total Firebird sales.

CAPSULE COMMENTS

THE GTO and LeMans Sport will be offered as options on the LeMans series. The GTO, available on the two-door hardtop and coupe models, includes side splitters on the performance dual exhausts, an Endura front end, a distinctive hood with air scoops, new air extractors on the front fenders, and G70-14 black tires.

The Sport features front bucket seats, trick interior and exterior trim. It's available on the LeMans two-door hardtop.

A special handling package is optional on all two-door intermediates except the Sport convertible. It includes fast variable-ratio power steering, G60-15 white lettered tires on 15x7-inch wheels, GTO high-rate springs, firm shocks, and 1⅛-inch front and rear stabilizer bars.

Two styling packages — the GT and Endura front end option — offer special equipment and distinctiveness.

The Endura option, available on all LeMans and LeMans Sports, includes the following GTO front end features: energy-absorbing bumper, grille, hood with scoops, headlamp arrangement, valance panel, parking lamps and front fenders with air extractors.

The GT package is optional on the LeMans two-door hardtop and Sport convertible with a V-8 engine. Included are a three-speed heavy-duty manual transmission with Hurst floor shifter, performance dual exhausts with side outlets, G70-14 white lettered tires and 14x7-inch Rally II wheels, special side striping, a GT decal on the deck lid and body colored outside mirrors.

Easily recognized by its fiberglass hood with long dual air scoops, the Formula is offered as a 350, 400 and 455, depending on the engine. The Formula 350 has a 350 two-barrel, the

Formula 400 comes with the 400 four-barrel and the Formula 455 is powered by the high-performance 455 HO. Standard transmissions are: three-speed floor shift for the 350, four-speed wide-ratio floor shift on the 400 and four-speed close-ratio for the 455. Turbo Hydra-matic is optional on all three.

All Formula Firebirds feature a special handling suspension consisting of a large 1⅛-inch diameter front stabilizer bar, firm springs and shocks and a ⅝-inch rear stabilizer bar. All also have performance dual exhausts with chrome extensions, F70-14 black sidewall bias belted tires, body colored outside mirrors and custom cushion steering wheel.

Available in blue with white stripe or white with blue striping, the Trans-Am provides the ultimate in performance and handling. Powered by the 455 four-barrel HO engine, this car has a long list of standard equipment, including: Four-speed floor shift or Turbo Hydra-matic, fast variable-ratio power steering, power front disc brakes and a handling package consisting of high-rate rear springs, a 1¼-inch front stabilizer bar and ⅞-inch rear bar.

Also standard are a through-the-hood rearward facing Ram Air scoop with throttle-operated valve, F60-15 white lettered tires, Rally II wheels, front and rear spoilers, wheel opening spoilers, rally gauges, and clock set in an instrument panel trimmed with engine turned (swirl-finished bright metal), aluminum performance dual exhausts with chrome extensions, engine compartment extractors on the front fenders and special identification.

The 400 cubic-inch four-barrel is standard on the Firebird Forumla 400, Grand Prix and GTO. This engine is optional on all other intermediates, the Catalina, Catalina Brougham and Safari. It has a net horsepower of 200 with single exhaust. Net horsepower with duals is 250. Dual exhausts are standard on the Grand Prix and GTO.

The 455 HO four-barrel is standard on the Formula 455 and Trans Am. It is optional on two-door LeMans, LeMans Sport and GTO. Net horsepower with standard dual exhausts is 300.

All 400 and 455 engines have a compression ratio of 8.2-to-1, except the 455 HO which is 8.4-to-1.

There was no GTO convertible in 1972 and GTO sales looked as though the supercar market had dried up. GTO 455-HO production included 3 four-speed and 7 automatic coupes and 310 four-speed and 325 automatic hardtops. Nice decals, exhaust splitters and functional air extractors didn't help.

When it comes to handling, it's almost impossible to beat a Trans-Am with a stock production car. Photo was taken at GM's Black Lake slalom course.

1972 PONTIAC HIGH-PERFORMANCE ENGINES

CUBIC INCHES	BORE	STROKE	HORSEPOWER	COMPRESSION	INDUCTION
400	4.12	3.75	250 @ 4400	8.20-to-1	Four-barrel
455	4.15	4.21	230 @ 4400	8.20-to-1	Four-barrel
455	4.15	4.21	250 @ 3600	8.20-to-1	Four-barrel
455	4.15	4.21	300 @ 4000	8.40-to-1	Four-barrel

This is one of the 5,250 Formula model Firebirds sold in 1972. It's powered by the Ram Air 455 engine, making it one of the strongest street machines of its time.

Pontiac upped production for the 1972 model year and Grand Prix sales went to 91,961. It had become a serious luxury GT car and part of a whole new marketplace.

THE GREAT REAR SPOILER DEBATE!

GTO freaks have been arguing for years about
the so-called "available" rear spoiler on 1972 Goats.
Early ads showed it, dealer brochures
listed it and some people actually
claim they own one. According to Jim Wangers,
Pontiac never went into production on it.
Here's the pre-production prototype

If you own a 1972 GTO with one of these spoilers you have a very rare car. According to Pontiac, not one was ever built. However, over the years we have heard rumors of such cars and the spoiler was shown in full color in sales brochures in 1972. We'd like to hear from any owners of spoiler-equipped '72 Goats.

FIREBIRD CAFE RACER, STAGE II

This one-of-a-kind Trans-Am served as a rolling test lab in 1972 for the SD-455 powertrain

Sporting Manufacturer's tags, this one-off Trans-Am was fitted with BFG Radial T/A tires mounted on special alloy wheels. If you look closely, you can see the padded roll bar which was not a factory option that year! Car was built and tested by the group of engineers headed by Herb Adams.

Obvious rear end mods set this car off from the production '72 Trans-Am. The LeMans fuel filler mounted in the center of the trunk lid was hooked up to a special fuel cell in the trunk.

Car 386 in line on the GM Proving Grounds skid pad with a brace of other Trans-Ams. Note that the lead car does not have the conventional rear fender flares.

Pontiac's Herb Adams makes a pass through the pylons on the Proving Grounds "Black Lake" slalom course. Performance was unreal and the car handled like a real race car.

1973 — SAVED BY THE SUPER-DUTY!

The GTO gets CARS Magazine's coveted award and a 455-inch Super-Duty engine establishes Pontiac as the year's performance leader. While originally announced as an option in the GTO and Grand-Am, the SD-455 appears *only* in the Formula and Trans-Am Firebirds

Rendering of the 455 GTO used on the cover of the award issue of CARS Magazine in 1973.

Prototype of Super-Duty 455 Trans-Am built by Herb Adams and his crew to introduce new engine package to the Press in 1972. Car had trick suspension, special alloy wheels, roll bar and quick-fill tank mounted in the trunk.

Firebird production started to pick up in 1973 with the Trans-Am accounting for an impressive 4,802, more than one-third of base car sales. The Formula with its twin-scoop sold 10,166 units and Esprit hit 17,249 mark.

This is the pre-production prototype of the GTO which almost didn't make it. Car looked really tough with Moon-style hubcaps and fat 60-series tires. By today's standards it is a killer car!

Pontiac built 25 455-inch automatic coupes and 519 automatic Sport Coupes. The 400 was the best performance choice and powers the detailed-to-perfection model shown here.

After presenting Pontiac with the CARS Magazine award, the author went out and bought a 455-inch Sport Coupe for daily transportation. After being tuned by Nunzi (he's the one doing the driving) it was tested at the strip. The author sold it in 1980.

CAPSULE COMMENTS

RECIPIENT of the coveted CARS Magazine Top Performance Car of the Year Award, the Pontiac GTO sports new styling for 1973. However, the GTO is still an option on intermediate coupes.

Listed under Order Code 341, the GTO option includes a blacked-out grille, NASA hood scoops, super-firm shocks, GTO decals and trim, HD 1.25-inch front and 1.00-inch rear sway bar, 7-inch steel wheels with Moon-style hubcaps shod with Goodyear G60x15 tires, dual exhausts, three-speed manual transmission and a 400-inch four-barrel engine.

The addition to the intermediate line is the stunning new Grand-Am which incorporates classic styling with unique ride and handling characteristics. A distinctive body-colored front bumper and flexible rubber-like urethane front end panel combine functional styling with engineering to give an improved bumper system.

Two new major options are offered for 1973. Radial ply tires are standard on the Grand Am and Grand Prix SJ, and are available on Formula and Trans Am Firebirds, the Bonneville and the standard Grand Prix.

The new 455 Super-Duty engine is available on the Formula and Trans-Am Firebirds.

1973 PONTIAC HIGH-PERFORMANCE ENGINES

CUBIC INCHES	BORE	STROKE	HORSEPOWER	COMPRESSION	INDUCTION
400	4.12	3.75	200 @ 4000	8-to-1	Four-barrel
400	4.12	3.75	230 @ 4400	8-to-1	Four-barrel
455	4.15	4.21	250 @ 4000	8-to-1	Four-barrel
455	4.15	4.21	310 @ 4000	8.40-to-1	Four-barrel

The Super-Duty 455 Trans-Am was the only genuine performance vehicle being offered by any domestic producer in 1973. In effect it was a streetable race car that could be had with luxury and convenience options.

Pontiac received the Top Performance Car of the Year award from CARS Magazine for its '73 GTO. It signalled the last year for a real GTO.

Classic Grand-Am was Pontiac's attack on the luxury European GT sedans. It offered the buyer a good suspension, responsive engines, bucket seating and a lot of small extras normally associated only with expensive imports. They built 34,445 coupes and 8,691 sedans.

Original plans called for the SD-455 engine to be offered in the Firebird, GTO and Grand-Am lines. They actually built pre-production SD-455 cars, such as the one shown here. However, the Trans-Am and Formula were the only cars to get production engines.

More restyling for the Grand Prix netted Pontiac with an impressive sales tally on its personal car. Grand Prix sold 153,899 units for its most dramatic year yet.

PART ONE OF A TWO-PART SERIES

SD-455—THE MYTH AND THE MAGIC!

The definitive technical presentation covering everything you could possibly want to know about the 1973-'74 Super-Duty 455 engines and cars

By Gary C. Menin

THE SD-455 engine was *supposedly* available as a production option in the Trans-Am and Formula Firebirds during the years 1973-1974. In 1972 Pontiac announced the option for use in the GTO and Grand-Am and did built such prototype cars. However, it was reserved only for production Firebirds. During 1973-1974 model runs, Pontiac Motor Division (PMD) assembled only 1,295 Firebirds with this option and acquiring one at the time was not that easy. Because of the limited availability and high performance, these cars have been in high demand in recent years.

So what is the big deal about the SD-455? Consider the following factory stock specifications: Forged connecting rods (strongest available from PMD), forged TRW pistons, greatest cylinder head air volume flow rate of any PMD head except for the Ram Air V, 800-cfm Quadrajet (50 more cfm than stock), 80-psi Ram Air V-style oil pump and the least restrictive dual exhaust system of any production Firebird.

Also consider the quarter-mile drag strip performance of stock SD-455 Firebirds tested by major newsstand automotive magazines. *Car & Driver* and *Super/Stock* magazines tested the following cars: 1973 model with automatic and 3.42 gears ran 103.6 mph in 13.8 seconds and a 1974 model with 3.08 gears and automatic clocked 100.93 mph in 14.25 seconds.

In the 1973 model year there were 180 automatic and 72 stick T/As and 43 Formula Firebirds and in 1974 PMD produced 731 auto, 212 stick and 57 Formula models. The grand total is 1,295 cars.

Aside from the performance characteristics of SD-455 Firebirds and the visual differences of cylinder heads and exhaust manifolds, SD-455 Firebirds can be identified by specific numbers, codes and labels. On the top left side of the dash is the vehicle serial number which must show an "X" as the fifth digit. The front right hand side of the block, just below the head, must have a stamped two-letter code with "ZJ" for stick cars and "XD" for

What could be more impressive than four immaculate Super Duty cars lined up all in a row? The lead car belongs to the author and is a rare Formula SD-455. It's used for daily driving yet still looks showroom new!

SD-455

It takes more than decals on the "shaker" scoop to make an SD motor. This is the Real McCoy in Gary Menin's highly-detailed Formula. Motor has been rebuilt.

auto cars in 1973 and "W8" or "Y8" for 1974 production. A stamped two-letter code of "6H" must appear on the machined pad on each head, above the exhaust ports and below the rocker arm cover. The front portion of the intake manifold has a cast code of "LS2" or "LS2X". A cast code of "16" must be on the center exhaust runner on each head. A color-matched SD-455 decal is on each side of the "shaker" hood scoop. All scoops were of a non-functional design.

Next check out the PCV valve in the left rocker cover. The oil filler cap on the left rocker cover of all SD-455 engines is modified to accept a PCV valve and hardware. On other Pontiac engines the PCV valve is located in the lifter valley cover. This difference is necessitated to preclude excessive oil consumption (due to the high-pressure pump) since the lifter valley gets a shower of oil and thus a PCV valve located there would actually suck oil and not just fumes into the induction system.

At the top rear of the left hand rocker cover is an ID label (red, silver & black) which provides oil usage and connecting rod nut tightening data. This label is not currently available from PMD. However, through the extensive efforts of Robert Warden, 3225 Hastings Road, Department T/A, Huntsville, Alabama 35802 (205-881-4229), excellent quality reproduction labels are available for $10.00 each or $7.50 each for members of the Pontiac-Oakland Club International.

The reader is cautioned that the existence of any one of the above ID features of the SD-455 when considered alone does not constitute the existence of an *original* SD-455 car. Decals and labels are especially meaningless in this regard. In addition one should match the last eight digits of the VIN with the stamped numbers on the engine (located on the block adjacent to the lower right hand corner of the timing chain cover) to match the engine to the car as original equipment. Note that this engine block number will start with "2".

After several years of maintaining a Formula SD-455 Firebird (including a complete engine overhaul) the writer has experienced various idiosyncrasies of the SD motor (not applicable to most other PMD engines) which can be extremely useful to the SD owner who wants to keep his or her engine 100-percent streetable. These unique characteristics are not spelled out in either the owners manual or service book but can be critical to maintaining a tuned and trouble-free SD motor.

The upper two rocker arm cover hold-down bolt holes and the rocker arm stud holes for the intake valves break into the intake passages. If thread sealer is not used on these holes, vacuum leaks can result which in turn can cause a rough idling engine. In addition, oil consumption may be increased via oil loss through the non-sealed intake valve rocker arm stud lower threads.

The oil gallery on the inside of the block has a pipe plug at the rear. This plug (which is adjacent to the distributor and cam gears) has a drilled-hole for distributor and cam gear lubrication. This plug (Allen head) must not be interchanged with any of the other oil gallery pipe plugs which are of the conventional Pontiac 5/16-inch square-socket-type for obvious reasons.

All stock SD-455 engines utilize all-rubber Perfect Circle valve guide oil seals (PMD #9790618) on the intake valves *only*. They tend to harden over the years and thus lose their effectiveness. It is recommended that one should utilize instead the all-Teflon PC seals (TRW #VP-66) on both intake and exhaust valves for both greater longevity and reduced oil loss via the valve guides. Contrary to popular opinion, tests have shown that inertia, gravity and vacuum can cause oil losses past exhaust valve guides as well as intakes. In a typical road test, oil economy dropped from 2100-miles-per-quart to 450-miles-per-quart when the only variable was removal of the PC seals from the exhaust valves *only*.

Unlike most other Pontiac engines, SD-455 motors do not utilize the metal valve spring shields (PMD #9778779). As long as valve lift is not significantly increased over stock, it is recommended that the SD-455 owner install these shields to further reduce oil loss via the valve guides.

All SD-455 engines are equipped with 80-psi oil pump relief springs. They tend to cause higher oil consumption and even cause the rupture of oil filters on cold days. It is recommended that one should replace the 80-psi spring assembly with a 60-psi spring and retainer assembly from a Pontiac 400 Ram Air IV unit which is interchangeable.

It should be noted that most of the above maintenance suggestions relate to oil consumption. The PMD Service Manual states in this regard, "The oil economy of an SD-455 will most likely be less than 1000-miles-per-quart due to the nature of this engine". The writer considers from first hand experience that the factors listed above are the major reasons for such "accepted" poor oil economy. This high consumption is not only not necessary, but it is also not good for the engine. It contributes to carbon buildup on the valves and in the combustion chambers. By adhering to the forementioned suggestions the writer has reduced the oil consumption in his Formula SD-455 from 250-mpq to a level acceptable for any common passenger car without any adverse affects.

They only built 57 Formula SD-455 Firebirds in 1974, making the author's a rare bird. The factory does not have the four speed/Turbo-Hydro breakdown. A total of 1,295 SD-455 Firebirds were built in 1973-1974.

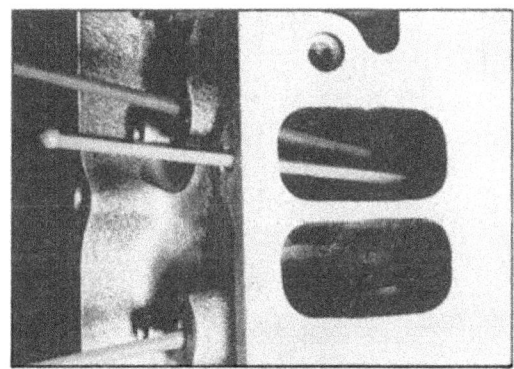

The stamped 6H and cast 16 identification numbers, left, can be found on either right or left cylinder head. Swizzle sticks illustrate that the upper rocker cover hold down bolt holes and the rocker arm stud holes for the intakes break into the intake passages. Thread sealer is required to stop oil seepage, vacuum leaks.

PART TWO OF A TWO-PART SERIES

SD-455—THE MYTH AND THE MAGIC!

Gary Menin wraps up his definitive research and documentation "white paper" on Pontiac's ultimate street supercar

By Gary Menin

The Super-Duty Firebirds were unquestionably Detroit's last examples of the golden days of the Supercar. When everyone else gave up, Pontiac made a last ditch effort to keep performance alive. And, they pulled it off for two model years!

EVEN THOUGH the SD-455 is certainly a unique and powerful engine by any standards, its rarity has created a generation of various hopeful but false myths.

It has been stated in numerous performance publications that the SD-455 engine came equipped with a forged crankshaft. This is not true. Unlike the early Sixties Super-Duty 389-421 engines, the crankshaft used in the SD-455 motors is a nodular cast iron affair. The shaker scoop is one other area of confusion. Regardless of what has been written, all Super Duty equipped Firebirds came through with *non-functional* hood scoops. The last functional shaker scoop came through on '74 Pontiac Ventura GTO models. The rear plate on the scoop of SD-455-equipped 1973-'74 Firebirds—and all Trans-Ams since 1973—was blocked off to meet California "drive-by" noise standards. It is common knowledge that the blocking plate on the 1973-'74 Firebird scoops can be removed simply by drilling out three pop rivets!

Most performance publications have listed the 1973 SD-455 as rated at 310 hp while listing the 1974 SD-455 as rated at 290 hp. Both ratings are at 4000 rpm. The difference in ratings stemmed from *intended* camshaft usage. The 1973 grind was supposed to be of Ram Air IV characteristics, while the 1974 grind was a milder Ram Air III type. From all available information, it is considered that the vast majority of 1973 models and all 1974 models came with camshaft PMD #493323. Characteristics of this cam at the valve with 1.50 ratio rocker arms are .406-inch intake lift at 301 degrees duration and .406-inch exhaust lift at 313 degrees duration. These are far milder specifications than the Ram Air IV grind.

As far as I have been able to determine, Pontiac Motor Division did intend to install the more radical camshaft in 1973 for the 310 hp rating. In fact, several engines were assembled with the high-lift cam, but these engines failed to meet Federal emission standards and thus the milder grind had to be substituted. The part number for the Ram Air IV grind for the SD-455 application (never released for consumer use) was #480737. Its specifications are intake lift of .470-inch at 308 degrees duration and exhaust lift of .470-inch at 320 degrees duration. The only difference between the Ram Air IV cam and the #480737 grind is in the size of the distributor oil pump drive gear.

Some early SD-455 engines in 1973 were assembled using the hotter grind cam. Estimates in this area are a dozen or so with no documentation indicating where the cars were shipped. The only way to positively identify the 310-hp 1973 cars is to check for a "K" stamp at the forward snout of the camshaft. This will, of course, require partial engine disassembly.

And then we have the myth surrounding the rocker arms used in the SD-455 motors. All SD engines came through with 1.50 ratio rockers. This is true even though original plans called

The author's Formula SD-455 is street-driven yet detailed enough to show. Display material is used to educate spectators on the Myth & Magic of the SD-455!

Even with "Federal" front and rear bumpers, the '74 SD-455 Trans-Am looked like a Café Racer straight from the factory. John Clegg's Super/Stock race car was built around a zero-mile, super-rare Formula SD-455 Firebird. It walls

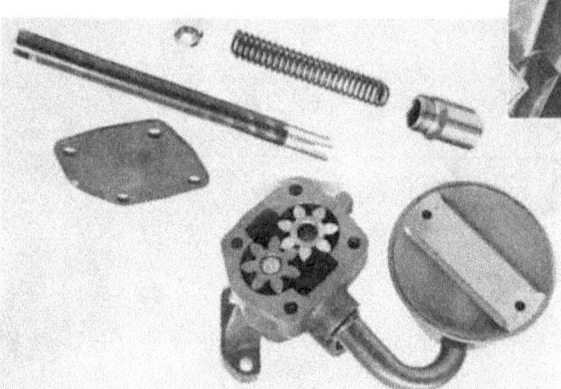

Original SD-455 rods still bring a top buck at swap meets and car shows. Pontiac recently got back into the SD rod business and they are available. Early batches had some failure problems, however. SD lube goodies are popular with hot street engine builders. Contrary to popular belief, the SD-455 shaker scoop was not functional. Dynamite!

for the Ram Air IV camshaft. The 1969-'70 Ram Air IV engine is the most recent Pontiac engine to come factory equipped with the 1.65 ratio rockers.

It has been stated that the SD-455 engines were designed to use racing clearances. Except for the piston-to-bore clearance (expressed in mils—6.4 to 7.2 for the SD and 2.1 to 2.9 for the standard 455) rod and main bearing clearances overlap with those of the standard motor. Thus by staying on the tight side of the clearance range for an SD-455, one would achieve essentially the same clearances as for the standard station wagon 455!

With regard to the piston-to-bore clearance listed, it is obvious that the SD-455 is intended to make use of a tighter fit. However, this is not unusual for any type of engine which is equipped with forged pistons. Forged pistons because of their greater molecular density than cast pistons, expand more than cast pistons for a given temperature increase.

It should be noted that piston-to-bore clearance is dependent on where the piston OD is measured. For the clearances shown this measurement is taken at the top of the piston skirt. If the measurement is taken at a lower point on the piston, the permitted clearance will be less. Note that the piston OD measurements must always be taken perpendicular to the pin axis.

At this point I would like to add some information about my particular Formula SD-455. Its VIN is 2U87X4N128475. The first digit indicates that the make is Pontiac. The second digit—U—indicates that the model is a Firebird Formula. The combined third and fourth digits—87—indicate body style of hardtop coupe. The fifth digit—X—tells you the engine is an SD-455. The sixth digit—4—indicates that the year of model is 1974. The seventh digit—N—specifies the assembly plant, Norwood, Ohio. The last six digits—128475—represent the sequence number. Since the first digit—1—is always used, it is my understanding that the last five digits indicate the manufacturing sequence which translates into my car being the twenty eight thousand, four hundred and seventy-fifth Firebird manufactured in the 1974 model year.

My car was originally delivered to Osborne Pontiac in Monsey, New York. The cost at that time for the Super-Duty option was $675.00. Adding Turbo-Hydro transmission added $242.00 to the base price. The car was optioned out with power front disc brakes, GR70 steel-belted radial tires, HD battery, 3.42-to-1 Posi, rally gauges. It was not ordered with air conditioning or power windows and the sticker price was $5,600.00. Who says those weren't the good old days? T/A

HOW TO DOCUMENT AN SD-455

It takes more than decals to make a real Super-Duty. Here's how to spot a fake!

1. The VIN or Vehicle Identification Number on the top of the dash, left side, will show an X for the fifth digit on 1973 & 1974 Firebirds.
2. The front right hand side of the cylinder block (just below the head) will have a two-letter code: ZJ on four-speed motors; XD on automatics for 1973. In 1974 the code is: W8 for four speed; Y8 for automatic.
3. The machined pad on each head, above the exhaust ports and below the rocker arm covers, has a stamped two-letter code. It must show 6H.
4. The front portion of the intake manifold must have a cast code of LS2 or LS2X.
5. The center exhaust runner on each head must have cast code number 16.
6. The Shaker hood scoop has exterior color-matched decals (SD-455) on each side. All SD-455 Trans-Ams and Firebird Formulas were equipped with non-functional Shaker-style scoops as close as we have been able to document.
7. The PCV valve is in the left side valve cover, adapted to the oil filler cap as opposed to normal Pontiac V-8 lifter valley cover mountings.
8. The top rear of the left side valve cover has a red and silver ID label regarding oil consumption and connecting rod nut tightening data. Reproduction labels are available.
9. One should match the last eight digits of the VIN with the stamped numbers on the engine block adjacent to the lower right hand corner of the timing chain cover to match the engine to the car as factory produced. The number on the engine block will be preceeded by the number 2.

SD-455 PRODUCTION DATA
1973 SD-455 Trans-Am: 180 Turbo-Hydro; 72 Four-Speed
1973 SD-455 Formula: 43 cars
1974 SD-455 Trans-Am: 731 Turbo-Hydro; 212 Four-Speed
1974 SD-455 Formula: 57 cars

Total Factory SD-455 Production: 1,295 Firebirds

SUPER-DUTY 455 REFERENCE

This action photo was taken at the GM Proving Grounds in June 1972 prior to the introduction of the SD-455 package. Racer Herb Adams was main man on this project.

Gary Menin's SD-455 engine is showroom stock and detailed for show use. He still street drives it and makes all the local POCI shows.

There's an impressive array of plumbing under the hood of an SD-455 Firebird (Formula installation) and it all works. Genuine stockers are becoming rare birds.

PARTS LIST FOR SD-455 ENGINE

AUTOMATIC TRANSMISSION		MANUAL TRANSMISSION	
Engine Part No.	487587	Engine Part No.	487583
Type 8.3 C. R. 455 S D Auto		Type 8.3 C. R. 455 S D Manual	
Cylinder Block	491948	Cylinder Block	491948
Camshaft	493323	Camshaft	493323
Crankshaft	490164	Crankshaft	490164
Flywheel Assy.	487651	Flywheel Assy.	9779234
Pressure Plate Assy.		Pressure Plate Assy.	3884598
Driven Plate Assy.		Driven Plate Assy.	482034
Rod Assy.	485225	Rod Assy.	485225
Piston and pin	493163	Piston and Pin	493163
Ring package for 1 piston (std.)	491212	Ring package for 1 piston (std.)	491212
Cylinder Head	485214	Cylinder Head	485214
Exhaust Valve	493142	Exhaust Valve	493142
Intake Valve	485222	Intake Valve	485222
Seal - Intake Valve	9790618	Seal - Intake Valve	9790618
Spring - Valve Inner	493144	Spring - Valve Inner	493144
Spring - Valve Outer	493145	Spring - Valve Outer	493145
Cylinder Head Gasket	488575	Cylinder Head Gasket	488575
Valve Lifter	5232265	Valve Lifter	5232265
Rocker Arm Cover	490028-29	Rocker Arm Cover	490028-29
Rocker Arm Gasket	9797580	Rocker Arm Gasket	9797580
Oil Pump Assy.	480246	Oil Pump Assy.	480246
Oil Pump Drive Shaft	9794305	Oil Pump Drive Shaft	9794305
Dip Stick Tube - Upper	9795830	Dip Stick Tube - Upper	9795830
Intake Manifold	494419	Intake Manifold	494419
Distributor Assy.	1112205	Distributor Assy.	1112205
Carburetor Assy.	7047346	Carburetor Assy.	7047339
Idle Stop Solenoid	1997432	Idle Stop Solenoid	1997432
E G R Valve	7040175	E G R Valve	7040175
Exhaust Manifold L. B.	490803	Exhaust Manifold L. B.	490803
Exhaust Manifold R. B.	490802	Exhaust Manifold R. B.	490802
Spark Plugs	5613302	Spark Plugs	5613302

FIREBIRD CAFE RACER, STAGE III

Herb Adams' SD-455 Mule car, originally built in 1971 and shown in 1972, was updated for 1973 for more serious performance testing.

Super-clean frontal treatment still sports Manufacturer's tags. Interestingly enough, this car was used by Pontiac Public Relations to illustrate a stock 1973 model. No one noticed the roll bar and unique headrests which are attached to racing buckets. Pontiac emblem is missing from the grille.

A set of mysterious grille-style vents, one next to each tail blinker, served to vent the trunk compartment.

A LeMans-style fuel filler mounted in the center of the trunk lid is mated to a fuel cell mounted inside the trunk. It just about filled the whole compartment!

Non-stock alloy mags were retained, but the Shaker scoop was replaced with an "unmarked" one. Kelsey-Hayes supplied the aftermarket wheels.

Adams lightened the car as much as possible and retained the foam-covered roll bar.

Replacing the conventional Trans-Am buckets are lightweight fiberglass race seats covered in tufted black naugahyde. SD-455 engine was hooked up to a stock four-speed.

Basically the body was strictly carryover, but Trans-Am lettering was added to the spoiler to keep in tune with the times.

1974—
THE END IS HERE!

The GTO is reduced to a mere shadow of its former self, but Pontiac maintains its King of the Hill position with an SD-455 option for Firebirds

The last of a line of supercars. Pontiac ended its GTO program with a cosmetic supercar based on the Ventura or Nova body/chassis. The 350 engine was hooked up to a shaker-style hood scoop.

CAPSULE COMMENTS

A NEW offering is the 350 four-barrel which is standard on the GTO and optional on the Ventura and LeMans series. The 455 Super-Duty engine is available on the Firebird Formula and Firebird Trans Am.

Steel-belted radial tires with a Radial Tuned Suspension system are available on all models and are standard on the Grand Am and the Grand Prix SJ. The package consists of steel-belted radial tires, a tuned suspension including Pliacell shock absorbers, stabilizer bars, tuned suspension bushings and jounce restrictors and special "RTS" identification on the instrument panel. The RTS objective is to give the Pontiac driver increased steering response with controlled vertical motion and a minimum of impact harshness. Improved roadability and traction are the results of Radial Tuned Suspension.

The compact Ventura carries

With Federal bumpers front and rear, the Trans-Am looked a little bulky, but ride, handling and performance were outstanding for the times.

through distinctive Pontiac identification highlighting new twin ports on the grille that accent the sporty youthful look of this series. An exciting new option for 1974 is the GTO which is available on Ventura, Ventura Custom Coupes and Hatchbacks. GTO features include a three-speed floor shift manual transmission (except California), the new 350 cubic-inch four-barrel V-8 engine with dual exhausts, special suspension and Rally II wheels. Distinctive styling features are a specific black grille with parking lamps, outside sport mirros, a shaker hood and GTO identification on the front, side and rear. The GTO option is being discontinued on the LeMans series. Venturas are built on a 111-inch wheelbase and are 199.4.

The 1974 Firebird has been dramatically restyled in both front and rear. Frontal surfaces have been canted back for a modern aerodynamic appearance. The distinctive twin ports have been maintained and two new functional air scoops have been added beneath the bumper.

The top-performance Super-Duty 455 engine is still available in Formula and Trans-Am Firebirds.

The Grand-Am represented the new breed of precise handling intermediates pioneered by both Oldsmobile and Pontiac. The dark car is a customized model while the white car is factory stock. Production of coupe hit 3,122; sedan hit 13,961.

With Radial Tuned Suspension, the Grand Prix handled like a smaller, lighter car. Still an impressive road car worthy of its name tag.

The Firebird line started looking really good on the charts as the Trans-Am hit 10,255, the Formula 14,519, the Esprit 22,583 and the base Firebird 26,372.

The ultimate street performance car for 1974 — the Super-Duty Trans-Am. Under all that plumbing and fixtures rests a race-bred motor that really does come on strong.

1974 PONTIAC HIGH-PERFORMANCE ENGINES

CUBIC INCHES	BORE	STROKE	HORSEPOWER	COMPRESSION	INDUCTION
400	4.12	3.75	225 @ 4000	8-to-1	Four-barrel
455	4.15	4.21	250 @ 4000	8-to-1	Four-barrel
455	4.15	4.21	290 @ 4000	8.40-to-1	Four-barrel
350	3.88	3.75	200 @ 4400	7.60-to-1	Four-barrel

END OF AN ERA

The '74 GTO represented the end of 'the good old days' and a decade of high-performance supercars

THE '74 GTO represents Pontiac Motor Division's last ditch attempt to save the nameplate which over the years had become synonymous with the words *Supercar* and *Musclecar*. The GTO started the Supercar Revolution in 1964 and ten years later ended up as a limited-production, mostly-cosmetic option on the Ventura, a compact car that Pontiac inherited from Chevrolet. The GTO of 1974 signaled the end of an era for Pontiac.

The handwriting had been on the wall and the factory figured that if they could repackage the GTO and price it right, the concept of a youth market performance car could be salvaged. The Ventura was priced right and sized right, but the factory did little to promote what could have become another cult car. The factory chose to put its performance dollars into the Trans-Am/Firebird line, letting the GTO die a quiet death.

"You can't inherit a name like GTO. You have to earn it. And we built our compact '74 GTO to do just that. The new GTO is a quick-handling, agile Wide-Track. It comes in either a two-door Coupe or roomy Hatchback Coupe.

The man behind the wheel of the '74 GTO that's on its way thru the clocks at Raceway Park in Englishtown, New Jersey is Nunzi Romano. This run netted him a 15.72-second/88-mph time slip. He also ran the '64 (389/325) GTO below which ran consistent 15.64-second/90-mph times. Both cars were stock. Listing out at $4500, the '74 Goat cost more than $1000 more than the original. The '64 GTO is owned by Tony Celantino, Brooklyn, N.Y.

Dimitrie Toth, Jr. owns a black '74 GTO complete with L-76 and Ram Air graphics on the Shaker hood scoop. Black was a very rare $97 option in 1974. He uses this car for daily transportation. Adding approximately $450 to the sticker price of a Ventura gave you the last GTO option offered by the factory.

"There's a blacked-out grille with inset parking lamps. Pontiac's tough-looking functional *shaker* hood scoop. Body-colored mirrors. Mag-type Rally II wheels. And contemporary GTO I.D. GTO's beefy suspension includes front and rear stabilizer bars and firm shocks. A special Radial Tuned Suspension with steel-belted radials is also available.

"GTO's performance comes from Pontiac's new 350 four-barrel V-8 teamed up with a tough floor-shifted three-speed and dual exhausts. 1974 GTO. The tough little road car that's earned a big name for itself." So said the agency copywriters in 1974.

Pontiac's sales pitch for the GTO-ized Ventura Sprint was certainly a far cry from the Jim Wangers-influenced copy from the days of The Great One!

The 111-inch wheelbase GTO Ventura outsold the '73 GTO (which had options up to the healthy 455-inch big-block) and could have become the supercar of the Seventies. They built 7,058 GTO compacts during the 1974 model year and then the factory quietly buried the nameplate. The 185-hp (at 4000 rpm) four-barrel 350-cube small-block had all kinds of potential and the size of the car was right on target for the times. They picked up 30 additional horsepower via dual exhausts and four-barrel induction and a bunch more was available via solid tuning techniques. GTOs destined for California delivery could be had only with the three-speed automatic due to California's tighter emission standards. Pontiac certainly wasn't going to spend more money trying to get a stick model certified for West Coast deliveries.

The big questions today are will Pontiac ever bring back the GTO nameplate and if they do, what size car will it be. If they do bring it back, you can rest assured it will be on a car with a smaller wheelbase and overall length than the last one. There is no market for a Seventies-sized supercar in the Eighties!

GTO SPOTTER'S GUIDE AND HIGH-PERFORMANCE PONTIAC REFERENCE GUIDE

GTO—"A Device For Shrinking Time & Distance"

GTO PRODUCTION 1964 THROUGH 1974

YEAR	HARDTOP	CONVERTIBLE	JUDGE COUPE	JUDGE CONVERTIBLE	TOTAL
1964 Option	25,806	6,644	N/A	N/A	32,450
1965 Option	64,041	11,311	N/A	N/A	75,352
1966	84,148	12,798	N/A	N/A	96,946
1967	72,205	9,517	N/A	N/A	81,722
1968	77,704	9,980	N/A	N/A	87,684
1969	58,126	7,328	6,725	108	72,287
1970	32,737	3,615	3,629	168	40,149
1971	9,497	661	357	17	10,532
1972 Option	5,807	N/A	N/A	N/A	5,807
1973 Option	4,806	N/A	N/A	N/A	4,806
1974 Option Ventura	7,058	N/A	N/A	N/A	7,058

*N/A denotes not available

1964 GTO

THE '64 GTOs had either the standard Bonneville engine—389 cubes, 325 horsepower with a single four-barrel Carter AFB, 273/289 camshaft—or the same engine with three two-barrel Rochester carbs which raised the output to 348 horsepower. Other goodies available were a four-speed, rear axle gears, optional suspension on top of the already-stiffer standard GTO setup, and all the other comfort and performance options that had made Pontiac's option list the envy of the industry.

1965 GTO

IN 1965, Pontiac increased the rating of the four-barrel engine to 335 horsepower but brought out a hot new engine option. It was still 389 cubes, but a new cam that had 292 degrees intake duration, 302 degrees exhaust duration and more streamlined cast-iron exhaust headers added up to 360 horsepower.

In addition to the engine stuff, there was also a Ram Air, fresh air package offered late in the model year. To cure the braking problem—Pontiac offered finned aluminum drums with harder organic linings. For still more abusive driving, they also carried over the metallic lining option.

1966 GTO

IN 1966, Pontiac made some improvements to the engine. They went to larger carbs on the tri-power option, using Rochester 2GC carbs at all three locations. There was also a cold air package on top of the tri power setup. The single four-barrel engine was unchanged, still 335 hp at 5,000 rpm and 431 foot pounds of torque at 3,200 rpm. The tri power engine was still rated 360 hp at 5,200 rpm and 424 foot pounds of torque at 3,600 rpm even with larger carburetors. The optional Ram Air setup didn't change the horsepower rating.

Naturally, this made it easier for GTOs to dominate their class at the drags since the engine was actually putting out just about its advertised horsepower.

More horsepower wasn't the big story for 1966. It was the new body style. It looked sharp, youthful, sporty and luxurious all at the same time. It was everything you could want in an automobile.

Pontiac sold 96,946 GTOs in 1966, the largest sales year in the GTO's history. The new body added size, weight and rear overhang. As a way of reducing weight, you could special-order a '66 GTO with all the sound deadener and sealers removed. This saved a lot of scraping if you were going racing, but made for a leaky car that rattled on the street.

1967 GTO

THE '67 GTO marked the beginning of Pontiac's de-emphasis on all-out performance. Gone was the tri power engine option. The hottest setup available was a single Rochester Quadrajet on a high-rise manifold. Pontiac axed the 389 engine and introduced a bored-out version which displaced 400 cubic inches.

In addition many new pieces had been developed since 1964 and were introduced on 1967 engines. A new set of cylinder heads was designed. The

1965 GTO—"Our Thing, Wide-Track Pontiac Tiger—GTO."

PART NUMBERS FOR ARM, BALL, PUSHROD PACKAGE

APPLICATION	RATIO	PUSHROD	PART NUMBER
1960-'62 SD	1.65-to-1	None	540832
1963 421	1.75-to-1	None	540831
1961-'67E all V-8	1.50-to-1	546695	9780053
1967L-79 all V-8, Exc. 301	1.50-to-1	9789677	546104
1968 RA II	1.50-to-1	9794043	9794325
1969-'70 RA IV	1.65-to-1	9782370	9798429
1961-'78 Rocker ball	—	—	538134

PONTIAC GTO PERFORMANCE

Year	Model	Displacement Cubic Inches	Horsepower hp	Torque Foot Pounds	Transmission	Rear End	0-60 mph Seconds	0-100 mph Seconds	Quarter-Mile mph/secs.
*1964	Royal Bobcat GTO	389	385	450	four-speed	3.90	4.6	11.8	115/13.10
1964	GTO	389	348	428	four-speed	3.23	6.6	14.5	99/14.60
1965	GTO	389	360	424	four-speed	4.11	5.8	14.5	101/14.40
1967	GTO	400	360	438	turbo-hydro	4.33	6.1	14.0	102/14.50
1968	Royal Bobcat GTO	428	390	465	turbo-hydro	3.55	5.2	12.9	104/13.80
1968	GTO	400	360	445	four-speed	3.90	6.6	14.6	99/14.50
1970	GTO	455	360	500	four-speed	3.31	6.6	15.8	97/15.0

*Prepared car running on slicks

RARE GTO SUPERCARS

Year	Model	Engine	Transmission	Production
1968	Convertible	400 Ram Air	four-speed	92
1968	Convertible	400 Ram Air	turbo-hydro	22
1969	Convertible	Ram Air IV	four-speed	45
1969	Convertible	Ram Air IV	turbo-hydro	14
1970	Convertible	Ram Air IV	four-speed	20
1970	Convertible	Ram Air IV	turbo-hydro	13
1971	Convertible	455-HO	four-speed	21
1971	Convertible	455-HO	turbo-hydro	27
1972	Coupe	455-HO	four-speed	3
1972	Coupe	455-HO	turbo-hydro	7
1973	Coupe	455	turbo-hydro	25

*Source: The Gas Can, GTO Association of America, Billings, Montana 59104

1966 GTO—"Speak Softly And Carry A GTO."

Rows of '67 Pontiacs and Tempests waiting to be loaded on trains or truck carriers for delivery to dealerships.

1967 GTO—"Now You Know What Makes The Great One Great."

1968½ PONTIAC GTO RAM AIR-II ENGINE

Option may be ordered on the GTO model by specifying code XW or WY on car order form. Manual transmission order should specify 358 close-ratio four-speed manual transmission (2.20 First gear) and 3.90 or 4.33-to-1 axle ratio.

ENGINE SPECIFICATIONS

400-Cubic-Inch Displacement
Bore 4.1200 - 4.1244-inch   Stroke 3.746 - 3.754-inch
Compression Ratio: Nominal 10.75-to-1, Maximum 11.4-to-1
Horsepower 366 at 5,400 rpm   Connecting Rods: Arma Steel
Torque 445 at 3,800 rpm   Bearings: Moraine 400A
Cylinder Head Volume 65.0 cc (Minimum)   Crankshaft: Arma Steel
Deck Clearance 0 (0 to .034-inch Below)   Crankshaft Bearings: Moraine 400A
Flat pistons with valve-clearance notches Hydraulic valve lifters
Four-barrel Rochester Carburetor   Rocker Arm Ratio 1.5-to-1
9794041 Camshaft

TIMING
Intake opens 42 BTC closes 86 ABC: Duration 308 degrees
Exhaust opens 95 BBC closes 45 ATC: Duration 320 degrees
Lift: Intake .480-inch
Exhaust .475-inch

Standard Inner and Outer Valve Springs

	Dual Springs
Total Spring Load Closed:	107-123
Total Spring Load Open:	303-327

Intake Valves:
GM-8440 Aluminum treatment on face—chrome-plated stem
5.198-inch Long   2.113-2.107-inch Head Diameter   .34-inch Stem Diameter

Exhaust Valves:
21-2 Steel—Aluminum treatment on face—chrome-plated stem
5.212-inch Long   1.773-1.767-inch Head Diameter   .34-inch Stem Diameter

heads were sorely needed and replaced the antique heads which were originally designed for the 287 cube V-8. The new heads sported clean chambers and ports, 2.11-inch intake valves and high flow capacity. Pontiac felt that the increase in displacement plus the new heads warranted a retention of the 360-hp rating despite the drop from three two-barrels to one four-barrel carb. The 360 hp was the high-performance option with the HO cam and long branch exhaust manifolds.

Halfway through the model year, Pontiac introduced a new Ram Air option which had a fresh air intake system and special internal components. A special block with four-bolt main bearings and Moraine 400 bearings were used along with forged rods and pistons, lightened, swirl-polished valves, stiffer valve springs and a Ram Air cam with 301/313 degrees duration. Pontiac rated the new engine 360 hp at 5,400 rpm and 438 foot pounds of torque at 3,800 rpm. They kept the horsepower rating at 360.

Styling of the '67 GTO was similar to the '66, only cleaned up. There were less loose pieces of chrome and less gimmicks.

1968 GTO

THE '68 GTO was all new from the chassis up. Sales rose to 87,684 for 1968 but the personality of the car had changed and it would never be the same again. The '68 GTO was on a 112-inch wheelbase, down from the 115 of previous years. And styling was more sporty than ever before. The engine lineup remained unchanged for 1968, as all the available effort went into the new body and chassis.

GOLDEN OLDIES
SPECIAL PERFORMANCE 389 PONTIAC ENGINES

APPLICATION	HORSEPOWER	SPECIFICATIONS	CODE	TRANSMISSION
Special	318 hp	10.75-to-1, Tri-Power	C-4	Manual
Special Police	303 hp	10.25-to-1, Four-Barrel	P-4	Manual
Special 425-A	333 hp	10.75-to-1, Four-Barrel, Four-Bolt-Mains	F-4	Manual
Special 425-A	348 hp	10.75-to-1, Tri-Power, Four-Bolt-Mains	M-4	Manual
Special	303 hp	10.25-to-1, Four-Barrel	B-1	Auto
Special	318 hp	10.75-to-1, Tri-Power	C-1	Auto
Special Police	303 hp	10.25-to-1, Four-Barrel	P-1	Auto
Special 425-A	333 hp	10.75-to-1, Four-Barrel, Four-Bolt-Mains	F-1	Auto
Special 425-A	348 hp	10.75-to-1, Tri-Power, Four-Bolt-Mains	M-1	Auto

HIGH-PERFORMANCE INTAKE MANIFOLDS

YEAR	DISPLACEMENT	CARBURETION	CASTING NUMBER	MATERIAL
1959	389	Tri-Power	532422	Cast-Iron
1960	389	Tri-Power	536194	Cast-Iron
1961	389	Tri-Power	541690	Cast-Iron
1961	421	Dual-Quad	9770859	Aluminum
1962	389	Tri-Power	542690	Cast-Iron
1962	421	Dual-Quad	9770859	Aluminum
1961½-1962	421-SD	Dual-Quad (plus one-barrel)	9772390	Aluminum
1963	389	Tri-Power	9770275	Cast-Iron
1963	421	Tri-Power	9770275	Cast-Iron
1963	421	Dual-Quad	9770859	Aluminum
1963	421-SD	Dual-Quad	9772128	Aluminum
1964	389	Tri-Power	9775088	Cast-Iron
1964	421	Tri-Power	9775088	Cast-Iron
1965	389	Tri-Power	9778818	Cast-Iron
1965	421	Tri-Power	9778818	Cast-Iron
1966	389	Tri-Power	9782898	Cast-Iron
1966	421	Tri-Power	9782898	Cast-Iron

One of the neat things about the '68 GTO body was its Endura front end. It was a Polyurethane material painted the same color as the body so that it looked like the car had no front bumper. In awarding the Car of the Year award to the GTO, *Motor Trend* termed the GTO's bumper "the most significant achievement in materials technology in contemporary automoative engineering."

Halfway through the 1968 Pontiac model run, Pontiac introduced a revamped Ram Air option that really put out power. They called it the '68½ Ram Air package. The '68½ Ram Air engine rated 370 horsepower at 5,500 rpm and 445 foot pounds of torque at 3,900 rpm. This was on the 400-cube block. The engine used a 308/320 hydraulic camshaft with 1.50-to-1 rocker arms, light valves and new heads with round exhaust ports for much better breathing.

1968 GTO—"The Great One."

1969 GTO JUDGE—"The Judge Can Be Bought."

HIGH COMPRESSION GTO & FIREBIRD ENGINES

YEAR	DISPLACEMENT	COMPRESSION RATIO	HORSEPOWER
1967	400	10.75	325
1967	400	10.75	325
1967	400	10.75	335
1967	400	10.75	360
1968	400	10.75	330
1968	400	10.75	335
1968	400	10.75	350
1968	400	10.75	360
1968	400	10.75	366
1969	400	10.75	330
1969	400	10.75	335
1969	400	10.75	345
1969	400	10.75	350
1969	400	10.75	366
1969	400	10.75	370
1970	400	10.25	330
1970	400	10.25	350
1970	400	10.50	345
1970	400	10.50	366
1970	400	10.50	370
1970	455	10.25	360

1969 GTO

THE '69 Goat was unchanged from its award-winning predecessor except for minor trim shuffling. And the engine lineup was almost unchanged at the beginning of the model year. The HO engine was now called the Ram Air III because it had open scoops on the hood. The rating was now 366 hp at 5,100 rpm. Midway through the model year, Pontiac made two changes. First they added the Judge model to the car lineup. The Judge was a GTO with a wing on the back and bright orange paint and strips. This was at the height of popularity of Rowan and Martin's "Laugh In" TV show.

In the performance department, the '68½ Ram Air package was updated and called the Ram Air IV engine for 1969. New heads gave better breathing and 1.65-to-1 rocker arms replaced the 1.50s, to give a full .520-inch lift. Horsepower and torque ratings were unchanged, however.

1970 GTO

FOR 1970, a much-needed rear sway bar was added. The width was ⅞-inch in diameter in standard form but an optional handling package was available on all GTOs. It included fast, variable-ratio power steering, G60-15 white lettered tires on 15x7 wheels, high-rate springs and shocks and 1⅛-inch front and rear stabilizer bars. This package put the GTO on a par with anything in its class.

The standard engine was the 400-cube, 350 hp, four-barrel engine with 10.25-to-1 compression. The rating was 350 hp at 5,000 rpm and 445-foot pounds of torque at 3,000 rpm. The Ram Air IV engine was still available as a limited-production option. The Ram Air III engine was also available and still rated 366 hp at 5,100 rpm. Near the end of the model year, both Ram Air III and IV engines were dropped and the optional engine became a 455-cubic-inch, 360 hp engine which was nothing more than a low-performance bored and stroked version of the 400. The 360 hp rating was at 4,300 rpm but the engine's torque rating was 500 foot pounds at 2,700 rpm.

As a last gasp toward capturing some of the lost performance, Pontiac announced the availability of a Ram Air V engine for *optional* installation in GTOs. It was almost a completely new engine. The heads featured round intake and exhaust ports for super top end breathing. The aluminum high-rise manifold mounted a 780-cfm Holley four-barrel. The camshaft was a 308/320 degree unit with solid lifters. Plus the engine had special beefed rods; four-bolt

1970 GTO—"The Quick Way Out Of The Little Leagues."

1970 GTO JUDGE—"For People Who Think Driving Should Be Fun."

mains was extra webbing for increased high-rpm durability. None of these engines was ever installed on the assembly line but it was possible to purchase a complete Ram Air V engine at any Pontiac dealership.

1971 GTO

A GM management edict lowered all compression ratios so that all '71 engines could run on low-lead or no-lead gas. The standard 400-cube GTO engine had an 8.2-to-1 compression ratio and rated 300 hp at 4,800 rpm with 400 foot pounds of torque at 3,600 rpm. Optional was a low-compression 455 four-barrel with 8.4-to-1 compression, 335 hp at 4800 rpm and 480 foot pounds torque at 3,600 rpm.

PONTIAC INTAKE MANIFOLD GUIDE

YEAR	MODEL	DESIGN	PART NUMBER
1967	GTO-400	Cast Iron	9786285
1968-1970	Four-Barrel-400	Cast Iron	9799068
1969-1979	Ram Air IV-400	Aluminum	9799084
1969	Ram Air IV-400 GTO	Aluminum	9796614
1971	HO-455	Aluminum	483674
1972	HO-455	Aluminum	488945
1973	SD-455	Cast Iron	494419
1974	SD-455	Cast Iron	495103
1969-1970	Ram Air IV-400	(1965-1971 Heads)	9796395
1971	HO-455	(1965-1971 Heads)	9796395
1972	HO-455	(1972-1976 Heads)	488983
1969	Ram Air V-400	Aluminum	545288

HIGH-PERFORMANCE PONTIAC BLOCKS

YEAR	DISPLACEMENT	BORE	STROKE	MAIN BEARINGS
1967-1969	400CID	4.120	3.750	3.000
1967-1969	428CID	4.120	4.000	3.250
1970-1976	455CID	4.150	4.210	3.250

PONTIAC HEAD GUIDE

YEAR	MODEL	CHAMBER CAPACITY	PART NUMBER
1967	Closed Chamber-400	72cc	9788067
1967	Ram Air-400	72cc	9783657
1968	D-Port-400/428	75cc	9791559
1968-1969	Ram Air & HO-400/428	72cc	9790118
1968	Ram Air, D-Port-400	72cc	9792700
1968	Ram Air II-400	72cc	9794040
1969	Ram Air, HO, D-Port-400/428	72cc	9795043
1969	Ram Air IV, Round Port-400	71cc	9796721
1969	Ram Air V, Tunnel Port-400	67cc	546534
1970	Ram Air III, HO, D-Port-400	72cc	9799496
1970	D-Port-400	72cc	9799497
1970	Ram Air IV, Round Port-400	71cc	9799498
1970	HO, D-Port-455	87cc	9799362
1971	D-Port-400	96cc	481760
1971	455	114cc	483714
1971	455-HO	111cc	481758
1972	D-Port-400	96cc	485316
1972	455	114cc	494995
1972	455-HO	111cc	485319
1973-1974	SD-455	111cc	485214

RAM AIR V PONTIAC TUNNEL PORT ENGINE SPECIFICATIONS

Type: 90-Degree V-8 Overhead Valve
Bore: 4.120 Inches (Nominal)
Stroke: 3.750 Inches (Nominal)
Displacement: 400 Cubic Inches (Nominal)

BUILD-UP SPECIFICATIONS

Piston To Bore Fit .... .0055-.0065-inch
Piston Ring End Gap .... .020-.038-inch
Pin To Piston Fit .... .0007-.0010-inch
Pin To Rod Fit .... .001-inch Press
Main Bearing To Journal Fit .... .0023-.0028-inch
Rod Side Clearance .... .018-.026-inch
Rod Bearing To Journal Fit .... .0028-.0033-inch
Crankshaft End Play .... .003-.009-inch
Piston-To-Block Deck Height .... .000-.010-inch

RAM AIR V COMPONENT SPECIFICATIONS

CYLINDER BLOCK #545686
Material, Type Cast Iron, Four-Bolt Center Mains, 90 Degree V-8
Bore 4.120 Inch Nominal (Fit To Pistons)
Bore Finish 3-4-Microinch, Or As Smooth As Possible
Distributor Hole Diameter 1.636-1.637-inch
Main Bearing Bores 3.1880-3.1890-inch

CRANKSHAFT #545671
Material .... SAE 4640 Fine Grain
Main Journal Diameter 2.9983-2.9993-inch
Rod Journal Diameter 2.2483-2.2493-inch
Stroke 3.750-inch

CONNECTING ROD #545855
Material .... SAE 8640, 5140 or 3,140
Center-To-Center Length 6.624-6.626-inch
Rod Bearing Bore 2.3745-2.3750-inch
Piston Pin Bore .... .9796-.9798-inch
Big End Thickness .... .9895-.9905-inch
Rod Weight (Approx.) .... 900 Grams
Rod Bolt Torque .... 65 Lb./Ft.

PISTON #545856
Material .... Forged Aluminum
Skirt Diameter 4.114-4.115-inch
Piston Pin Bore .... .9808-.9810-inch
Piston Pin Height 1.725-1.739-inch
Piston Weight (Approx.) .... 580 Grams
Piston Pin Offset .... None

PISTON RINGS
Type 9789691 Top Compression   Moly Filled, Barrel-Face
Type 9786616 2nd Compression   Moly Filled, Taper-Face
Rod 9786628 Segment
     9786634 Expander (Oil)   Low Tension
Width: Top & Second   5/16-inch
       Oil   3/16-inch

CYLINDER HEAD #546534
Type .... Overhead Valve, With
                                    Integral Valve Guides
Material .... Cast Iron
Valve Clearance .... .0016-.0033-inch Intake
                                    .0021-.0038-inch Exhaust
Valve Seat Angle .... 30 Degree Intake
                                    45 Degree Exhaust
Combustion Chamber Volume .... 72-cc (Nominal)

INTAKE VALVE #545718
Material .... Hollow Stem Steel

EXHAUST VALVE #545710
Material .... Hollow Stem Steel
                                    Filled With Sodium
Head diameter
  Intake 2.180-inch
  Exhaust 1.700-inch
Valve Face Angle
  Intake .... 29 Degree
  Exhaust .... 44 Degree

VALVE TRAIN
VALVE SPRINGS #545706
Type .... Single Spring And
                                    Damper Asm.
Spring Loads & Heights ....
  Closed .... 100 Lb. @ 1.82-inch
  Open .... 288 Lb. @ 1.32-inch
Free Height 2.085-inch
Spring Rate .... 375 Lb/In.

ROCKER ARMS #9783989
Type .... Ball & Socket
Ratio 1.65-to-1

PUSH RODS #545703
Type .... Hollow, With
                                    Hardened Ball Ends
Length, Overall 9.62-inch

CAMSHAFT #545713
Type .... Mechanical, Flat
                                    Follower
Timing: (Events Based On End Of Opening Ramp And Start Of Closing Ramp)
Intake Opening .... 42 Degrees BTC
Intake Closing .... 86 Degrees ABC
Intake Curation .... 308 Degrees
Intake Cam Lift .... .303-inch
Exhaust Opening .... 95 Degrees BBC
Exhaust Closing .... 45 Degrees ATC
Exhaust Duration .... 320 Degrees
Exhaust Cam Lift .... .303-inch
Overlap .... 87 Degrees

1971 GTO JUDGE—"Pure Pontiac."

1972 GTO

IN 1972 Pontiac, like the rest of the industry went to SAE Net horsepower ratings.

Thus the standard 400 GTO engine now rated 250 hp at 4,400 rpm and 325 foot pounds of torque at 3,200 rpm. Optional was a 455 four-barrel that rated 250 hp at 3,600 rpm.

But Pontiac did sneak in a ringer. Deep down in the option sheets was a little goodie called the 455 HO engine option. It was essentially a 455 block but chock full of the old Ram Air goodies. The new horsepower rating

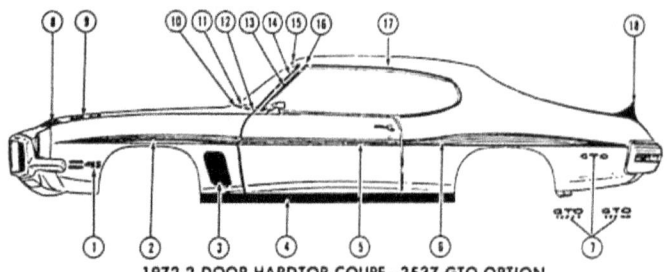

1972 2-DOOR HARDTOP COUPE—3537 GTO OPTION

Key	Qty.	Part No.	Name	Group No.
1.	2-	479185	EMBLEM, "455"	8.147
2.		487488-89	STRIPE, Fender - Black	8.147
		487490-91	STRIPE, Fender - White	8.147
3.		486400-01	EXTRACTOR, Fender	8.147
4.		479164-65	MLDG. PKG., Rocker	8.304
	2-	9777710	CLIP PKG.	8.309
5.		487492-93	STRIPE, Door - Black	12.112
		487494-95	STRIPE, Door - White	12.112
6.		487496-97	STRIPE, Quarter - Black	12.116
		487498-99	STRIPE, Quarter - White	12.116
7.		479917	DECAL, "GTO-455 C.I.D." - Black	12.116
		479919	DECAL, "GTO-455 C.I.D." - White	12.116
		479920	DECAL, "GTO" - Black	12.116
		479922	DECAL, "GTO" - White	12.116
		9790503	DECAL, "GTO-455 H.O." - Black	12.116
		9790505	DECAL, "GTO-455 H.O." - White	12.116
8.		483927-28	ORNAMENT, Hood	8.030
9.		454257	DECAL, "Ram Air" - Black	8.030
		454258	DECAL, "Ram Air" - White	8.030
10.		483540	MOLDING, Hood - Rear	8.054
11.		7731088	MOLDING, W/S - Lower	10.093
12.		479151-52	MLDG. PKG., Fender - Upr. - Rear	8.147
	2-	9790369	CLIP PKG.	8.148
13.		7726067-68	SCALP, Pillar - Drip	12.075
14.		7725634-35	MOLDING, W/S - Side	10.093
15.		7726034	MOLDING, W/S - Upper	10.093
16.		7660172-73	ESCUTCHEON, Roof - Drip	12.075
17.		7723586-87	SCALP, Roof - Drip	12.075
18.		486325	SPOILER, Lid	12.181
		486326-27	EXTENSION, Spoiler	12.181

1972 GTO—"Pontiac's Great Road Car"

was 300 at 4,000 rpm with an 8.4-to-1 compression ratio. Torque output was a true 415 foot pounds, at 3,200 rpm. It was the strongest street engine available for 1972.

1973 GTO

For 1973, all GM intermediates were completely redesigned and the LeMans body got new skin too. The GTO, now just an option that could be added to any LeMans body, was one of the sharper looking '73 intermediates.

At the Press Preview for the '73 GTO, Pontiac engineers announced a new engine option called the Super-Duty 455 to replace the 455-HO. The Super-Duty designation had a long tradition at Pontiac, first used in 1959½-1963 for the top performance option available. The engine was unreal. Not only did it have all the 455-HO goodies but it also had such niceties as new cylinder heads which flowed at least 10 percent more than any other previous Pontiac production cylinder head.

The original plan was to make the Super-Duty 455 an option in both GTOs and Firebirds. But a change in Pontiac's top management closed down the Super-Duty project and the engine was never released as an option for the GTO.

1973 GTO—"Top Performance Car Of The Year."

1974 GTO

TEN years after the GTO started the entire Supercar Scene, the '74 GTO is an option on the smaller and sportier Ventura rather than being an option for the larger LeMans. The Ventura is more in keeping with the original concept of the GTO which was small, light car with enough power to move it out in style. The LeMans series had simply become too heavy and luxurious and the GTO concept was lost in the process.

For there is only one GTO engine. It's a 350-cubic-inch four-barrel engine rated 200 hp at 4,400 rpm and 295 foot pounds of torque at 2,800 rpm. All GTOs come with a fresh air shaker hood scoop as standard equipment plus such other goodies as heavy-duty suspension with front and rear anti-sway bars, wide tread tires and styled wheels.

1974 GTO—"Pontiac's Tough Little Road Car."

THE GRAND AM THAT NEVER WAS!

If Pontiac had followed through and actually produced the Can-Am model, they would have started the Supercar Revolution all over again

The CA or Can-Am Grand-Am, based on the intermediate model car, featured a 400-inch Trans-Am powertrain and suspension. This could have been the Supercar of the late-Seventies. It was built in 1977-'78. Photo was taken at GM's "Black Lake" skid pad at the Milford Proving Grounds.

After testing and evaluation for possible production status, the CA was turned into a show car. Note the open-roof treatment and extensive detailing. It then received Pearl paint and glitzy interior appointments.

Large rectangular Quartz headlamps work well with the bold front end treatment. At this stage the roof was chopped and conventional Grand-Am emblems were reinstalled on the front fenders. They were later dropped in favor of the unique CA trim. Trans-Am-style front spoiler looks good on this intermediate-size car.

The interior of the CA boasted such goodies as a Trans-Am steering wheel, sporty bucket seats, four-speed floor shifter, full instrumentation and even micro switches for built-in timing equipment which could read out elapsed times, etc. The read-out was built into the rear section of the hood scoop in plain view of the driver and passenger. Additional instrumentation was fitted to the dash below the glove compartment.

The CA lined up with a bunch of Trans-Ams on GM's skid pad. This was part of maximum handling testing by members of the Press and Pontiac Engineering.

Panic stop on the slalom course shows need for an anti-drive suspension! Rear spoiler is striped and decked-out with unique Grand-Am CA trim.

Two-tone paint treatment with dark trim on the lower end make the CA look lower than it actually is. The front and rear sway bar suspensions boasted special spring and shock rates plus wide alloy wheels with 60-Series Radials. Small molded-in fender flares in front of the front and rear fender wells were pirated from the Trans-Am.

Flip-up rear side windows (gull-wing-style) give access to the rear stowage section. The Type-K Trans-Am wagon project was started shortly after the debut of the '70½ Firebird and was actually executed in 1977. The original plan called for the limited production of K-wagons in Italy. However, the project was cancelled because of the projected mid-$20,000 price tag.

PONTIAC WAGONMASTER!

With a little help from GM Styling and Pininfarina in Italy, Pontiac turns the Trans-Am into a family Ponycar

From the front the K-wagon looked like any other Trans-Am. All graphics were production Pontiac. The prototype for the program was built around a standard Firebird out of fiberglass. Under a contract with GM's William Mitchell, Pininfarina in Italy built two all-steel wagons. One was Silver with a Red interior; the other Gold with a Tan interior. Both cars toured show circuits here and in Europe.

The designation Type-K stands for Kammback, referring to the styling of the flat rear end treatment. The quality of the two prototypes was in keeping with the Pininfarina reputation. However, over the years there have been some replicas built for sale in this country that have left a lot to be desired. It's not easy trying to mate station wagon form and function with swoopy Ponycar styling.

Wall-to-wall style tail blinkers and a wide glass area are both safety features as well as styling plus-features. The rear bucket seats can be folded down individually to increase cargo area, turning the Trans-Am into a truly utilitarian vehicle. The Trans-Am Type-K logo was designed by the General Motors Design Staff.

The K-wagon project was not exclusively Pontiac, as Chevrolet had a hand in it with plans for a Camaro version if it was successful. The project was headed by Dave Holls, executive designer of the GM Styling Studio, with Jerry Brockstein in charge of details. The cars were built around '78 Trans-Ams, later updated to 1979 model trim for the second year on the auto show circuit.

THE BANSHEE TRILOGY

A trio of Firebird-based sports cars that personify the Ponycar concept

Highlights of the first Banshee include gull-wing T-tops, fully-instrumented console integrated into the dash, and sleek fastback roof treatment.

The first Banshee was this '66 Firebird-based sports coupe. The word Banshee was one of the name choices for the Firebird, but was later discounted because of negative translation (Irish Folklore — "Wailing woman is a sign that someone will die).

The Second Generation Banshee was based on a 1973-'74 Trans-Am and powered by a Super-Duty-455 engine hooked to a Turbo-Hydra-Matic transmission. Faired-in glass housings hide the Quartz lighting. Front scoop is functional.

The Third Generation Banshee was simply updated from the original with minor customizing and trim features. Color is Candy Apple Red over Gold Metalflake. Flip-open vents in the windows are a must as windows do not roll down. Note updating of tires to GT Radials and early mags to later Snowflake Trans-Am alloy hoops.

These two views show some of the rear end modifications. The First Trans-Am had a smooth rear deck with recessed LeMans filler cap and two exhaust tips per-side. Later the rear venting (ten per-side) with built-in tail blinkers was executed and the rectangular exhaust tips were added.

THE FIREBIRD PHENOMENON

Three generations of fantastic sports machines for those who demand more than just transportation from their cars

1969 TRANS-AM Convertible

1969 TRANS-AM Coupe

THERE IS A car on the streets and highways of America today that says a lot, just by its presence, about what a growing number of people really want in an automobile. The car is the Pontiac Firebird, the performance-oriented hardtop coupe that is offered for people who want something more from automobiles than just basic transportation.

Introduced in 1967 as a performance car designed to capture a share of the industry's most rapidly expanding market segment—the youth-dominated specialty car market—the Firebird has successfully evolved into today's performance car featuring a combination of good acceleration, superb riding and handling while maintaining good fuel efficiencies.

Early in 1978—during several ten-day sales periods—the Firebird was the top seller among all Pontiac car lines—a first in Pontiac divisional history.

1970 FIREBIRD

The first Firebirds went on sale February 23, 1967 and were available in two styles—a hardtop coupe and convertible. Five engines were available including the Pontiac Overhead Cam Six-cylinder as standard up to the optional 400 cubic inch V-8. Standard equipment included: bucket seats, three-speed manual transmission (four-speed manual and two-speed and three-speed automatic optional) and all-vinyl interior trim.

A number of performance and comfort features were offered such as a hood-mounted tachometer and a revolutionary space-saver spare tire provided as standard equipment. The first Firebird was built on a 108-inch wheelbase with an overall length of 188.8 inches.

The name Firebird came from the legendary Indian symbol which promised action, power, beauty and youth. The name was first used in 1954 on GM's dramatic gas-turbine-powered car, Firebird I.

The nation's press, especially the auto enthusiast magazines such as *Car & Driver* and *Road & Track,* reacted very enthusiastically to the new Firebird. The concensus of opinion appeared to be that Pontiac had created an exciting new line of products which phsyically and psychologically projected a personality of youthful exuberance.

The car was an instant success with 82,560 Firebirds being produced the first year. Market studies showed that styling and performance were two key features in establishing youth appeal in the auto market—and these were the two main reasons cited by buyers for favoring the new Firebird.

In 1968, the Firebird's successful styling was unchanged but there were some engineering improvements in the suspension and ventilation systems plus the HO (high output) option on the Firebird engine was based on the newly-introduced 350-cubic-inch power plant. The Ram Air package on the 400-cubic-inch engine had ratings of 335 horsepower and 430 foot pounds of torque.

Popularity of the Firebird continued in its second year as production jumped to

1971 TRANS-AM

over 107,000.

The '69 Firebirds took on an added distinction with fresh styling and a lower appearance. Exterior styling was highlighted by front bumper extensions made of new, tough body-color plastic. For the first time a three-speed automatic transmission was available for all Overhead Cam Six-cylinder engines and the 350-cubic-inch V-8s. Standard engine was the 250-cubic-inch Overhead Cam Six-cylinder. Optional engines included the OHC-6 Sprint with 230 horsepower and the Firebird 400 which included an optional HO version and two Ram-Air packages with hood scoops that could be opened or closed by the driver.

A Pontiac engineering group had been working on a special street package Firebird and in the Spring of that year the package was formally introduced as the ultimate "performance ponycar" of the day—the Trans-Am.

The newest Firebird was an impressive handling car with staggered shocks, a one-inch anti-roll bar in the front, quick steering and seven-inch wheel rims. It was powered by the 400-cubic-inch 335-horsepower Ram-Air engine, and was available only in white with blue stripes or blue with white stripes.

Exterior appearance items on the Trans-Am included side scoops, functional scoops on the hood, special decals and a rear spoiler which Pontiac engineers said kept a 100-pound downward load on the car at 100 miles per hour.

Just 697 Firebird Trans-Ams were produced that first year (1969) with total Firebird production dipping to 87,000 units.

In 1970, the Firebird line was all-new and was expanded and offered in four models: the standard Firebird, the luxury Esprit, the high-performance Formula and the Trans-Am. Emphasis was placed on the Formula which featured a specially-molded fiberglass hood with distinctive air scoops, a 400-cubic-inch engine with a dual-snorkle air cleaner and dual exhausts on the Formula 400 and the Trans-Am with Ram-Air engine, four-speed floor-mounted transmission, power front disc brakes and rally gauge package with an instrument panel tachometer and clock. Front air dams on each of the wheel openings along with a full-width spoiler across the rear deck added special distinctiveness to the Trans-Am.

The '70 Second Generation Firebirds all featured the new long-hood short deck theme with the overall length being increased to 192.3 inches. New Endura front bumpers, optional concealed windshield wipers and hidden radio antenna were other significant features.

Special attention was given to chassis tuning with a different state of chassis tune being offered as the customer went

1972 FIREBIRD FORMULA

1973 SD-455 TRANS-AM

1974 FORMULA & TRANS-AM

1975 TRANS-AM

1976 TRANS-AM

1977 TRANS-AM

1978 TRANS-AM

1979 TRANS-AM

up the scale from the base Firebird to the Trans-Am.

Car & Driver magazine called the '70 Trans-Am "a hard muscled, lightning-reflexed commando of a car, the likes of which doesn't exist anywhere in the world, even for twice the price." Firebird production totaled 48,000 in 1970.

In 1971, a 455-cubic-inch engine was released for use on two Firebirds with the 455-HO standard on the Trans-Am. Ratings were 335 horsepower at 4,800 rpm and 480 foot pounds of torque. New interior styling was highlighted by high-back bucket seats with integral head rests.

Firebird production increased slightly to 53,000 in 1971.

Firebird changes in 1972 were minimal with the top engine option remaining the 455-HO. Standard equipment on the '72 Trans-Am included vinyl bucket seats, formula steering wheel rally gauges with tachometer, special handling package, dual exhausts, 455-HO engine, four-speed transmission, power disc brakes, and limited slip differential.

Positive media reaction continued with Martyn L. Schorr at *Cars* Magazine calling the '72 Trans-Am "the best handling American car ever made."

Firebird production dipped to its lowest level ever in 1972 with a total of 29,951 cars being made.

Early in 1973, many of the nation's top automotive writers were saying that the Firebird was on its last wheels, but remaining firmly convinced that a market still existed for a car featuring excellent appearance and superb ride-and-handling, Pontiac management decided to continue the car line and to improve it.

The Super-Duty 455 engine was introduced in 1973 as perhaps the only true high-performance engine to come out of Detroit since regulated emission laws went into effect. A limited number of the basically hand-built engines were produced during the model year. The SD-455 had a new version of the Ram Air IV cam with 380/320 timing, improved Ram-Air IV heads, a stronger block with provision for dry sump oiling and a number of other improvements.

1973 also saw the introduction of the now famous Trans-Am hood decal and a production increase to over 46,000 Firebirds.

Steel-belted radial tires became standard on all Firebirds in 1974. Trans-Am sales exceeded 10,000 for the first time in 1974 despite the gasoline shortage and limited advertising. Suspension systems were improved even more with the coil spring front suspension and the leaf spring rear tuned to a fine degree.

Firebird front bumpers were of urethane foam cast over a stamped high strength steel retainer, while in the rear the impact bar was a low density flexible urethane casting.

Firebird production increased dramatically to nearly 74,000 in 1974.

In 1975, the Trans-Am accounted for one of every three Firebirds sold and was well on its way to becoming the top sports car in America.

Steel-belted radial tires with Radial Tuned Suspension became standard on all Firebirds. The RTS concept provided a suspension system with components specifically modified to take advantage of the performance characteristics of the steel-belted radial tires.

Engine availability for the '75 Firebird ranged from the 250-cubic-inch Six-cylinder to the 355-cubic-inch V-8.

Firebird production took another big jump in 1975 to over 84,000—with the Trans-Am becoming the top seller in the Firebird line for the first time in history (27,274).

In 1976, the Trans-Am topped the Corvette in sales for the first time and became the number one domestic sports car in America. The Trans-Am featured a standard 400-cubic-inch four-barrel engine and an available 455 engine option.

Among the new options for '76 Firebirds were a fuel economy indicator, a canopy top, and a bold, new appearance package available on the Formula.

All Firebirds featured new, body-colored urethane bumpers on front and rear.

Cars Magazine named the '76 Trans-Am the "Top Performance Car of the Year." A Limited Edition black and gold Trans-Am was introduced at the Chicago Auto Show in February of 1976. A gold Firebird ensignia across the hood and removable roof panels were just two features of the limited edition.

Production totaled over 110,000 in 1976 with the Trans-Am accounting for 46,000 of the build.

Bold new front styling with dual rectangular headlamps highlighted the '77 Firebirds. Engine availabilities ranged from the 3.8-Litre V-6, standard on the regular Firebird and Esprit, all the way to the optional T/A 6.6-Litre engine, available on the Formula and Trans-Am. The T/A engine option included a 3.23 axle ratio; higher compression ratio; specific camshaft; chrome-plated rocker covers, and 20 more horsepower than the standard 6.6-Litre engine.

1980 TURBO TRANS-AM

Production reached an all-time high of 155,000 units in 1977—nearly 69,000 of those were Trans-Ams.

For 1978 the Firebird Phenomenon continued. A new gold Special Edition became one of the big attractions at the major auto shows across the country. A "Redbird" appearance package was offered on the Esprit.

Also new for 1978 was a special Trans-Am performance package (WS-6) which included a revised T/A 6.6-Litre engine, special handling components and eight-inch cast aluminum wheels. Also offered on Firebirds was a new integral AM/FM/CB radio and an AM/FM stereo radio with cassette tape player.

In 1979 the Firebird took on a bold new look with individual recessed rectangular headlamps in front and, on the Trans-Am, innovative black-tinted tail lamps in back. Also, four-wheel power disc brakes became available for the first time. The exclusive 10th Anniversary Edition was the first Firebird to feature eye-soothing aircraft-style red instrument lighting in the cockpit.

1981 TURBO TRANS-AM

The 1980 Trans-Am, with a new 4.9-Liter Turbo engine, was chosen as the Indianapolis 500 Pace Car, and about 5,700 turbocharged Pace-Car replicas were produced for sale to the public. Similar cars also paced NASCAR Grand National stock car events throughout the season.

For 1981 the standard Trans-Am engine was a 4.9-Liter four-barrel V-8 with Electronic Spark Control, while the Turbo version was optional in both Trans-Am and Formula.

As you see, the new Firebird is clean and contemporary, a road-hugging, wind-cheating aerodynamic wedge, reflecting an aircraft sort of design philosophy that we feel is just right for the sophisticated sports-car buyer of the Eighties.

1982 TRANS-AM

There are three great Third Generation Firebird models. The first-level Firebird, which is clean and simple in appearance, affordable in price and, with the standard electronically Fuel-Injected Four-Cylinder engine, surprisingly peppy yet economical to operate.

The new, subtle and sophisticated, international-flavor S/E. This is the discerning gentleman's or lady's sports car, high in content, tasteful in color, and featured with the 2.8-Liter V-6 engine.

And the precise, contemporary performance-look Trans-Am. More subtle than in the past, it is also vastly more aerodynamic, more fuel efficient, and—with its standard carbureted or optional Fuel-Injected 5.0-Liter V-8—offers performance comparable to or better than last year's turbocharged model.

DESIGNING THE THIRD-GENERATION FIREBIRD

John Schinella, Pontiac's Chief of Exterior Styling, talks about what went into the state-of-the-art Firebird and Trans-Am

RIGHT OFF you'll notice that it looks very new, yet maintains the Firebird tradition. The ultra-low nose, twin venturi air intakes and smooth contours . . . the soft, undulating "S" shape over the wheels . . . the subtle "bone line" through its middle, accentuating its downward wedge thrust.

Design development of this machine began way back in 1975 when a number of drawings and scale models were produced in my Pontiac Studio as well as in Chevrolet and Advanced Studios. At that time, we were looking primarily at a front-wheel-drive car, trying to get a feel for what the next-generation Firebird should be. Should it be dramatically different or evolutionary? Basically, we were trying for a clean, aerodynamic, aircraft sort of look.

The program progressed for a while, but then it was temporarily halted because of workloads on the new J-cars and other projects. Also, more inputs on weight targets, size and cost were needed. Many, many concepts were evaluated.

By early-1978, we were rolling again with some new direction. Based on market research and engineering rationale, it was decided to retain the Firebird's rear drive and V-8 power capability. Roger Hughet, an assistant in the Advanced Studio, came up with the rendering that management felt would set the concept for the 1982 F-body.

John Schinella is the man responsible for the bird graphics on Trans-Am hoods and for the most exciting Ponycar to come down the Pike in years.

A scale model was sculptured from the rendering, still featuring the smooth, undulated all-glass upper. And soon after, we received the full-size clay model as a concept. It was a great theme, but our challenge in the Production Studio was to take this concept and develop the three distinct series of new Firebirds in keeping with Pontiac's new image.

We accentuated the undulating S-shape along the front fender, belt and rear deck, which was developed from the original design and from aerodynamic testing; and the overall wedge shape, which was important to the total stance and aggressive character of the new Firebird.

Both front and rear were proportioned to accommodate the latest engineering inputs and to establish the new Firebird identity. Bumpers were sculptured to enhance the theme while meeting the required five-mph impact mandates. Many management reviews and careful design adjustments were carried out to achieve the eventual production version.

We spent a lot of time developing the Firebird character, especially in the front. We decided that the car should have hidden headlamps for a clean, low, uncluttered look. We worked with both dual and single retractable lamp units trying to capture the ultimate frontal appearance.

The front evolved into the familiar, well-proportioned twin air-intake scheme. In the wind tunnel, the nose and air-dam were developed so that the major air intake volume would flow down and then up through the radiator from underneath . . . more of a "Bottom Breather." Above the twin air intakes, we designed two small slots that would house the park, signal and headlamps. Twin lines were developed by subtle surfacing, starting at the air intakes and tapering rearward over the hood to accent the cockpit.

It was a tough battle for Pontiac and us

to sell the hidden headlamp motif to the Corporation, but eventually everyone realized that this treatment would give Pontiac a leading edge in uniqueness and design sophistication.

Another tough aspect of the new F-car theme to translate into production was the compound-curved hatch glass, and a great deal of credit is due the glass companies for finding a way to build it in spite of a lot of moaning and groaning that it couldn't be done.

We also had fun designing a decent-looking optional louvered sunshade, especially important in sun-belt climates, to fit it.

The removable roof hatches were sculptured many times, and there were many precise adjustments from engineering, before we settled on this high-quality and visually well-balanced design for production. Considerable effort also went into the rear wing—not a solid rear spoiler as on other cars, but a real aerodynamic *wing*—which is standard on T/A models and optional on the S/E.

Again, Pontiac wanted uniqueness in the Firebird, and this wing has Pontiac heritage. It actually reduces drag while increasing downforce. The rear design evolved into a high motif, which helped the aerodynamics and location of the neutral density black tail lamps.

Obviously, a great deal of wind-tunnel development went into this machine, and the result is an outstanding drag coefficient for the Trans-Am, as measured in our tunnel at EPA-required height and attitude, of 0.323.

No other production car we've tested, foreign or domestic, has topped that, and we're damned proud. Even the standard Firebird has an excellent drag coefficient of 0.333. The car is almost a perfect aerodynamic wedge and very sensitive to its attitude in the wind, and if you lower the nose about an inch, the Trans-Am's coefficient drops to below 0.30! Unfortunately, because of bumper-height and ride-travel requirements, Pontiac can't sell it that way or use that figure.

Notice that the lower, aerodynamic devices are hardly visible because they've been integrated below the body break, just in front of the wheels front and rear. The front air dam is as low as it can be and still clear the curb and meet ramp angle requirements, and it completely covers the radiator support before turning toward the wheels.

Even the flush aero covers on the Turbo cast-aluminum wheels are a result of extensive wind tunnel development. Deep-dish and offset wheels by themselves may be lightweight, but they don't pass through the air as well as a flush surface.

The idea of flush-type wheels or covers is exploited by professionals in Land Speed Record cars and other racing

Roger Hughet turned out this rendering of the '82 Trans-Am in 1976. The styling project actually started in 1975.

The first of the new F-car line was chosen as the official NASCAR Pace Car for use at the Daytona 500. It was a natural both because of the car and Pontiac's long time relationship with the racing body.

Full-size clay model of the new generation Trans-Am, photographed inside Pontiac's Exterior Styling Studio.

1982 FIREBIRD TRANS AM
Aerodynamic Air Flow & Features
0.323 C$_D$

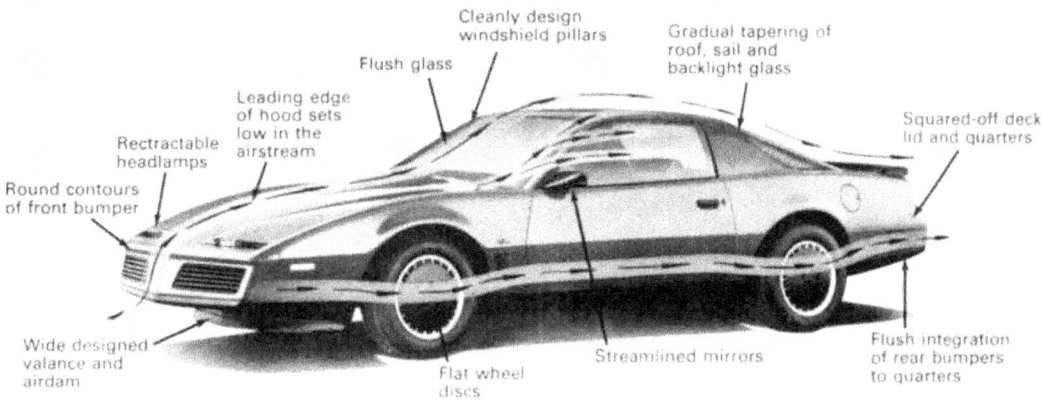

One of Pontiac's major concerns when designing the Trans-Am was to come up with as low a coefficient of drag as possible. This was one of the early CD ratings, later changed to reflect reduced drag. In 1983½ they reduced drag even more via aerodynamic panels.

Tom Goad, long time Pontiac performance freak and product planning engineer at Pontiac, was instrumental in coming up with the streamlining panels used on the '83½-'84 Trans-Ams. He also built the first five-speed injected T/A with panels and BBS wheels.

Tom Goad's Café Racer at speed at the GM Proving Grounds. This was the first T/A fitted with the "aero package" along with five-speed and injected motor. The car also boasted a lot of suspension work and some gear changes. It was easily quicker than a Corvette.

machines, and you will be seeing a lot more of this practice coming out of Europe. In this case, our Turbo covers are worth several counts in drag coefficient, and that's why they're there.

The Trans-Am of the past, while it was right for its time, hasn't been the cleanest car in the world with its scoops and flares and graphics. But the premise, the challenge that we took on this one, was to design the smoothest, most-aerodynamic, most-fluid, most-precise piece of machinery we have ever done—a very clean, pure, high-tech look in keeping with the new Pontiac image.

With the S/E sharing the Trans-Am's wheel design and certain other elements, we were also faced with the challenge of creating two very different identities for

Sharing the Pace Car limelight was this '82 Trans-Am which served as the SCCA Pike's Peak Hill Climb official car. Powering this car in its race to the clouds was a throttle body injected 305-inch V-8.

them. To accomplish this, we designed the S/E to be beautiful, subtle and sophisticated, as well as contemporary, to stand right at the top of the International sports car market. We came up with a subtle, tone-on-tone concept, like the blend of colors and form you might find in *Vogue* or *Gentleman's Quarterly*. It doesn't jump out at you, but you know it's tasteful.

If you take the Gold car, for example, the upper surfaces are light Gold, the lower surfaces dark Gold. The Turbo wheel covers, the optional wing, the mirrors and door handles are all Gold, even the S/E lettering is Gold-On-Gold.

The Trans-Am, on the other hand, we look to the opposite extreme. Instead of all the appendages of the past, this car has its aerodynamics built-in. It's very smooth to begin with, so we couldn't shout about that. Instead, we took a very "mechanical" approach with bright, high-intensity colors.

All the elements that identify it as a Trans-Am are in high-tech structural-look black—the Turbo wheel covers, dual mirrors, wing, door handles, grilles, and functional air extractors. Just rearward of the front wheels, the lettering, graphics, accent along the lower body—all these features are precise and functional.

The unique asymetrical hood, which is available on the Trans-Am, sports functional fresh air induction.

A program like this takes a lot more than one or two individuals to put it together. It is very much a total team effort, and in our case the team is composed mostly of enthusiasts. We *love* this car! We know that the Firebird is all about. We've driven it, and we *feel* it and enjoy it. You have to have direction from above; but believe me, you have to be turned on to give it that little extra edge. And this team is turned on!

Key pqople on the team at Design Staff are John Wagner, chief engineer; Dick Schell, assistant chief engineer; Jim Haberek and Illene Mazura, design engineers; John Folden, assistant studio chief; Bill Davis and Bob Menking, designers; Bill Traicoff, chief modeler, and Jim Clara, Hugh Hartman, Harvey Robb, and Tony Campagna, modelers.

HIGH-OUTPUT TRANS-AM

A serious Supercar from the folks who invented the word!

A HIGHER-output (HO) V-8 engine option for Firebird Trans-Am added a new dimension of excitement to the popular Pontiac sporty model in 1983½-1984.

Featuring a standard five-speed manual transmission and a 3.73 rear axle ratio, the 5-liter HO V-8 powerplant offers zero-to-60 performance at around seven seconds. The HO engine is rated at 190 horsepower at 4,800 rpm and achieves its peak torque rating of 240 foot pounds at 3,200 rpm.

Improved output of this HO engine over the 5-liter V-8 four-barrel version is attributed to: a higher-lift, higher-rpm camshaft; a new free-breathing exhaust system; electronic spark control which optimizes the spark advance for maximum performance; V-8 CrossFire 9.5-to-1 pistons and cylinder heads; fresh air hood induction system, and usage of an electric-motor-driven fan in place of an engine-driven fan that would normally absorb about 10 horsepower.

The WS-6 special performance package is standard with the HO engine option. This includes four-wheel disc brakes; 3.73-to-1 axle ratio with a premium material gear set and P215/60R15 Goodyear Eagle GT tires on 15 x 7-inch turbo-aero aluminum or turbo-finned aluminum wheels.

Specific suspension tuning includes a larger 32-mm front stabilizer bar and a 21-mm rear stabilizer bar; higher-rate bushings in the control arms and track bar; specific shock absorber calibrations; added body-to-frame structural reinforcements, and a faster 12.7-to-1 power steering gear with a higher rate torsion bar.

A stiffer torque arm, connecting the transmission to the rear axle, has been added to the rear suspension. The gain in stiffness and strength is achieved by eliminating the lightening holes.

The combination of the HO V-8 engine option with the WS-6 special performance package, fresh air hood induction system and the wind-cheating aerodynamic exterior of the Trans Am provides the enthusiast with a true driver's car that offers quick acceleration, balanced braking, and excellent ride and handling.

With its Formula-style snorkle air intake climbing up the rear window and over the roof, the Fiero pacer looks ready to take on the world. Replicas are sure to become instant collectibles.

PONTIAC SETS THE PACE

The first American-produced mid-engine sports car
is also the first mid-engined car
to pace the Indy 500

ON November 16, 1983, Pontiac announced its revolutionary, mid-engine Fiero designed to be the official pace car for the 68th Indianapolis 500 Mile Race on May 27, 1984. The all-new Fiero was the first four-cylinder car to pace the Indy classic since 1912 when the field was paced by a Stutz.

"Fiero represents a bold new thrust for Pontiac in designing expressive, fun-to-drive cars for today's expanding markets," said Pontiac General Manager and GM Vice President William E. Hoglund. "During the Fiero's first month on the market, dealers delivered a record 80 percent of their availability. Fiero is the right car for the markets of the Eighties and this Indy pace car is further evidence of the versatility in designing specific cars for customer needs."

The Fiero Indy pace car is white with a silver lower accent. The aerodynamic appearance is enhanced with a new aero package which highlights the improved ground effects of the car. A new integral front provides a noticeable and more aggressive appearance than current production cars. The pace car air intake has been relocated lower in the front fascia to provide better air flow for the Super Duty 2.7-liter, four-cylinder (165 cubic-inch) engine which powers the pacer.

New side and rear skirts and a functional rear-deck wing add to the aerodynamic efficiency of the car.

The most dramatic touch on the pace car is a futuristic rear air scoop which stretches up above the rear window and provides an efficient way of getting fresh air into the engine system. The integral safety light at the back edge of the air scoop eliminates the aerodynamic drag usually associated with add-on lighting systems, and marks the first time a high-intensity strobe light of this type has been used in pace cars. The system was adapted from lighting used on the wing tips of the Boeing 747 aircraft.

The body changes on the Fiero Indy pace car point to the flexible body concept provided by the car. The idea of a driveable chassis, with easily removeable bolt on body panels, provides for easy after-market styling changes such as flared fenders, air dams, rear spoilers, and even completely new and different bodies.

The powerplant in the pace car is a 2.7-liter four-cylinder engine that cranks out 232 horsepower at 6,500 rpm. Torque rating is 210 foot pounds at 5,500 rpm. The pace car engine is an adaptation of the full Super-Duty package of aftermarket components Pontiac offers for serious off-road enthusiasts. The foundation of the SD pace car engine consists of a Super-Duty engine block; a steel forged, fully counterweighted crankshaft; and a special high-performance cylinder

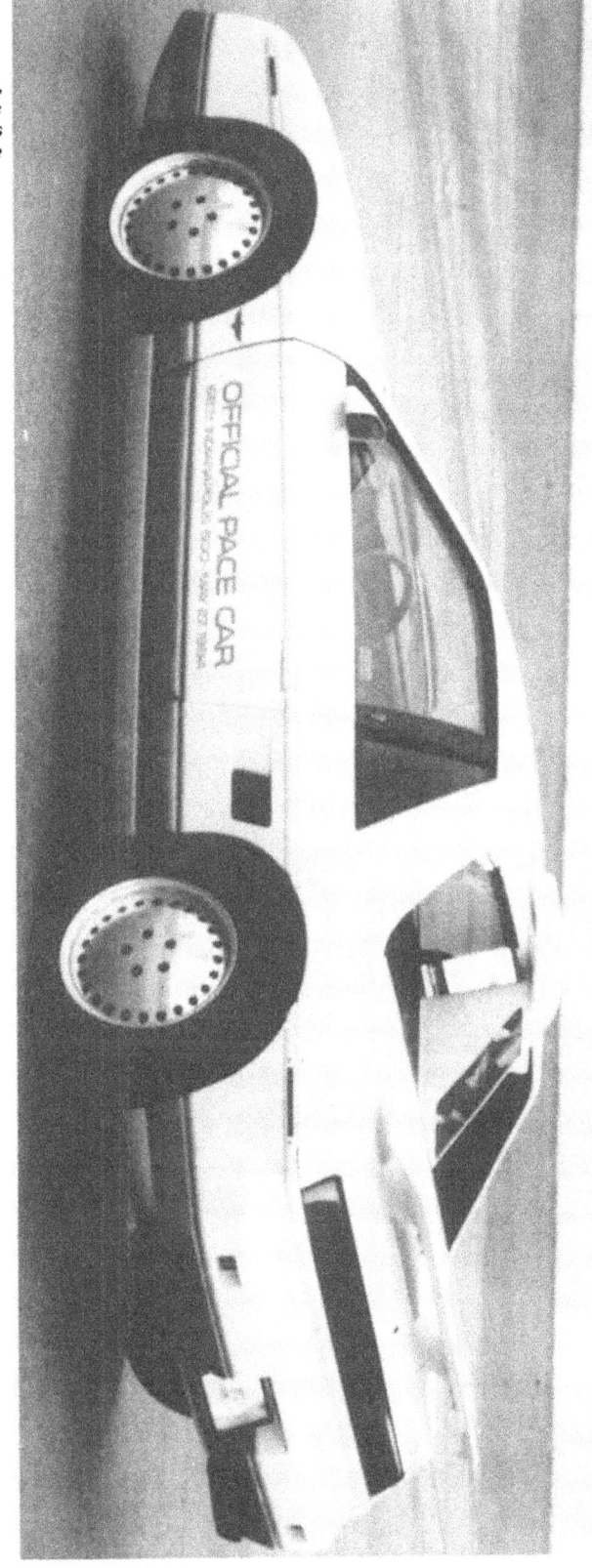

Finished in white with a silver accent lower panel, the Fiero Pace Car is one of the most aerodynamic cars ever to pace the classic race. Power comes from a Super Duty Four making it one of the fastest pace cars to run at Indy.

head.

In tests at the Indianapolis Motor Speedway, the Fiero pace car has turned an average speed of better than 136 miles an hour—one of the fastest pace cars ever to run at Indy, and faster than the 1959 Indianapolis average winners speed which was 135 miles per hour. Pontiac's last pace car at Indy—a Turbo 301 Trans-Am—hit an average speed of 127 miles per hour in 1980.

Chassis features on the pace car include: a special racing transmission featuring a close-ratio design with a higher torque capacity to handle the higher-performance engine; a high-torque capacity axle shaft; high-performance wheel bearings, based on Pontiac's successful STE model; higher rear spring rate; added structure to the engine cradle; Delco/Bilstein high-pressure shock absorbers; Delco electric power-master brake system with four-wheel disc brakes with vented rotors; and a specific exhaust system with a four tube header design into a low resonation exhaust system. Wheels on the pace car are new high-tech polished aluminum (front 16x7-inch rear 16x8-inch), and the tires are Goodyear Eagle GT 205/50VR16 (front) and GT 225/50VR16 (rear).

Pontiac offered 2,000 replicas of the Fiero Indy Pace Car at dealerships in April, 1984, which are very similar in appearance to the actual pace car.

The interior is highlighted by slate gray leather seats with red cloth inserts. Also included are: spoiler, power sport mirrors, leather wrapped steering wheel and ETR AM/FM stereo with cassette and five-band graphic equalizer.

The powertrain on the Indy replicas is the 2.5-liter four-cylinder engine with swirl port head that spirals the fuel charge for faster and more efficient combustion. A four-speed manual transmission is standard, while an automatic transmission is available.

The four-speed with a 4.10-to-1 axle ratio offers excellent overall performance along with 40 mpg EPA highway driving. The Indy replica engine has a special silver valve cover and silver air cleaner with unique black graphics. Red ignition wires are also a part of the engine package. Wheels on the car are special white high-tech cast aluminum with a red accent around the rim.

THE FIERO STORY

It's a Super-Duty revolution all over again as Pontiac launches its mid-engined sports car

John Schinella holding futuristic Fiero rendering, discusses Second-Generation designs with Design Studio Two Staff.

The Fiero is America's first mid-engined sports car and a marvel of engineering and design. This is a T-type version built by Cars & Concepts to showcase its new Skylite T-Roof.

AS AMERICA'S first production two-seat mid-engine sports car, Fiero was designed to appeal to a very special group of people.

Market research indicates that by 1990, one-third of the U.S. population will be between the ages of 25 and 44. This generation will be the largest and will have the greatest spending power in U.S. history.

Fiero is targeted directly at two segments of that group. The first segment consists of younger, well-educated consumers who are very interested in small personal sports cars. The second buyer group consists of consumers looking for a uniquely-styled second or third car with exceptional fuel economy for commuting purposes.

With those two groups in mind, Fiero's philosophy was clearly defined for both the General Motors advanced engineering and advanced design staffs at the beginning of this project: create a lower-priced, personal sports car to appeal to those two principal buyer groups through quality engineering and fun-to-drive, high-tech Pontiac styling.

The Fiero concept was turned over to the General Motors Design Staff under the direction of Irv Rybicki, vice-president, and Chuck Jordan, assistant executive. And in early 1979, Dave Holls, executive in charge of the Advanced and Experimental Design studio and Ron Hill, chief designer of the Advanced III studio were assigned to the Fiero project. They received the initial engineering drawings and chassis specification for Fiero—a two-seat, mid-engine sports car.

Hill and his staff worked on initial sketches for a design concept based upon a wedge-type aerodynamic shape. Just as important, however, the design had to have a challenging, "drive-me" styling.

From the initial design sketches, Hill and his designers created full-size renderings and then clay models of the car. The designers molded numerous clay studies of Fiero to achieve the right shapes and forms for optimum aerodynamic numbers in the initial wind tunnel testing at the California Institute of Technology.

The initial stage—Block One Fiero—was very well-received by General

One of the early Styling Studio prototypes with European-styled wheels, razor-edged lines and radical raked windshield.

Motors management on April 16, 1980, and the go-ahead was given to proceed with further development. On April 24, 1980, Fiero was assigned to the Pontiac II design studio under the direction of Chief Designer John R. Schinella, who followed Fiero through to production.

The first challenge facing the Pontiac II design staff was to give Fiero a pure Pontiac identity, like Firebird. That meant Fiero simply had to be one of the most exciting, fun-to-drive machines on the road.

Jack Humbert, GM executive designer for automotive exteriors, assisted in shaping and directing the initial concept to include traditional Pontiac design characteristics. All concept details were reviewed and then selectively incorporated into the initial Fiero design sketches by John Folden and Bob Menking. These sketches illustrate how Fiero began to take on a true Pontiac identity with styling characteristics such as dual blacked-out impact pads in the front and rear of the car as well as concealed headlamps integrated into the front-end styling.

Pontiac II designers worked closely with Pontiac engineering staff and key suppliers to carefully study characteristics of the new car. A main consideration was the new "Enduraflex" material or skin for the car. This material was so special the designers found it gave them a unique opportunity to explore new shapes for Fiero.

General Motors and Pontiac management selected the theme sketch for Fiero in May, 1980, setting the direction for the development of aero clay models. The sculpture team, under the direction of chief sculptor Bill Traicoff, skillfully carved and blended the outer surfaces—front, side and rear—of Fiero.

In clay, Fiero's design had a relatively low frontal theme, sweeping to a high

The Fiero SD4 was built for the auto show circuit to showcase the super-high-performance Super-Duty Four engine. It's a full-bore IMSA racer with parts available from Pontiac dealers.

Behind the scenes at the Design Studio Two during the building of the full-size clay Fiero. Some prototypes carried the "Pegasus" nameplate.

rear, creating a well-balanced wedge shape. The car was designed to be a "bottom-breather." The design staff found through aerodynamic studies that the best place for air-intake was below the nose so this function was incorporated into the Fiero's front-end appearance.

Fiero designers then used a rub strip to completely surround the car, accentuating its racy wedge-type shape. The designers incorporated many of the Fiero's built-in features into the rub strip including the front and rear side-markers, door handles and locks. In addition, engine exhaust louvers were integrated into the rear deck lid. Thoroughly Pontiac twin-black impact graphics were integrated with the rub strip into the rear of the Fiero.

During Block Two Fiero, the design staff moved the cockpit forward and increased the windshield angle to 63 degrees. They then shortened the nose, keeping Fiero's shape taunt. These changes gave Fiero better weight distribution and better aerodynamic numbers which improved fuel efficiency.

This stage of design and wind tunnel testing was completed by 1981. Further development on Fiero was slightly delayed as General Motors and Pontiac Motor Division management reviewed the marketplace conditions and rescheduled the introduction of Fiero for September, 1983.

To keep the exterior design of Fiero clean, unornamented and high-tech in appearance, Pontiac graphics were de-bossed in the left headlamp door and rear fascia of the car. The jewel-like Pontiac 'V' crest was inset into the black side pillars. And the Fiero design team pioneered an all-new Fiero 2M4 decal by using 3M solar film transferred into black to transmit a deep, shiny quality.

Many of Fiero's shapes and forms were guided by extensive wind tunnel testing at Lockheed and the General Motors Technical Center. Testing on full-size running models began shortly after the introduction date—September, 1983—was set. The combination of hours of aerodynamic testing and computer-uided design, under the direction of Design Studio Engineer John Wagner, helped fine-tune Fiero's shape.

The luggage rack, designed especially for Fiero, was integrated into the aerodynamic shape of the vehicle. The designers moved the body side molding, located over the rsar of the car, and increased the wheel opening shape for better fit and finish. In addition, an air intake scoop was integrated into the left rear quarter panel to bring fresh air to the engine.

Fiero's upper sail panels were kept to a minimum shape for the best management of weight and space. The rear taillamps, made of a black neutral-density

One of the more-radical Fiero designs to come out of Schinella's Design Studio Two team. Super-wedge design is ready for the street, race track or even Bonneville.

PONTIAC SUPER-DUTY 2.5-LITER FIERO COMPONENTS

SUPER-DUTY CYLINDER BLOCK (semi-finished cylinder bores):
- Solid 19mm main bearing bulkheads
- Oil pan rail section doubled
- Cylinder bore wall increased to 8.5mm (minimum) and siamesed
- Cylinder deck thickness increased (13mm minimum)
- Cylinder heat bolt bosses deepened (46mm)
- Lifter boss height increased for roller lifters
- External ribbing and boss diameters increased
- Front and rear flange sections increased
- Main oil gallery diameter—no change
- Head bolt bosses tap drilled, but not tapped
- Semi-finished cylinder bores 100.88mm (3.962-inch diameter)

SUPER-DUTY CYLINDER BLOCK ASSEMBLY INCLUDES:
- Align-bored Super-Duty block
- Maleable iron two-bolt main bearing caps
- Production 11mm main cap bolts
- Camshaft bearings
- Engine block water jacket plugs
- Water tested jacket

SUPER-DUTY CRANKSHAFT (semi-finished):
- Forged steel
- Fully counterweighted
- Common 1982 production main bearing diameters
- Crankshaft front and rear common with 1982 production
- Accepts Chevrolet performance connecting rods—(5.7 and 6-inch)
- Cross drilled main and rod journals
- Rolled fillets
- Rod arm cleanout traps
- Available in 3.0 and 3.25-inch strokes from single forging
- Rod and main journals semi-finished to 0.25-inch oversize (sold unbalanced)

SUPER DUTY CYLINDER HEAD (semi-finished):
- Revised intake and exhaust ports (enlarged, raised and recontoured for 1.94-inch intake and 1.60-inch exhaust valves)
- Deck and chamber wall thickness increased to 8mm
- Blocked EGR passage
- Enlarged combustion chamber (unshrouded intake)
- Valve seats and bowls machined for production valves
- Pushrod clearance holes not machined
- Rocker arm stud tap drilled 3mm shallower (1.12-inch tap drill changed to 1-inch—8 places)

material, have a high-tech grid design inside. And the rear taillamps were mounted flush to the body surface and extended the full width of the rear to maintain Pontiac heritage.

Two cast-aluminum wheels were designed under the direction of Dick Shell, design studio assistant chief engineer, to complete Fiero's fast, contemporary appearance. The entry level 13-inch steel wheel is silver with black air slots and a black center. It is offered with an optional chrome trim ring. Fiero's exterior designers also created an aluminum 13-inch finned turbo wheel. This wheel is very mechanical in design and has bright machined ribs and rim.

An even more daring look is created with the use of Fiero's optional 14-inch high-tech wheel. This wheel was designed to appear flush to the surface of the body in side view and its asymmetri-

Aircraft-styled Fiero interior combines high-tech with tried and true sports car function to come up with a dynamite cockpit layout.

PONTIAC DEALERS: AVAILABLE PRODUCTION PARTS

WINDSHIELD WIPER SYSTEM
- Motor Asm. 22030809
- Transmission-RH 22039336
- Transmission-LH 22039337
- Arms 20302338
- Blades 20364747

TRANSMISSION CONTROLS
- Control Asm.–Transmission 10026655
- Knob–Trans. Control Lever 10030989
- Cable Asm.–Trans. Control 10026619
- Cable Asm.–Trans. Control 10026626

CLUTCH SYSTEM–HYDRAULIC
- Slave Cylinder 10026326
- Bracket–Slave Cyl. to Trans. 10028098
- Lever Asm.–Clutch Fork 10030026

WHEEL BEARINGS
- Bearing Asm.–Wheel 14035594

FRONT BALL JOINT
- Ball Joint Kit–Front LCA 9767113

DRIVE AXLE SHAFTS (FIERO RACE CAR ONLY)
- Axle-RH 7845336
- Axle-LH 7845337
- Axle Seal Kit 7842034
  (RH & LH Outer)
- Axle Seal Kit RH Inner 7842040
- Axle Seal Kit LH Inner 7842039

ENGINE MOUNT "BUSHINGS"
- Bushing Asm. 10000953

WINDSHIELD 20479012
STEERING WHEEL 17980171
STEERING WHEEL HUB 10028355
TAIL LAMP HOUSING 16500453/54
TAIL LAMP OUTER LENS 16500461/62
TAIL LAMP INNER LENS 16500457/58
6 SPRINGS REQUIRED 5949351
BACK UP LENS 16500460

PONTIAC DEALERS: AVAILABLE OFF-ROAD PARTS

SUPER DUTY BLOCK 10027633
SUPER DUTY CYLINDER HEAD 10027776*
SUPER DUTY CRANKSHAFT
  (AS FORGED) 10027777
SUPER DUTY CRANKSHAFT
  3.00-inch STROKE 10027778
SUPER DUTY CRANKSHAFT
  3.25-inch STROKE 10027779
SUPER DUTY HEAD GASKET 10031324
SUPER DUTY EXHAUST VALVE
  1.600 inches 10031325
SUPER DUTY INTAKE VALVE
  1.94 inches 10031326
SUPER DUTY EXHAUST VALVE
  1.625 inches 10031338
SUPER DUTY INTAKE VALVE
  2.020 inches 10031339
SUPER DUTY ROCKER COVER ASM. ... 10031327
SUPER DUTY ENGINE BUILD PKG. 10031328**
SUPER DUTY INTAKE MANIFOLD
  RACING 10031330
SUPER DUTY INTAKE MANIFOLD
  STREET 10031340
SUPER DUTY 5.7-inch CONNECTING
  ROD (CHEV) 14011090
SUPER DUTY 6.0-inch CONNECTING
  ROD (CHEV) 14011091
SUPER DUTY REBUILT WATER PUMP ... 12309677
SUPER DUTY DAMPENER 10031581
SUPER DUTY CAM BEARING 14002525
SEE CYLINDER HEAD PREP. SECTION
STARTER 1109533

10027776 discontinued after October '83 (PN10031322 W/O EGR) (PN10031323 W/EGR). These new parts will not require pushrod sleeves or exhaust sleeves. PN10031322 valve seat not machined. PN10031323 valve seat machined for 1.94-inch intake and 1.600-inch exhaust. Engine build package gives you all of the necessary fasteners and sheetmetal parts to complete engine build. See illustration: All parts marked "4" come in kit.

PONTIAC SUPER DUTY PARTS

- SD Engine Block 10027633
- SD Cylinder Head 10027776
- SD Crankshaft .... 10027778 (3.00-inch stroke)
- SD Crankshaft .... 10027779 (3.25-inch stroke)

The following manufacturers produce parts for Super Duty engines

Fel-Pro	Head Gaskets	Local Outlets
Mr. Gasket Co.	Gaskets	(216) 398-8300
B.H.J. Products	Torque Plates	(419) 797-6780
A.R.E.	Dry Sumps	(916) 929-0496
Moroso Performance	Oil Pans, Bolt Kits	(800) 243-6536
Hamburger Oil Pans	Oil Pans	(201) 240-3888
Melling Tool Co.	Oil Pumps	(517) 787-8172
Quartermaster Ind.	Clutch and Drive Systems	(312) 593-8999
Edelbrock Corp.	Manifolds	(213) 323-7310
Red Line, Inc.	Weber Carbs	(213) 538-3233
Brooks Racing Co.	Pistons	(714) 893-0595
Arias Racing Pistons	Pistons	(213) 532-9737
Crane Cams, Inc.	Cams and Valve Gear	(305) 457-8888
Hooker Industries	Headers	(714) 983-5871
E.V.M. Injectors	Fuel Injection	(414) 793-4467
Autotronic Controls	MSD Ignitions	(915) 772-7431
Speed Pro	Piston Rings	(616) 724-5011

Diversified Glass Products, Inc.
(313) 373-7575

- Complete Body Asm. 84PCBA
- Roof Cap & Windshield Sun-around 84PRWS
- Front Center Bumper 84PFCB
- Right Front Fender 84PRFF
- Left Front Fender 84PLFF
- Center Lower Spoiler 84PCLS
- Right Door w/Rocker 84PRDR
- Left Door w/Rocker 84PLDR
- Right Rocker Panel 84PRRP
- Left Rocker Panel 84PLRP
- Right Rear Fender W/Sail 84PRRFS
- Left Rear Fender W/Sail 84PLRFS
- Rear Engine & Vent Cover 84PREVC
- Front Hood & Headlight Cover 84PFHH
- Rear Center Bumper 84PRCB
- Rear Deck Spoiler 84PRDS
- Air Intake Scoop 84PAIS

Goodyear Tire Company
- Front 23-11.5x16
- Rear 25-12.5x16

cal surface is very contemporary and unique to Pontiac.

Interior themes for Fiero were first created in 1979 under the direction of George Moon, executive designer of Automotive interiors at the GM Technical Center Interior Concept Studio with the aid of Assistant Executive Designer George Angersbach. So the philosophy of creating the ultimate interior for the "driver's car" was set even before Block One Fiero. Both men brought their design experiences in sports car interiors from the Corvette and F-body cars.

The Fiero project was assigned to Group Chief Designer John Schettler and his staff. Assistant Chief Designer Marvin Fisher created the first original interior sketches. From those sketches, Chief Designer Corwin Hanson, Fisher and Designer Dan Nelson created a three-dimensional foam-core sketch of the all-new interior. This method of interior design, from theme sketches directly to three-dimensional foam-core sketches, is relatively new and the interior design team found it especially successful for Fiero.

Hanson, Fisher and Nelson began with an instrument panel space and seat structure, then built up the instrument panel and door panels. Then they worked toward the rear to complete the first interior model which strongly resembled an aircraft cockpit.

The functional essence of aircraft interiors gave direction to the overall Fiero interior theme. The designers found that the instrument panel shape provided extra interior space for the passenger. In addition, the driver-oriented instrument cluster and hand controls were ergonomically placed in relation to the driver's seating position making it especially easy to control the car. The interior designer used a high-quality speedometer and tachometer in a floating-pod cluster for optimum packaging and easy serviceability.

The outer tunnel between the passenger and driver provided a convenient platform for several items once located on the instrument panel including the radio, heater, air controls and rear storage compartment. The center arm rest provided the correct elbow height, matching that provided by the door arm rests. In addition to serving as a platform, the tunnel houses the fuel tank and service lines.

In the spring of 1980, the Interior Concept Studio transferred the project to the Pontiac Interior Production Studio headed by Pat Fuery. Marvin Fisher stayed with the project and had the opportunity to see Fiero through to production.

In 1981, Bill Scott became the chief designer of Pontiac interiors and worked on Fiero until production. One of his chief

This is the one-off Schinella-designed Fiero roadster which came out of Design Studio Two. It was the net result of a brainstorming session that Schinella had with chief engineer Jay Wetzel, Jack Folden, assistant chief designer and Ron Rodgers, Fiero project manager. It too was put on the auto show circuit to test consumer appeal.

assignments was developing a unique seating direction emphasizing proper contour, lateral and lumbar support for the driver. This, Scott and his crew accomplished by using special foam padding in critical seat sections.

Early developmental test trips aided Scott and his designers in the fine-tuning of other interior details. Design changes were made on the interior door panel including the use of a pull-grip armrest on a new molded door panel instead of the original design which had horizontal pullstraps unattached to the armrest.

In addition, Fiero's interior originally was dark charcoal with insert-color accents on the seats. The color scheme was changed under Scott's designer to two-medium value interior colors increasing the spacious feeling of the cockpit. The use of plush Pallex fabric completed an interior atmosphere which combines function with comfort for a contemporary high-tech look.

All new instrumentation graphics were added during Block Three of Fiero's interior evolution. New contemporary graphics emphasized clarity by using details such as white numbers which turn red at night for easy reading. Other details were integrated into the instrument panel and console design to combine safety ideas, with international flavor and a Pontiac identity.

As this Pontiac innovation took on shape and character, Pontiac searched for the right name to capture the character of the car. In final decision-making meetings, the name Fiero—proud and dignified in the Italian language—won the competition. Upon investigation, it was found that Fiero was the name of a 1967 Firebird show car—an aerodynamic shape before its time. With that heritage, no other name seemed more appropriate. Thus, Fiero was given to a most unique project and commitment for General Motors and Pontiac Motor Division—the offering of America's first mid-engine two-seat sports car.

This is the Firebird IV, debuted at the 1964 World's Fair in New York City. It was designed to cheat the wind and run on a computer-controlled automated highway network.

CHEATING THE WIND

Pontiac and General Motors stylists have gone the 'aero' route to reduce drag and fuel consumption and increase efficiency and performance

Two engineers are dwarfed by the 43-foot diameter wind generating fan in GM Engineering's Aerodynamics Laboratory at the Tech Center. This is part of the first full-scale automotive aerodynamic wind tunnel in this country.

AERODYNAMICS literally means "air motion," and this fascinating science basically involves four fundamental factors—weight, lift, drag and thrust. By far the greatest in importance, as applied to the automobile, is DRAG. There are different varieties of drag, but they all add up to be "the resistance produced to a body moving through air."

Friction drag is caused by the extremely thin layers of air which are next to the surface of a moving body. Aerodynamic scientists call these the "boundary layers." As the body shape moves along, the thin layer of air in contact sticks to the surface. The next layer rubs against the surface layer and a third layer against the second and so forth. Near the leading edge, the frictional layer is smooth or to use aerodynamic language—LAMINAR. At some point on the surface, depending on its design, the boundary layer becomes turbulent in the way that smoke, after rising cleanly, breaks up into a whirling pattern. Similarly, boundary layer turbulence increases as the air moves rearward and the boundary layers reach their greatest thickness near the trailing edge.

Where the air is smooth, the drag force is considerably less than in the turbulent portion of the boundary layer. It is a fact that if "boundary layer" flow can be kept "laminar" then the least amount of drag will be produced.

Form drag is simply "the resistance of the air to the passage of a body through it." A blunt shape such as a box creates a great deal of form drag. The airstream curves around the front outer edges and flows along the sides so that a partial vacuum forms in the space behind. This partial vacuum will add greatly to air resistance and turbulence whereas a more streamlined air foil shape will allow the air to move smoothly over and around the body.

Car designers have always been somewhat aware of drag influence and streamlining is an old term as applied to cars. However, it was generally an appearance approach with very little scientific basis. In fact, at one time, we didn't believe that drag was of much importance at speeds below 80 miles per hour. It is now well recognized that even at 40 mph, the air resistance can be greater than the mechanical rolling resistance of the car, and that drag rises rapidly as car speed increases.

The simplest calculations for determing air resistance to a vehicle shape can be stated as follows:

The *drag force* (R) applied to a vehicle in motion is directly proportional to:
- (C) Drag coefficient
- (A) Cross-sectional area of vehicle
- (V_2) Velocity of vehicle squared or
R v CAV_2

Herb Adams built this radical Trans-Am road racer using swoopy fiberglass T/A panels over a tubular chassis. Dubbed "Quicksilver," it was one of the slickest, most radical cars in its class. He went to great lengths to come up with an aerodynamic racer without having the benefit of a wind tunnel at his disposal.

During the mid-to-late-Seventies, the Trans-Am was a pretty slick production car. This is a modified '77 Trans-Am built by Herb Adams. Fender flares and spoilers helped cut down on drag.

PONTIAC FIREBIRD TRANS AM AERODYNAMICS

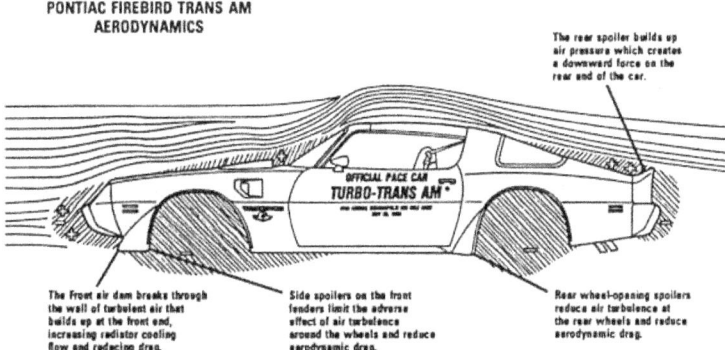

Pontiac started pushing aerodynamics with the '80 Trans-Am which was the Indy 500 Pace Car that year. It was the first time that a manufacturer tried to explain the benefits of aerodynamic styling to the public. This was the start of something big.

Herb Adams took advantage of the new features in 1980 and applied them to his Daytona road racer.

The world energy shortage and mandatory fuel economy ratings have quickly changed attitudes and true aerodynamic streamlining and other drag and friction-reducing techniques have become important factors in the design of a new automobile. All available power in the car must be utilized more efficiently to provide greater driving range and maximum payload capacity.

Historically, sufficient power applied to the wheels could pull some remarkably inefficient vehicles, but the more modern solution is to shape the vehicle's surfaces to produce the least amount of drag. This naturally requires some compromise in order to achieve a practical car. Considerations must be balanced between an ideal aero shape and size so that the payload of passengers, luggage, fuel and engine can be carried with convenience and mechanical efficiency.

Presently, we have found no ideal shape for a car, and we must continually search for the optimum profile to eliminate drag. In general, whenever shapes can be utilized that meet the air at an angle, the air will flow over the car's surface in the smoothest possible sweep and the boundary laters of air will not separate to become turbulent.

Blunt shapes, or "form drag," such as frontal areas, are especially difficult to handle on full-size cars, but we have been able to round off edges and slope the hood and windshield at greater to flush up the side and lower extremities. Flush windshield glass, side windows and moldings, flat wheel opening lips and protuberances have all helped to combat simple air resistance by making streamlining a practical reality. In some instances, front and side spoilers have been used to deflect the air so that it will not create turbulence and lift on the underside of the car where streamlining is not yet practical.

The reduction of drag has resulted in other bonus side effects. Controlled air flow eliminates windshield wiper lift, excessive wind noise and contributes to self-cleaning side windows and backlight areas. We have also achieved better handling and more stable cars in gusty and cross wind conditions.

As stated earlier, there is no ideal formula for automobile aerodynamics. Every design presents a new and sometimes unpredictable set of values. But now designers have actually been given a new element for creating newer and fresher esthetic forms, and the appeal of the cars of the future will surely reflect this "Science of Aircraft."

With the availability of new wind tunnels, technology and attitudes, we are optimistic that aerodynamics can be adapted and exploited for the benefit of our product, our economy and our consumers.

The aero option became reality in 1984 and included new front and rear fascia panels, larger air dam, door and rocker panel extensions, wide lower body strobe graphics, upper body color aero mirrors and rear body-colored aero wing. As far as most buyers were concerned, they bought the package for the cosmetic benefits!

One of the centers of attraction at the GM World of Motion exhibit at EPCOT Center in Florida, is the Aero 2000, the most aerodynamic automobile that GM has ever designed. It has sliding doors, top-hinged front wheel skirts and a speed-regulated rear foil to reduce costly air turbulence.

The Pontiac Fiero undergoing aerodynamics testing in the GM lab. This car got a good head start because it was conceived when aerodynamics played an important role in car design.

If you enjoyed this book, spread the word.

Tell your friends, recommend the book on your favorite message board, review the book on Amazon.com, or Tweet @stanceandspeed.

Stance & Speed is an independent company dedicated to serving enthusiasts.

To find out more, visit **www.stanceandspeed.com**

Also available in the Quicksilver Supercar Series

www.ingramcontent.com/pod-product-compliance
Lightning Source LLC
Chambersburg PA
CBHW080540170426
43195CB00016B/2623